NAKED
AMBITION

NAKED AMBITION

WOMEN WHO ARE CHANGING
PORNOGRAPHY

EDITED BY CARLY MILNE

CARROLL & GRAF PUBLISHERS
NEW YORK

NAKED AMBITION
Women Who Are Changing Pornography

Carroll & Graf
An Imprint of Avalon Publishing Group Inc.
245 West 17th Street • 11th Floor
New York, NY 10011

AVALON
publishing group incorporated

Copyright © 2005 by Carly Milne

Introduction © 2005 by Carly Milne • ". . . on experiencing boot camp on the road to becoming an adult video expert" © 2005 by Violet Blue • ". . . on revamping Playgirl Magazine" © 2005 by Jill Sieracki • ". . . on bringing porn into the world of lad mags" © 2005 by Laura Leu • ". . . on how sex and technology come together" © 2005 by Regina Lynn • ". . . on helping debunk the pervert myth surrounding porn through mainstream media" © 2005 by Jayme Waxman • ". . . on being the managing editor of one of the world's most recognizable porn magazines" © 2005 by Lisa Massaro • ". . . on covering the porn beat for the Hollywood trades" © 2005 by Dana Harris • ". . . on launching Playboy Radio" © 2005 by Tiffany Granath and Juli Ashton • ". . . on following in her mother's footsteps to become an erotic photographer" © 2005 by Holly Randall • ". . . on crossing the line to create feminist porn" © 2005 by Tristan Taormino • ". . . on becoming and being a porn star" © 2005 by Tera Patrick • ". . . on directing the hardest of hardcore" © 2005 by Mason • ". . . on transitioning from a performer to a director" © 2005 by Stormy Daniels • ". . . on making porn that's titillating, educational and feminist" © 2005 by Jackie Strano • ". . . on launching reality porn from a woman's perspective and becoming a mother in the process" © 2005 by Shane • ". . . on pioneering the hardcore How To video" © 2005 by Nina Hartley • ". . . on marketing adult content on the Internet" © 2005 by Katy Smith • ". . . on mining the Internet for good adult content" © 2005 by Jane Duvall • ". . . on starting a sexual revolution in the UK through Internet publishing" © 2005 by Emily Dubberley • ". . . on how a longtime interest in vintage porn launched the most unique site on the Internet" © 2005 by Hester Nash • ". . . on learning how to launch the most popular adult Web site from working at a strip club" © 2005 by Danni Ashe • ". . . on being a feminist with a porn site" © 2005 by Joanna Angel • ". . . on taking the amateur porn approach to the web" © 2005 by Seska Lee • ". . . on running an adult specialty store" © 2005 by Sheila Rae • ". . . on helping restructure the Hustler empire" © 2005 by Theresa Flynt • ". . . on helping create the sex toys that make it into your bedroom" © 2005 by Jennifer Martsolf • ". . . on being one fifth of the Club Jenna team" © 2005 by Linda Johnson • ". . . on wearing many different hats behind the scenes, from PR to sales and almost everything in between" © 2005 by Joy King • ". . . on the decision to front an ultra hardcore porn company" © 2005 by Jewel DeNyle • ". . . on promoting some of adult's most recognizable brands" © 2005 by Lainie Speiser • ". . . on lending an artistic eye to the industry" © 2005 by Jodi Marie Lindquist

Library of Congress Cataloging-in-Publication Data is available.

ISBN: 0-7867-1590-1
ISBN-13: 978-0-78671-590-9

Book design by Maria E. Torres
Printed in the United States of America
Distributed by Publishers Group West

CONTENTS

INTRODUCTION · xi
CARLY MILNE

PORN PURVEYORS
THE WOMEN WHO SHAPE WHAT WE CONSUME
BY THEIR MEDIA COVERAGE

LAURA LEU · 1
. . . ON BRINGING PORN INTO THE WORLD OF LAD MAGS.

JILL SIERACKI · 9
. . . ON REVAMPING *PLAYGIRL* MAGAZINE.

VIOLET BLUE · 21
. . . ON EXPERIENCING BOOT CAMP ON THE ROAD
TO BECOMING AN ADULT VIDEO EXPERT.

REGINA LYNN · 31
. . . ON HOW SEX AND TECHNOLOGY COME TOGETHER.

JAYME WAXMAN · 43
. . . ON HELPING DEBUNK THE PERVERT MYTH
SURROUNDING PORN THROUGH MAINSTREAM MEDIA.

LISA MASSARO · 53
. . . ON BEING THE MANAGING EDITOR OF ONE
OF THE WORLD'S MOST RECOGNIZABLE PORN MAGAZINES.

JULI ASHTON AND TIFFANY GRANATH · 59
. . . ON LAUNCHING PLAYBOY RADIO.

DANA HARRIS · 69
. . . ON COVERING THE PORN BEAT FOR THE HOLLYWOOD TRADES.

EROTIC ENVISIONERS

THE WOMEN WHO ENABLE OUR VIEWING HABITS

TRISTAN TAORMINO · 87

. . . ON CROSSING THE LINE TO CREATE FEMINIST PORN.

HOLLY RANDALL · 99

. . . ON FOLLOWING IN HER MOTHER'S FOOTSTEPS
TO BECOME AN EROTIC PHOTOGRAPHER.

TERA PATRICK · 109

. . . ON BECOMING AND BEING A PORN STAR.

MASON · 125

. . . ON DIRECTING THE HARDEST OF HARDCORE.

STORMY DANIELS · 139

. . . ON TRANSITIONING FROM A PERFORMER TO A DIRECTOR.

JACKIE STRANO · 149

. . . ON MAKING PORN THAT'S TITILLATING, EDUCATIONAL, AND FEMINIST.

SHANE · 157

. . . ON LAUNCHING REALITY PORN FROM A WOMAN'S PERSPECTIVE AND
BECOMING A MOTHER IN THE PROCESS.

NINA HARTLEY · 169

. . . ON PIONEERING THE HARDCORE HOW-TO VIDEO.

WANTON WEBMISTRESSES

THE WOMEN WHO CHANGED THE FACE OF ONLINE SMUT

JANE DUVALL · 181

. . . ON MINING THE INTERNET FOR GOOD ADULT CONTENT.

EMILY DUBBERLEY · 189

. . . ON STARTING A SEXUAL REVOLUTION IN THE U.K.
THROUGH INTERNET PUBLISHING.

KATIE SMITH · 199

. . . ON MARKETING ADULT CONTENT ON THE INTERNET.

HESTER NASH · 207

. . . ON HOW A LONGTIME INTEREST IN VINTAGE PORN LAUNCHED
A UNIQUE SITE ON THE INTERNET.

DANNI ASHE · 221

. . . ON LEARNING HOW TO LAUNCH THE MOST POPULAR ADULT WEB SITE
FROM WORKING AT A STRIP CLUB.

JOANNA ANGEL · 233

. . . ON BEING A FEMINIST WITH A PORN SITE.

SESKA LEE · 245

. . . ON TAKING THE AMATEUR PORN APPROACH
TO THE WEB.

SEX SELLERS

THE WOMEN BEHIND THE COMPANIES WE BUY FROM

THERESA FLYNT · 255

. . . ON HELPING RESTRUCTURE THE *HUSTLER* EMPIRE.

LINDA JOHNSON · 263

. . . ON BEING ONE-FIFTH OF THE CLUB JENNA TEAM.

JENNIFER MARTSOLF · 275

. . . ON HELPING CREATE THE SEX TOYS THAT MAKE IT
INTO YOUR BEDROOM.

SHEILA RAE · 289

. . . ON RUNNING AN ADULT SPECIALTY STORE,
BOTH ONLINE AND BRICK-AND-MORTAR.

JOY KING · 295

. . . ON WEARING MANY DIFFERENT HATS BEHIND THE SCENES,
FROM PR TO SALES AND ALMOST EVERYTHING IN BETWEEN.

JEWEL DE'NYLE · 307

. . . ON THE DECISION TO FRONT AN ULTRA HARDCORE PORN COMPANY.

LAINIE SPEISER · 313

. . . ON PROMOTING SOME OF ADULT'S MOST RECOGNIZABLE BRANDS.

JODI MARIE LINDQUIST · 329

. . . ON LENDING AN ARTISTIC EYE TO THE INDUSTRY.

ABOUT THE CONTRIBUTORS · 343

NAKED
AMBITION

INTRODUCTION

"YOU'RE CRAZY," HE SAID TO me, rolling his eyes. "Women don't watch porn."

I'll never forget when one of my good male friends said that to me. I looked at him from across the table that held our lunch and thought about how the previous night I had ordered an entertaining little fuck flick starring Stacy Valentine called *My Funny Valentine* off pay-per-view and watched it while my then beau was sleeping. Usually I would walk down the street to my favorite sex store, Come As You Are, to rent porn for the both of us to enjoy (he was too embarrassed to do it himself), but that night I was feeling lazy. So when my friend said this to me, I was a little stunned. Last I checked I was a woman, and *I* watched porn. So what on earth was he talking about?

"What on earth are you talking about?" I finally asked. "I watch porn!"

He waved his hand dismissively as he dug into his salad. "Yeah, but you're weird."

I couldn't accept that as an answer, and I found it nearly as insulting and short-sighted as his initial declaration. So while I was certainly on my own personal crusade to understand and explore my own sexuality, my friend unwittingly put me on a path that led me to deconstructing my own initial revulsion-turned-interest in porn. And that path led me directly to the heart of the adult industry.

When porn first appeared on the pop culture radar, it was as an underground phenomenon that took over movie theaters in red light districts across the globe. Titles like *Deep Throat, Behind The Green Door, Misty Beethoven,* and *Insatiable* became household names, as did women like Linda Lovelace and Marilyn Chambers. The 1980s brought the home video revolution, and— constantly adapting to new technologies—porn went right along with it, launching a number of powerhouse video companies that furnished the world with smut they could view in the comfort of their own homes. This was also when toy companies as we know them today truly started appearing on the map, bringing "sexual aids" to the masses. And then there were the '90s, which brought along the Internet revolution, another charge led by the adult industry as companies and stars alike flocked to the World Wide Web, some becoming multimillionaires almost overnight. Soon after, the writers followed, bringing forth a batch of sex-positive females whose mandate was to make sexuality and pornography comfortable for everyone. And while the history of the adult industry's meteoric rise to popularity is certainly interesting, it's the women behind it who make it more interesting.

Initially, I was completely perplexed by them.

My own consumption and acceptance of pornography has led me down a long and rocky road, as has my sexuality. When I was a teenager I had a distinct interest in seeing images of naked people getting it on, but my friends thought it was gross and disgusting, therefore I thought it was gross and disgusting too . . . out loud. Internally, I was filled with guilt and shame, wondering what the hell was wrong with me. So when I saw those images peering out over the black shields that were used to hide the content of those magazines in the top row at the newsstand, I felt revulsion and couldn't comprehend what on earth would make a woman want to get involved in such a sleazy and degrading industry. I rationalized that they must have been forced by some overbearing male figure, or were emotionally stunted—or just plain stupid.

A wise person once said to me, "Find your fear, then go there." So, because I feared pornography and my sexuality to such a great degree, when the opportunity arose to enter the porn industry, I took it. I took it because I knew that I wanted to write about it from the inside, although I didn't know what it was that I wanted to say. I knew when I started collecting data for what would eventually become a book that I wanted to show a cross-section of my experiences, and I expected that my experiences would be bad based on all the propaganda I had been fed over the years. What I didn't expect was that I would meet a multitude of smart, strong, and driven women—in front of, behind, and not having anything to do with the camera at all—who challenged my thinking and forced me to grow spiritually as well as sexually.

I learned that in the beginning, women were little more than the eye candy that helped drive the eyeballs to a product—you saw them in adult magazines, on box covers, and naked on your TV screen, and for the most part they answered to men. But as porn evolved with the times in terms of technology and consumer demand, it also encouraged more sexual equality both in front of and behind the cameras. Not only are the female performers taking charge of their careers, but women are running the companies people purchase movies from, opening stores that porn purveyors patronize, and writing thoughtful, analytical commentary on America's most favorite pastime since baseball. And this generation of women in and around the adult industry is helping shape and change society's views on sexuality.

For well over a decade now, women sex writers and pornographers have brought strong women to pornography and pornography to strong women, changing the ways we look at both pornography and women's thoughts on it. Women such as Susie Bright and Annie Sprinkle helped open the adult film field to other women, including women viewers, allowing for a new interpretation of what's erotic and what's taboo. This first wave of women pornographers led to a cultural revolution in the 1990s, when younger women took inspiration from the sex pioneers of the 1970s and '80s, thereby setting off a new wave of women pornographers that reaches all the way up to today.

No book before has charted the evolution of this body of work, much less in the voices of those women responsible for it. Thus, *Naked Ambition* charts this course by inviting thirty-one of the leading women involved in adult entertainment and the proliferation of it to share their ideas, experiences, histories, and passions so that we might better understand the profound influence that porn—a social force that feminists and others on the left for a generation espoused as dangerous and degrading to women—had in helping a newer, younger generation of women claim their sexual selves on their own terms.

Carly Milne
Los Angeles, California
May 2005

PORN PURVEYORS

THE WOMEN WHO SHAPE WHAT WE CONSUME BY THEIR MEDIA COVERAGE

LAURA LEU

MY JOB IS JUST LIKE any other in corporate America. All day, I sit at a cluttered desk in front of a computer slathered with Post-It notes and struggle to get work done because the phone keeps—

Ring, ring.

"Hello, this is *Stuff* magazine, Laura Leu speaking."

"Hey, Laura. It's Dylan with Doc Johnson Toys. I'm just checking to make sure you received the shipment of products we sent you and wondered whether you could fit the Jenna Jameson pussy mold into your section."

Oh, yeah, and I have a porn star's vagina stashed in my desk drawer. So maybe my job as a sex writer and editor at a national men's magazine doesn't quite fit into corporate American standards. After all, my computer's home page is set to NewsForPerverts.com. Post-It notes are scribbled with "Call guy about vibrating nipple clamps." And that clutter on my desk consists of photos of half-naked women wanting to grace the pages of *Stuff* magazine. And then there's the massive amount of porn I receive. S&M, golden showers, girl-on-girl, girl-on-girl-on-girl-on-guy . . . you name it, and it's in a box under my desk—right next to the dildos and butt plugs.

When I tell people about my job and the perks that come with it, I am inevitably asked one of two questions: 1) Can I have your porn? Or 2) How did you prepare for a job where you work closely with a misogynistic industry that objectifies women as sexual play toys? To which I respond: 1) Sure. And 2) I just went to college. For it was in college that two important milestones occurred: I received a degree in journalism, and I was introduced to the Worst Porn Ever. That might not seem like sufficient preparation, but allow me explain.

At the tender age of twenty-two, when I was a senior at the University of Wisconsin (and a porn neophyte), I was bar-hopping with my roommates when my friend Menia wobbled over to the curb and picked something up.

"Look what I found!" she squealed, as excited as Veruca Salt discovering her golden ticket to Willy Wonka's chocolate factory. There, in the impeccably clean hands Menia used to pray with every night, was a movie called *Finger My Ass*. The box was covered with naked girls. The naked girls were covered with semen. And the semen was covered with taglines like "Watch these cum-loving sluts get their assholes pounded by huge cocks." How perfectly appropriate that it was found in a gutter.

That night, my four roomies and I slid *Finger My Ass* into the VCR and giggled and *eww*'d our way through forty-five minutes of raunchy, low-quality porn. There were things my virgin eyes had never seen before: giant anal beads, vaginas at *that* angle, and ugly people fucking even uglier people. But the climax (and a multiple one, at that) was the wedding-slash-orgy scene circa 1970, complete with a not-very-blushing bride screwing five groomsmen, bridesmaids eating wedding cake off each other's roly-poly bodies, and more bush than in the last sixteen years of presidential elections. When the credits finally rolled, my mouth was as agape as those cum-loving sluts' assholes.

Finger My Ass popped my porno cherry and, in doing so,

created such low expectations that any adult film in comparison would have looked like *The Sound of Music*. So when I became the new sex scribe at *Stuff* a few years later, I felt prepared for any smut movie thrown my way. And there were certainly a lot of them. The production companies that sent them drooled at the thought of being reviewed in a mainstream magazine, but the truth is, it rarely happened at *Stuff*. Even though horny twenty-something-year-old guys make up the bulk of our audience, we rely on celebrities to appear in the magazine and advertisers to buy our pages, and neither would want to be associated with such a sexually explicit form of entertainment.

Still, I knew it was something we couldn't ignore. The porn industry was exploding—and not just on young starlets' faces. Seymour Butts had his own TV show and Ron Jeremy was speaking at universities. And when, pray tell, was the last time you heard someone ask, "Jenna *Who?*" It was evident that porn had become more than a dirty movie you hid between the couch cushions whenever company came over. In fact, all I needed was a weekend in Manhattan to realize that pornography had gone from taboo to trendy. The proof was in my journal:

> Friday night, Downtown: Got retarded drunk at Pop Burger, a hip new bar in the Meat-Packing District that plays vintage porn on plasma screens. There was also a curtained booth, which looked like a photo booth, but instead of a camera, there was a small TV screen showing people doing the nasty.

> Saturday afternoon, Midtown: Checked out the pornography exhibit at the Museum of Sex. It was a nice change to see women as they were when adult film first started appearing in 1907 (i.e., not full of laxatives and silicone).

> Sunday morning, Uptown: Read the *New York Times* while sipping my latte amongst debutantes and ladies who lunch at an Upper East Side café. I was the only woman there without a string of pearls and a sweater tied around my shoulders.

You could say the last entry isn't very pornographic, but you can bet that under each of those uptown girls' khakis was a small, skinny strip of perfectly coifed pubic hair. Now how do you think that style came into vogue?

With this realization that porn was more than just masturbatory fodder, that it was trendy and something all the cool kids were doing, I decided that maybe it was worthy for *Stuff*. I brought that notion to my boss along with a story idea: I wanted to be an extra in an adult movie and write about the people, procedures, and porking that happens on the set, and the camaraderie that goes on behind it. It'd be like a documentary, I told him, only in print form. After a brief moment of hesitation, either from fear or shock, he gave my fuckumentary the green light.

"Oh, heavens to Betsy!" my mom cried in true church-lady fashion when I told her I was about to make my X-rated debut in Wicked Pictures' *Lover's Lane*.

"Mom, relax. I'm not actually having sex in it. I'm playing the crime-scene photographer—it's a non-sex role, and I'll be fully clothed," I assured her.

"Don't you let them make you drink alcohol or do drugs, Laura Ann," she pleaded. "Pornographic movie sets are littered with those kinds of hallucinogens, you know."

I wish my mother had been right, because I really could have used a drink when I arrived on set at that day. But the production company prohibited Fucking While Intoxicated, and thus, any drugs or alcohol on set. Not that I needed it—my nerves were calmed nonalcoholically when I met the gracious cast and crew, who welcomed me with open arms. (Conversely, I was sent off with open legs when I left during the last sex scene twelve hours later.) My scene, the first one that day, featured eight lines of dialogue and took over an hour to film. I managed to get through it and played the best crime-scene photographer in the history of adult cinematography (or so I like to think). Not that anyone would notice, since people will fast-forward through it to get to the humping parts anyway.

It was a strange thing, being on the set of a porno. Not strange as in, "Wow, I'm surrounded by butts and boobies and boning, oh my!" More like, "Wow, I'm on the set of a porn, and it's about as sexually charged as a family reunion." I guess I had certain expectations: of the actresses, being depressed shells of people who felt like their vaginas were all they had to offer; of the all-male crew, walking around with permawood, swapping sex tips like muffin recipes. But I was wrong. The actresses (Devinn Lane, Jessica Drake, and Kimberly Kane, to name three) were strong, bright businesswomen, who, unless they were in a scene giving a rim job, seemed more like girls next door than girls gone wild. And the crew was friendly, but not in that I-wanna-get-in-your-pants sort of way. When the cameras weren't rolling, they'd gather around the proverbial water cooler and gab about politics, family, and sports. But as soon as I'd try to interject sex talk, they'd clam up faster than New England chowder. Because, as it turns out, they weren't oversexed; they were just over sex.

Sex is business for these people, after all. For the same reasons plumbers don't want to sit around during their off-time discussing how to fix a drippy faucet, pornographers don't want to chit-chat about the mechanics of making a woman squirt. And even during the sex scenes, the enthusiasm of the crew was equivalent to that of students in a geometry class. I remember one particular scene where a female star ordered her male counterpart to go to third base with her. Or as she eloquently put it:

"Stick your fingers in my tight, little pussy and wiggle them around." Right after she barked her command, one of the lighting gaffers turned to me, rolled his eyes and whispered, "No girl would *ever* say that in real life." That's why the crew was good at what they did: they were just jaded enough to not let an erection get in the way of the job at hand.

When I left the porn set that day, I was a different person than when I arrived. A porn star, for one. But I also learned a few important lessons along the way:

1) Porn stars are just like regular people—only a little stickier.
2) You can have sex when you have your period as long as you have a make-up sponge or ice-cold douche handy.
3) It is possible to have too much of a good thing.

Those three points were summed up nicely in the thirteen hundred or so words I submitted to my editor. It covered the ups and down, the ins and outs, the tops and bottoms, and everything in between. Some of it was edited out, deemed—ironically—too pornographic. There were certain things I fought for, like the war story recounted by a porn star turned makeup artist from when she first started out in the biz. Her story involved a lesbian anal scene with a dildo attached to an electric drill. Long story short: the dildo recipient didn't get an enema beforehand and shit sprayed everywhere. I won the battle to keep it in, as long as I agreed to tone it down.

As a sex writer, toning it down is something I've had to deal with a lot—not just in my articles, but in everyday life. Some-times, after being at work all day writing about oral-sex etiquette, I'll go to a dinner party and forget that it's not polite to talk about cunnilingus in front of strangers. I've absorbed so much sex knowledge over my career that I'm certain I've grown a new area in my brain reserved specifically for sex. I'm not a pervert or a nympho, but as an occupational hazard, I have a dirty mind and I can't help it. When a friend tells me she's going to get a facial, I immediately think bukkake. When I see a hamster, my mind flashes to felching. One time, during a trip home to visit my family in Wisconsin, my jacket was dirty and my mom told me, "You look like a DP."

"I look like a double penetration?" I asked, confused.

"No, a displaced person," she said. "What's double penetration?"

"It's a term for when a girl is having sex with two guys and they penetrate each of her orifices at the same time, Mom."

"Oh, heavens to Betsy, Laura Ann! I'm taking you to church."

Oh, great, I thought. *On my knees again . . .*

The final lesson? You can take the girl out of Wisconsin, but you can't bring the porn back with her.

JILL SIERACKI

I'LL ADMIT IT—BEFORE I was asked to contribute to this book, I never really thought of myself as a sex pioneer, educator, or role model. I was just a creative woman who had stumbled into what many others consider a pretty interesting nine-to-five. However, as I sit here writing about what I do over those eight (which often seems more like 24) hours each day, I do feel pretty lucky. Working at *Playgirl* magazine has been the most rewarding, exhausting, inspiring, confusing, and motivating experience of my life.

Unlike many of the women who dreamed of working in the adult industry, I never had the goal of working at *Playgirl*. To be honest, I don't remember ever buying a *Playgirl* until I purchased one before my interview. I assume I had. After all, I lived in a sorority house in college and there was a tradition of "dirty" cards and gifts for graduating seniors, but I can't recall any specific issues, or models for that matter. When I graduated from the University of West Virginia with my advertising degree, I imagined moving to New York to write the next "Where's the beef?" or "Can you hear me now?" memorable tagline for whatever was the hot soda, shoe, or shampoo of the moment.

I did come to the "city" (as New Yorkers refer to it, as if it's the only city on earth) about a year after graduation, and accepted a position at a fairly prestigious book publisher. At the time, I didn't really consider myself much of a writer, and if I couldn't create the next Great American Novel, maybe I could discover it and put it on bookshelves, happily taking my accolades on the acknowledgments page. Later, I moved into magazine publishing, becoming an editorial assistant at the senior of the Seven Sisters, *Good Housekeeping*. I loved it. I was making more money and working for the entertainment editor. She was young and cool, and a force to be around. I wanted to be her. The occasions where I picked up the phone to hear Judge Judy or Lorraine Bracco's voice was just the icing.

However, I was a little older and certainly more ambitious than the other assistants. I wanted to write. I pitched story ideas and watched as they were handed off to more senior editors. I was separated from the entertainment editor because we "got along too well." I was bored and I wanted more.

One afternoon, as I joke, I wrote a snarky memo to the editors from their assistants, chiding them on their half-empty yogurt cups stinking up the fridge, their habit of emptying the candy jar and leaving it to the assistants to fill, and their lack of ability to master office machinery. And then, after all my coworkers had a good laugh, I—perhaps a tad impetuously—sent it to an industry Web site, where it quickly took on a life of its own. The next morning, it was the main headline on the Web site. I was fired. The infamous "Page Six" of the *New York Post* ran it as their banner item on my first morning of unemployment.

I'll admit that it was a rude and a foolish thing to write and an even more foolish thing to send it out into cyberspace, but all over New York, assistants were being treated to bagels from their bosses and being asked to do things "please," and for that, I'm not sorry. (In fact, three years later, a girl I had just met at a party of publishing people knew my name, shook my hand, and told me about how she keeps the article on her fridge and sends it to other frustrated media types.)

However, minor celebrity doesn't pay your rent, so I spent the summer freelancing, and lounging on Rockaway Beach. If I weren't so uptight, I would have to say that it was my best summer in New York. But really, I was sweating running out of money, and fearing I would never find another job, and having to return home to Pittsburgh and start again from scratch. Anyone who knows me knows I'd rather eat bugs on *Fear Factor* than admit I had failed at something. I'm half Polish and half Sicilian, a combination that equals one hundred percent stubborn.

At the same time, my friend Rachael's giftware magazine was about to fold. We started job hunting together. Mediabistro, the *New York Times*, Hot Jobs—we combed them all, and if you saw something that the other could be interested in, you passed it along.

One afternoon, Rachael forwarded me a listing from Monster.com. It was for an associate editor position (a step up from where I had been). I don't remember the exact wording other than "must be comfortable with nudity."

"Who would want this job???" Rachael wrote. Well, I'd been unemployed for nearly three months and I needed to get back into the game.

"I would!" I answered. The fact that I absolutely was *not* comfortable with nudity was just a speed bump. I was going to need to suck it up and get over it.

I sent in my résumé with an unconventional cover letter: I interviewed myself in the same style that *Playgirl* was interviewing their female celebs. I confessed my prior sins, but put a positive spin on them. I was sassy, creative—I was a *Playgirl*!

The interview and writing test are all kind of a blur, but I remember I was confident. The weekend after my first interview, I was heading home to Pittsburgh for my brother's twenty-first birthday.

"Adam, don't tell Mom and Dad, but I think I got a job. At *Play-girl*," I told him. And like good little brothers do, he told everyone. Starting with my parents. I was waiting for the bomb to drop. "Does it pay well?" they wanted to know. "Well, as long as you've got a job."

My dad thought it was hysterical. I couldn't believe they were so supportive.

At dinner that night, Adam told the rest of our friends. Of course, they thought it was awesome. "How's it feel—four years of college and your daughter works in porn?" one guy asked my dad. Everyone laughed and I felt relieved. After all, it was just a job to get me moving in the right direction. I wasn't actually going to stay there.

That was three years ago. I started out doing book, Web site, and adult movie reviews. My first real assignment was a phone interview with the December 2002 Centerfold. I was so embarrassed, and he was equally shy. After all, he knew I was staring at pictures of him naked while asking him questions about what turns him on and the length of his penis.

My first celeb interview was Jim Brickman. (Jim, if you're reading this, I apologize, but when I walked into that room, I'd never even heard of you.) But we talked about his CD and his concert tours, and I asked him if he'd ever had sex on a piano like they did in *Pretty Woman*. He was great, answered all my questions, and had a voice like warm brandy. Smooth, sexy, with gorgeous eyes. *I can't believe this is my job!* I thought. While answering one question, Jim talked about how he had to consider his tour schedule before he asked a woman out on a date. But the way he paused, I thought he was asking me out on a date. I panicked, forgot what he was saying, forgot what I was saying, debating if I would say yes or no. However, once he continued on with his story about bunking with Donny Osmond, I realized my mistake. I nearly burst out laughing; thank god I didn't, because he would really have thought I was a nut.

One of my favorite parts of my job is attending book parties and press events. It's fun talking to people and watching their reactions when you say you work at *Playgirl*. But at one of these events, I was met with the harsh reality of where I worked. It was at a Santa-themed book party in Chelsea. (It's considered Manhattan's "gay" neighborhood, but it has some of the best shopping and restaurants, so whatever you want to call it, I don't care. I love everything about the area.) Two former *Playgirl* models were there dressed in fuzzy red shorts and Santa hats, and women would sit on their laps and get a Polaroid taken.

Over the course of the night, I started chatting with some of the other guests, who just so happened to be gay men. "Wow, I can't believe you're actually a woman," one guy told me. "I always assumed it was gay men working there and they just used fake female names to hide it."

It was a quip I had heard before. Your magazine has a penis in it, what woman would want to see that? Only gay men want to see other naked men. And truthfully, when I had started at the magazine, I hadn't particularly wanted to see penises, let alone on a daily basis, but now, I was proud of the magazine I was working for. I was helping women have a fun fantasy life. If men can have a selection of dirty magazines, why can't women have something for themselves?

It's not the same thing, people insisted.

A few weeks later, I was at a New Year's Eve party and a single guy at the party seemed insistent on asking me every question he could about my job. "Do you think the reason you're single is because men are intimidated by your job?" I had never thought about it. Why would they be? It's not like I'm sleeping with the models, I'm just interviewing them. Truthfully, any man who would be intimidated by an 8x10, 98-page glossy magazine isn't exactly the knight in shining armor I dreamed of, but who the hell was this guy to insinuate it was either my job or coupledom?

Then he started polling all the other guests: Would you date a girl who worked for *Playgirl*?

"Sure, but I wouldn't bring you home to meet my mom," one guy answered.

Three. Two. One. Happy New Year.

I felt dirty, like what I was doing was wrong. My friends loved the vibrators, chick lit books, porn movies, and copies of *Playgirl* I brought them, but none of them said they would ever *buy* my magazine. I was starting to think that women actually didn't want a magazine like *Playgirl*. Maybe they were fed up with the penises attached to the men they already had at home, so why would they spend five bucks every month for an entire collection of them? Was I forcing on women a magazine that they didn't really want? Sure, *Playgirl* had had its peaks and valleys—like the high times in the '70s when it was Girl Power and equal sex for the sexes, and James Caan, John Travolta, and Paul McCartney were cover guys.

Or the '90s, when celebs like Wesley Snipes granted exclusive interviews. Our circulation was huge, we sponsored parties, and the editors went overseas to scout models. But maybe now was a "been there, done that" time. Women were still referring to *The Rules* and looking to please their men in bed. Did they really not care about their own satisfaction? Shows like *Sex and the City* were fun to watch, but no one actually wanted to be those girls.

But the soaring sales of the Rabbit after that one particular *Sex and the City* episode gave me hope. Women did want good sex—not just for their men, but for themselves! And *Playgirl* has a place in that. It's just a matter of finding it.

Not to get too far off the subject, but I have to share my own Rabbit story. About six months after starting at *Playgirl,* I started dating my current boyfriend, also an editor of an adult magazine. For my birthday, we were going to New Orleans, our first romantic trip together. We packed the Rabbit. But I didn't want

to have to face security for a vibrating bag, so I packed the batteries in my suitcase, and the actual "pink pleasure" in my
boyfriend's suitcase, wrapped securely in a plastic grocery bag.

In New Orleans, we got to our hotel and went to change
clothes. We open our luggage and it was a disaster. My makeup
bag was dumped out, our clothes were no longer folded, my eye-
glasses and his sunglasses were gone, and mixed in with my
boyfriend's things was a torn plastic bag.

"Honey, what did we have in here?" he asked. And I honestly
couldn't remember. Shampoo? Sun block? Oh my god, the
Rabbit!

I was pissed. I called the airline to report the missing items.
Thankfully, I got a woman on the phone. I told her about our
tossed suitcases, reported our missing glasses, and then told her
my vibrator had also been stolen.

"Your what?" she asked.

"My vibrator." I told her how my boyfriend and I were on our
first romantic vacation and that it's the Rabbit, like from *Sex and
the City*. The Rabbit.

"I totally understand," she commiserated.

She logged all our missing items into her computer, sent us the
paperwork, and Continental Airlines bought me a new vibrator.

So now you know about me, but really, what you're interested
in is what it's like to actually work at *Playgirl*. Fair enough.
Imagine a world where women actually see each other as team-
mates, not competition. Where there's a friend to tell you your
butt looks great in jeans, you openly discuss who's hot or not,
chocolate is readily available, and you never have some idiot guy
in the next cubicle eavesdropping on your "my boyfriend is
great/a jerk/a figment of my imagination/hung like a horse" conversations. Welcome to the offices of *Playgirl*.

I'd like to tell you that we have a vast corporation of women
working tirelessly to put out *Playgirl* month after month. That we

sit in a high-rise office in the latest designer fashions, or cruise the clubs in South Beach looking for the next Centerfold. That there are writers and editors and photographers coming in and out of our studios while shirtless hunks stand by at our beck and call.

I'd like to tell you that. But I'd be lying. Actually, there are just four of us on staff. My associate editor—now the editor in chief— and I writing/editing/conceptualizing the editorial, and two extremely talented and highly overworked designers, Diane and Dana, stylizing the pages. We're all pretty much blue jeans kind of girls. And our offices are on the eighth floor, just above National Public Radio, and just below a slew of law offices. No one has ever been shirtless.

I don't want to crush anyone's fantasy about what it's like being at *Playgirl,* because it truly is an amazing job. And another one of the things I love most about working for this magazine is the personal connection we have with our readers. If you call to look up the date of a past issue, either Michele or I will be taking your call. Write us a letter or send an e-mail, we all read it. Send in your picture to model, it's Diane or Dana sending you the guidelines. And I think this close contact with the people who read *Playgirl* is what has shaped it, and is continually shaping it, into the new and improved publication we're putting on newsstands today. We're not doing some sort of fanzine. We don't refer to massive online polls or what trend forecasters think women want to read about—we get it right from readers.

At the beginning of 2005 we massively redesigned *Playgirl.* The magazine was turning thirty-three that year and we had run into a bit of a format rut. Big, muscle-bound hunks, orgasm article, relationship article, erotic fiction—ta-da! But we had a core group of readers who had been subscribing for years, so no one had really felt the need to change anything. Then a few things happened.

First, we got word that *Playgirl* was launching a television channel, Playgirl TV, featuring woman-targeted adult programming (meaning softer porn: none of that spit-rainbow, tacky outfits/plots/dialogue, way-too-close close-up shots that none of us really want to see). There would be cross-promotion between the magazine and the television channel. We started writing press kits and voice-overs, and screening already existing films, while another team started shooting original footage.

To be honest, from a women's perspective, the first round wasn't all we had hoped and dreamed. Then a new team took over Playgirl TV and we were left to our own devices to run the magazine. And so we starting changing everything.

We added articles on women's health, something we had never done before. After all, we were advocating having good sex, so we should tell you what's going on with your body once you do have sex and the reasons you should be safe. We started featuring all types of men. "Real Men" was our most popular section, home snapshots of women's boyfriends naked—and very few of them had perfect bodies. Plus, none of us were sleeping with a gigantic muscleman, so we figured it was time to give the Above-Average Joe his layout. We threw away every neon Pantone chip we had. Our covers used to blend in with the men's adult magazines on the newsstands, with their neon pink headlines shouting double entendres at you from our cover. I don't know about you, but I haven't owned anything neon colored since 1984.

And we started treating both our readers and ourselves with a little more intelligence. You could read the "What's he thinking when he sees you naked?" article time and time again in those other women's magazines. (P.S. He's thinking—woo hoo! Naked woman! There, I just saved you $4.99.) Instead, we wanted to give you articles on why you need to have safe sex, how to love your body and find pleasure for yourself as well as your partner, and that the G-spot ain't all you thought it was supposed to be. (In fact, our health columnists are even working on a study to prove it doesn't really exist. Stay tuned, and in the meantime, enjoy clitoral orgasms for the wonderfully blissful thing that they are.) Our favorite new motto became "Smart is sexy."

As for the photographs of penises—yes, they're still there. But from listening to you (who just proved what we knew all along), women love the whole man, not just his penis. We're giving you a little more of the man. After all, 99 percent of the arousal process is the slow reveal, and the discovery process is . . . wow. Women are just as visual as men, but you need to appeal to our minds, not just our bodies.

The new issues are beautiful, and the letters from our readers tell us that people (both women and gay men) are putting the magazine on their coffee tables again. We feel better about ourselves putting out the *Playgirl* we do today, and people are responding. Women appreciate the sexy subtlety and actually do read the articles. Celebs are saying yes to interviews. It's a brand-new day. They say life begins at forty, but for us, it's starting anew at thirty-three.

Does the work ever turn me on? Yes, you bet. But not the pictures so much anymore. It's the erotic fiction our readers send in. It's the most time-consuming to edit and select, but it's by far one of my favorite sections in *Playgirl*. I don't know whether it's because I'm a woman or because I love words so much, but I'd rather someone set the stage for me and let me paint the picture. When I'm reading about the touching, kissing, caressing, I can almost imagine the feeling in my mind, and that's so much more erotic to me than seeing it being done. And some of the things our readers create are things I never would have thought of. But damn, am I glad they did.

Twenty years from now, I don't think anyone's going to remember my name like an Annie Sprinkle. However, I hope they still know *Playgirl*. I think times are changing again, and even in the face of "family values" and all the other ways politicians are trying to stuff religion down our throats while leading amoral lives themselves (read Jessica Cutler's *The Washingtonienne*—you'll see), people are still going to have sex. And if you're going to have sex, it should be good sex. Women will still fantasize, whether it's about the UPS guy or someone they knew in college, or even an erotic scenario they want to play out with their husband, boyfriend, or one-night stand.

I'm positive there is a place for *Playgirl* in all that. I'd like to think we're the spice in women's sex lives. Not a necessary ingredient, but a pleasure to have included. I want to think that the men we choose to feature and the articles we write give you a little extra naughtiness that makes you feel sexier for having read that issue. That it instills in women a sense of confidence that you can be a great lover, whether you're with your first partner or your fifty-first, and no matter what the number, that's OK too.

Men are experienced, women are sluts. It's too difficult to make a woman climax. Lingerie is only for women who look like lingerie models. A picture of a naked man is only for a gay man— it's all bullshit, if you ask me. I think the bedroom is the one place we're all on a level playing field. While *Playgirl* has always reflected these truths, we're just doing it better in our "dirty thirties." And I'm proud to be a "playgirl" who's gotten comfortable with nudity, is smarter about what's sexy, a little more adventurous than I was three years ago, and who feels I am just getting better with age.

See you on the newsstand.

VIOLET BLUE

. . . ON EXPERIENCING BOOT CAMP ON THE ROAD TO BECOMING
AN ADULT VIDEO EXPERT.

IN EARLY 1997, DURING WHAT was another long stretch of sexlessness in a now-defunct long-term relationship, I picked up a copy of an adult video catalog. I was living in a shoddy San Francisco neighborhood lovingly called the Goth Ghetto in reference to the large number of poor, black-clad denizens, and my roommates consisted of a stripper, a dominatrix, and a sexually-explicit performance artist. According to everyone around me, I was a modern girl—sexually open-minded and in a hot relationship where I had lots of hot sex all the time.

Alone late one afternoon, I browsed the porn catalog I had purchased for a dollar at a local women-run sex-toy store. The store had been a homegrown boutique-style shop with a colorful paint job, and hand-written reviews of the products on the shelves, and was known as a "clean, well-lighted place" for women to shop for sex products. There were many racks of adult videos. I was intrigued, and visited these racks often, but I hadn't brought anything home. It was a new world, full of promise and excitement.

I knew better about porn. I had watched a few porn videos before with boyfriends. Either they rented and brought the tapes home, or we ventured past the Western-style "adults only" doors together and did our best to make out the tiny pictures on the box covers, looking for even a hint of what we hoped to see. And no matter what, when we got all set in front of the TV with lube in hand, they were almost always bad. Really bad. Worse than made-for-TV movies, worse than art school movies your friends make.

But the catalog I got at the women-run store held a promise: handpicked videos from cultured, sex-happy female reviewers. Savvy selections by women like me, or at least women who hired punk chicks who could smilingly sell a dildo to women like me. The store featured porn directed by women, ostensibly created for women viewers. The catalog fed my fantasies of better sex—a better life—with videos described as having "high production values," "excellent plot," and "good-natured, unrestrained sex fests."

It left me believing that with a little guidance, porn could be good, and that it had the power to resurrect the dead.

Taking their advice I brought home tape after tape of grunting and sweating performers, and although once in a while I caught a glimpse of sexuality that turned my crank, the cornucopia of cartoonish porn stars, overstuffed and underfed starlets, and soft-focus "feminist porn" was clearly not the type of sex girls like me were having. Or at least wanted to have. Or wanted to see. Everything looked like it was from the 1980s, even the brand-new titles, and most especially the sex acts. It all seemed like it was for older women and men to watch. Much older. People who, though they might even be "feminist," still think sex is "dirty." No one ever told me what to think about porn before this, good or bad. But I was disappointed because I just wanted porn to look like real sex in the modern era. I wondered if this, the curated collection which now had me even more sexually depressed, was as good as it was ever going to get.

"Don't take it too hard," my stripper roommate told me after I confided my porn-watching woes, combing out the peroxide blonde wig she wore to cover her pink hair when she danced at the club. "Like, I've never seen a good porno. Unless you think 'good' means Miami Barbies or New Age hippies, and the same five or six gross old men in every video."

And not by coincidence, about a year later I found myself working in the very store I'd purchased the catalog from. I discovered the store's cache of adult video industry magazines and pored over the lurid, graphic pictures on my breaks. I was shocked by the photos, turned on by the range of sexuality presented (albeit a narrow one), excited by the women directors, disappointed by the female reviewers parroting the men around them, fired up by the ignorance about female pleasure, and appalled by the awful writing. I couldn't put it down. And while my employer had mandatory sex education training classes and a required reading list, I felt it my duty to go beyond the requirements for porn watching. With free rentals at the sex shop, I dug in and brought home as many VHS tapes as would fit in my motorcycle bag. I even saw a few good films at last. Though I sometimes found myself thinking, "I should get some porn to jack off to," forgetting that I was already watching a porn video.

My interest in porn and my reputation as a local 'zine writer landed me a job advancement; I became the company's porn reviewer. The problem was, the women who wrote the reviews up till then were the kind of people who wrote letters to porn directors about facial ejaculation being demeaning to women, urging them to stop this "humiliating" practice. These women were my new bosses.

I felt a quiet wave of shame roll over me whenever I found myself enjoying this activity onscreen; then I felt indignation for being shamed by other women about my sexuality, especially women who were supposed to be in the nonshaming corner womens sexuality. In no time, I was at odds with them. They wouldn't give me a desk or a computer. They were in charge of the department's payroll, and elected to pay me less than the hourly wage advertised for the position. I had never considered that being a young, female porn reviewer in a pro-woman, pro-sex environment would feel like accidentally walking into a gay bathhouse and not having a penis. I also had no idea how cruel women could be to one another until I started my job as a porn reviewer in an office full of "sex-positive" women. I had started out on a racy quest to find hot porn for myself and my boyfriends—and my other girlfriends too. Instead, I had entered boot camp for the female ego.

My first year was a battle. In fact, every year was a battle, and it stretched far beyond the borders of my desk job. Everyone in the adult business had an opinion about "what women like" in porn. But the more I talked to female (and male) consumers in the retail stores and in online forums and message boards, the more I realized that the porn industry was providing only a small slice of what both women and men wanted to see, and it wasn't as different between the genders as everyone thought. Women didn't want it softened, and men didn't want it dumbed down. No one wanted what they were getting.

But money and dogma will make any industry blind. The feminists in my office were pro-porn, but anti–male sexuality. The industry was pro-porn, but ambivalent about female pleasure (fakers don't count). The media in the outside world was anti-porn, unless they wanted ratings. Conventional feminist thinking that porn degrades women informed culture in the 1970s, and most people grow up thinking it's true, without understanding what that even means, or experiencing porn for themselves. Across the board, everyone seemed to take porn really seriously, while never really taking the consumer seriously at all. All of these attitudes somehow managed to show in every porn video I watched, whether it was an industry formula, Barbie-goes-though-the-motions video, or a female-directed, no-male-ejaculation video. I didn't fit in anywhere, but there were a lot of people like me. There was no consumer advocacy, just a war of ideology.

When you just want to jack off, all of this is enough to make a girl lose her boner. Amazingly, even though I was watching porn every day, I was finding porn that made me have to hit "pause" and run to get a vibrator. I thrilled to being able to (often accidentally) find authentic female orgasms and female ejaculations that had me gripping my thighs together in pleasurable erotic empathy. I saw passionate blow jobs that made my mouth water with envy. I watched pairs of women and men tear each other's clothes off with a passion that startled me. I watched films with gorgeous cinematography, natural lighting, and beautiful real people as performers, and a whole host of independent porn that blew my mind. Film noir porn, playful European porn, intelligently staged voyeur porn that aroused and inspired me. I still couldn't find any good bisexual porn or porn that doesn't see male anal penetration as "gay" or perverted, but I figured that eventually the high market demand would win out over old-school porn's puritanical perceptions of sexuality. After all, with around twelve thousand titles released a year, there was always hope.

In no time, my passionate porn reviews brought me much attention. Although the old-school women in my office disliked me for this, the salespeople in the stores were thrilled. The rest of the porn industry pretended that I, my company, and others like it, didn't exist.

My porn review Web site was popular, fan mail rolled in, and I got marriage proposals from three-hundred-pound Elvis impersonators. I waged a personal war on overused words like "nubs," spellings like "cum," and phrases like "a pop in the pooper." I made lots of friends on the fringes of the mainstream porn business, and some friends that weren't on the fringes at all. Well-known female porn directors sought my friendship, as did a few acclaimed female performers. I was being interviewed by cable news stations and glossy magazines about being a young female porn reviewer, and before I became completely deluged I wrote three porn columns that covered topics like awful porn music and porn recommendations for first-time viewers.

I was offered a book deal. And then several. I didn't know it, but book publishers had watched my writing for quite a while. They'd been using my quotes on book covers to promote their own sex books and keeping an eye on me. One afternoon I got a call at my desk for an offer of dinner from a well-known sex publisher, and that evening, I was asked if I had any ideas for books. Of course I did; having watched closely the adult book and porn industry and commenting on it for years, the idea of explaining sex and porn to people in practical, insightful, nonjudgmental, and exciting ways had become like little puzzles my brain was constantly trying to solve. I had lots of ideas: smart erotica for het couples, hip guides for oral sex, a porn primer for people like me, and more.

My first book *The Ultimate Guide to Cunnilingus* sold out within the first month; I couldn't believe it. The sales were off the charts, making me feel less like I was in a dream and more like I was totally awake. Intuition: correct. During all of this, I kept reviewing porn, and preparing for the book I'd wanted to write for half a decade.

I began work on an adult movie review guide, a book that would share everything I'd learned for five years as a reviewer, and let others—especially women—put it to some good use: Presenting porn without sexual shame. Showing that liking porn is a healthy way to experience masturbation. Showing that degradation is in the eye of the beholder. Pointing out porn's homophobic tendencies so viewers could decide for themselves what works for them. Taking a stand on the racism behind the lily-white porn world that typically sees black performers in an "interracial" context. Explaining the many genres, offering history to make sense of porn's genres and formulas—and hoping to begin a dialogue that could someday having this huge industry create porn that had what viewers might see as authenticity. I wanted to set up a challenge to anti-porn pundits and points of view by creating a wealth of viewers armed with self-knowledge about porn's positive effects on their sexuality, by beginning the breakdown of cultural myths about porn's degradation of women and its mythical ability to cause rape and child molestation, and to create "porn addicts." I felt that the more people—especially women—knew the truth about what porn really could and couldn't do to us, the less power people who perpetuated these myths would have a little less power over our freedom of choice. And our sexuality.

Although I had been watching porn every day for my desk job, writing a book meant that I now I had to watch it at night too. I joined more online forums and posted questionnaires and polls. Meanwhile friends working in porn stores gave me free rental memberships all over San Francisco. I visited porn shops in other states, in hick towns where my black clothing alone attracted stares. I joined online DVD porn rental sites. I needed firsthand knowledge of not only the viewing experience, but also the physical experiences that readers and viewers would have while looking for titles. I set to work in earnest. I had to watch it all, and that meant titles I would never watch for myself, or for my day job. My VCR gave out, my DVD player got a workout. My fast-forward button begged for mercy. My libido went on vacation but returned during nice weather for a few sporadic, porn-inspired visits.

Some things I saw made me feel like the Pollyanna of porn, and clouded the path to my goals. I watched a woman get fucked up the ass with a baseball bat. She seemed to like it. I watched gangbangs where the female performer was in too much genital pain and swelling to continue and "set the record." I saw scenes where the women seemed to be trying to get away from their male counterparts, even physically pushing them off on occasion. Clown porn. Angry, red, fresh augmentation scars on tender nipples. I watched a video where the women pretended to be teenage girls and were strangled with balloons, had their faces shoved in toilets, and were face-fucked until they vomited. In the middle of my book, suddenly porn made me very sick, very confused, and very sad. How could I explain *this*?

At the same time, I was discovering some of the best porn I'd ever seen in my career. I called in sick at work for an entire week. I had to sort things out. I was writing a book to help consumers—and would-be consumers—find the porn they think is hot, a book that gives the finger to the anti-porn arguments, a book that gives people a gateway to the products from an industry that sometimes offends their tastes.

I came to the conclusion that couldn't explain it; I could only provide tools for understanding and enjoying it. Nor could I explain the far-ranging (and I mean *far*) voices and opinions of the women and men in online porn forums about what porn they like to masturbate to. Sex is multifaceted, always changing and often unexplainable, as are we. Porn is about sex, and about people, though sometimes it doesn't seem like it, but that makes describing it even more complex. Some people want to make porn seem white, while others want to make porn seem black, and in reality it's gray.

I had high hopes when I sent the galleys of my book to the senior female editor at the adult industry magazine that was formative in my beginnings as a reviewer. I was shocked to get an angry message stating that she would never endorse my book, in any way. When I called her for an explanation and to get feedback before the book went to print, she was livid. She said there were problems but wouldn't tell me what the problems were. The ones she did specify seemed odd. She said I should have included movies that (when I checked at print time) weren't available for consumers, and complained that I mentioned her magazine's Web site's pop-up. But she told me that what really bothered her about the whole book, the big main problem, was that it was directed at female consumers. She told me to take out everything that spoke to women as viewers. I realized that it would be useless to explain to her that the book was in fact written for women and for couples that included women, and that was kind of the whole point.

The book did very well, and resulted in interviews on national news networks, and quotes and compliments from dozens of glossy national magazines. I reviewed for the women-run company for almost eight years in what became an amusing old-school vs. new-school battle on women and porn, with my taking arrows (and cheers) from both sides. I'm now the moderator of a porn club for women with over 350 members, and we have a review page on a porn forum with thousands of members—and lots of fans who watch, and make, porn. They want to know what we want to see. We've inspired sex makeovers for major women's magazines, whose editors confide that they "read every word" we write. Women are talking about porn with no restrictions, and other women are listening. What I learned in boot camp is that for women, watching porn is more about our relationships with other women than with men, and our lovers, whatever gender they may be. And that's a good thing.

REGINA LYNN

. . . ON HOW SEX AND TECHNOLOGY COME TOGETHER.

EVERY WEEK, I EXPOSE MYSELF to a hundred thousand people online and invite them to discuss it in a public forum.

They don't love me for my body. Hell, some of them don't love me at all. But they come back each week because they know they'll find a geek's-eye view of sex. If nothing else, I give them something to think about over the weekend.

It's a challenge, and I love it.

I started writing Sex Drive in early 2003 as a companion to TechTV's documentary series *Wired for Sex.* TechTV was reaching out to a more mainstream audience, and the Web team wanted to develop some strong Internet personalities distinct from the on-air talent. The producer of TechTV.com knew me well—I had hired him into a good job, once upon a time—and what's more, he knew about my explorations into the areas of the Internet everyone visits but no one talks about in polite company.

Our initial conversation went something like this:

Producer: So we're doing this doc series about sex and technology, and we need some Web content to go with it.

Me: You need me to write a weekly sex-tech column!

Producer: Can you start Monday?

When I tell people I write about sex and technology, they often look puzzled, cock their heads to one side, furrow their brows, and say something like, "Sex and tech? You mean like . . . online dating?"

Except in place of "online dating," some people say "Internet porn." And some say "cybersex." And some say "sex toys." Less common are "virtual reality" and "Webcams."

Given a moment to think about it, most people come up with an example of how technology infuses their own sex lives. Some send steamy text messages throughout the day, while others compose romantic e-mails that would do Cyrano de Bergerac proud. Sex toys are coming out of the closet, thanks to their relatively new accessibility. Now everyone in the world can visit women-friendly sexuality boutiques like Good Vibrations or Toys in Babeland. (Unfortunately, not everyone can have their purchases shipped to them—it depends on local laws. But we'll get there.)

Through chat rooms, e-mail forums, online personals, and role-playing games, we're finding kindred spirits and building relationships without regard to geographical or political boundaries.

And, of course, we have an abundance of porn. Porn on the Web, porn on DVD, porn on your PDA, porn on your cell phone. Technology is enabling a barrage of sexual content unlike anything the world has ever seen. It's a right wing crusader's wet dream to have so much to wage moral war against.

After TechTV's demise and a three-month hiatus, I pitched Sex Drive to *Wired News*. I sent the senior editor several sample columns and described my mission: to chronicle, and to help drive, the sexual revolution 2.0. We agreed to a four-week pilot, and if the column succeeded, I would sign an ongoing contract. I was stoked.

Up until this moment I had only written about porn peripherally. Sex Drive is about sex, I thought, not about porn. Only when *Wired for Sex* produced an episode about online pornography did I devote any serious column space to it. I had no objection to porn. It was just that I don't watch much porn and I had so many other topics to cover. But during those first four weeks at *Wired News*, porn dominated mainstream media headlines. Congress had invited four prohibitionists to testify in a hearing about whether we need more studies about pornography's effect on society and perhaps a public-awareness campaign, much like the ones warning us not to smoke or drink to excess.

Porn is heroin! the headlines proclaimed. *Porn is crack! Porn compels people to commit rape, to succumb to addiction, to become pedophiles!*

My new editor all but demanded I write about this.

And in researching that column ("Porn Prohibitionists Miss Point," *Wired News*, 11/27/04), I had to examine my own feelings about porn. Was I offended? Did I fear it? Did my sexual self-image change because of it? When I did view porn, what did I do with it?

When the Web first began to boom in the mid-1990s, I bought an electronic passkey of some kind that let me into any porn site that used the service. The idea was to keep minors out without putting too much of a burden on subscribers—you entered your passkey, rather than your credit card number, to verify your age at each site. It was cool to be able to look at as much porn as I wanted, of any flavor, without having to leave the house.

That, and I thought it was cool to be a girl looking at porn. Not that my parents ever mentioned porn, but somehow I learned early on that it wasn't for girls. (Ha!)

I caught myself clicking through to a gallery, taking in the contents with a glance, and backing out to click through to the next gallery. I didn't need to spend much time with the pictures to feel the titillation of porn.

That's what gives me a hint about how it must feel to be obsessed with online porn—that the search, as much as (or more than) the pictures, is really what turns you on. No individual picture or video can be as novel or exciting as you hope it will be, so you keep searching and looking, looking and searching. You're never satiated because if you just masturbated to any particular picture or video, you'd miss out on all those other ones.

Never mind that they, and thousands like them, will still be there for you tomorrow.

I browsed through a lot of genres just because I could, but what appealed to me most were group scenes and triple penetration. Fantasies I had not tried, but that could be possible (although not probable for most people) in real life. I learned that romantic, softly lit scenes of heterosexual couples did absolutely nothing for me. Neither did naked girls. But one woman with multiple men? Yes, please.

The novelty wore off and I did not renew my passkey when it expired. Yet I was aware that I had taken advantage of an opportunity not available to women until recently. Even among the Internet generation, men far outnumbered the women working the newsgroups for porn. It took the World Wide Web to bring us equal access.

I liked seeing women in sexual situations who enjoyed what they were doing, and wished I could find more of it. I came to terms with my own preference for being submissive in bed (although not anywhere else). I learned that being the sub meant being in control—and that being sexual meant so much more than I had heretofore experienced.

I rarely saw anything on the Web I would call degrading or damaging to women. I'm not saying it's not out there, only that I could usually avoid it. The actresses and models on the sites I chose to patronize were paid to be there, and they knew what they were getting into.

Hell, I have a fantasy of lying across a coffee table on my back, my hands wrapped around two different men's cocks, and my lips sealed around a third, while another man knelt between my thighs and yet another masturbated above my belly and breasts. If an actress in a similar scene is degraded, and represents the humiliation of all women by all men, what did it say about me that the image made me wet and achy?

Within months, I learned that most porn is boring. It's churned out without regard for quality and certainly with no thought to portraying female enjoyment. But when porn is good, it has a powerful effect on the senses. And when it's likely to appeal to women (which doesn't mean it's not explicit or "dirty"), it is often referred to as "erotica" instead.

While women like Danni Ashe and Tristan Taormino began to turn the porn world upside down in the 1990s, I looked elsewhere for sex.

In my teens and early twenties, my sexual actions did not live up to my sexual imagination. I was shy, inhibited, fearful, and had almost no libido. I'd find any excuse not to have sex, and I deliberately gained weight to keep myself "protected" from sexual behavior.

I had experienced inappropriate childhood sexual incidents, although I hesitate to label them "abuse" because on the scale of things it truly wasn't that bad. I could trace my negative responses to sex directly back to being six years old when I knew something was wrong and that I had absolutely no control or power over what was happening.

As an adult, my libido was drowned in shame and I managed to dissociate from anything more involved than a kiss. Two years of therapy during college helped me find peace and forgiveness, but I couldn't translate that mental state into a healthy and active sex life.

Enter cybersex.

One night, when porn wasn't doing it for me, I decided to try something different, something more interactive: adult chat. I picked the first HTML chat room that came up in a Yahoo!

search, called myself Aphrodite, and plunged in. I spent six hours in that chat room the first night, so involved in conversation and flirting that I didn't mind the clunky technology. But when another member told me about Internet relay chat (IRC), I dumped the HTML chat in favor of text-based IRC (a sort of "back door" to the same chat community). Then I went back the next day, and the next, and the next. . . .

It was transcendent. I had written sex scenes before, but never real-time, never with a man writing back to tell me how aroused he was, or continuing the fantasy with words of his own. The immediate response to my words turned me on like nothing else.

And the challenge of keeping it interesting, unique, and hot engaged my brain in ways real sex had not. It's hard to make love to a mind that's completely dissociated from the proceedings. But good cyber is all in the mind, even if you are also using your hands, cucumbers, or other convenient household objects for physical stimulation.

In training my brain to love sex, I found myself craving it outside the computer. I overcame my fears about oral sex and developed a newfound appreciation for penetration. I was in my late twenties, I had been in my relationship for twelve years, and for the first time I truly felt myself to be a sexual creature.

One of my childhood experiences involved being trapped against a wall while a neighborhood boy shoved a porn magazine in my face. I clearly remember a picture of two women extending their tongues on either side of a penis. "Just like licking an ice cream cone!" the boy said, and I could feel a heat radiating from him that had nothing to do with the weather.

I didn't give much thought to the picture, even though it was my first exposure to what adult males look like naked. This was in the 1970s, when men in porn didn't look like they do now. Alas.

But I instinctively knew I was trapped, vulnerable to whatever the big kid had in mind, and that I had to handle the situation very carefully if I were to escape unscathed. At that time I didn't have any specific knowledge of what might happen but I did know that it would be bad.

That incident and others, more serious, that followed imprinted on my brain one thing: penises are predators. It wasn't the pictures that taught me this, it was the way I was exposed to them. Never a secret, private perusal of the adult world; always an image thrust in my face, and yanked away again before I had a chance to process what I was seeing.

And yet when I hit my teens I always got along well with boys, and I could flirt with the best. Only when it came time to put all that energy into practice did I freeze. My mental warehouse door rolled down with the reverberant clang of metal on cement, and that was it. My mind was safe on one side, no matter what was done to my body on the other.

Cybersex blew that door to pieces. The computer provided two things that no amount of real-world behavior modification could: I was safe, because no penises were in the room with me, and I was intimate, because cowriting sex does not leave much room for dissociation.

If you've done it, you know what I mean. If you haven't, I probably can't explain it well enough for you to understand just how powerful it is. It's something that has to be felt to be believed.

My relationship was in trouble when I discovered cybersex, and spending all that time on the computer did not help. We eventually parted ways. (At least he benefited from my newfound sexual enthusiasm before we split up!) I found myself single for the first time in my adult life.

That year is still hazy in my memory. Too much happened in a short time. I changed jobs, moved to a new city, got a puppy. My mom was devastated about my breakup and we could hardly talk without one of us crying.

I traveled across the country to meet one of my cybersex partners in real life and we had earth-moving sex. I traveled up the coast to meet another one, and we had tide-changing sex. I met a guy at a country bar and we had sex.

Suddenly, I was Aphrodite_Offline. I kept condoms in my purse and a twinkle in my eye and I invited a few of my male friends to have sex with me. (Individually, over time, not one big orgy.) This was not "casual sex" per se, because I don't believe sex can ever be casual, but I made it clear that it was sex without a romantic relationship to frame it. Sex based on mutual affection and chemistry.

Eventually, I knew I needed to try dating formally, not just slutting around with my friends. It's too easy for boundaries to get blurred if you let those flings go on too long. (Not all of my sexual education was fun.)

I realized I had never actually dated. I met my ex when I was 15, and was dating him by the time I was 17. Here I was almost 30, and while I had slept with more than one person (finally!), I had never actually been on a first date. So I went after one the only way I knew how. I created an online personal ad and dated by the database.

Perhaps because my most powerful positive sexual experiences involved technology, I have incorporated tech into my sex life on a permanent basis. Or maybe it's just that I'm already a geek, with technology infusing every aspect of my life, including sex.

That's probably why my favorite sexual imagery involves tech. FuckingMachines.com and the sci-fi/fantasy sex at Pornotopia.com consistently stoke my fire.

The intersection of sex and tech happens on the communication side of things. Sure, we have all kinds of gadgets and doohickeys to use during intercourse, but it's the mental intercourse that best benefits from technology. You can have sex without any manmade tools at all; you can't whisper sweet nothings to a lover a hundred miles away without some sort of technology.

Mobile phones, with their video cameras and hands-free headsets, are essentials for any couple who spends time apart. Webcams and instant messaging enable long-distance sex, and show us that most of sex really happens in the mind. Women often tell me they had their first good orgasms in cyberspace.

Remote sex is getting closer to the real thing with products like the Sinulator. The Sinulator is a combination of hardware and software that connects your sex toy to the Internet for someone else to control. The control panel works with any browser and it looks like a game console, so if you're in the airport, no one can tell at a glance what you're doing.

The system even translates between a sleeve-style vibrator for men and a rabbit pearl vibrator for women. If he thrusts hard and fast, her toy vibrates hard and fast. If he goes slow and gentle, hers goes slow and gentle. If he gets up and walks away, her toy goes dormant. You can be thousands of miles away or in the same room, as long as both toys are connected.

Through it all, communication technologies keep you in tune. Cell phones and Internet telephony take the expense out of long distance, as does instant messaging and a Webcam.

The web also offers a wealth of sexual education, and I don't just mean porn. You can read up on sexual technique, sexual health, and sexual fantasy without having to hide a stack of books away every time your parents come to visit. Never before have we had access to this much information with this much privacy. It may not be as sexy to think about, but it's one of the great benefits that technology brings to our relationships and our sex lives.

And the anonymity conferred by a chat room handle gives you a comfortable arena in which to ask questions, practice flirting, and even have sex in ways you haven't had or won't have except in a fantasy setting.

When I was asked to contribute to this book, my first thought was, "Wait, I'm not in the adult industry." Then I thought, "If I'm associated with adult content, will my chapter be taken less seriously?"

That's when I realized I held prejudices about porn that I didn't know I had. I always said I had no problem with porn, whether or not I chose to bring it into my life. Yet by not wanting to be associated with it, wasn't I perpetuating the stereotype that Porn Is Bad, and particularly that Porn Is Bad For Women?

"Adult" encompasses so much more than porn. And porn itself is hard to classify. I love Laurell K. Hamilton's *Anita Blake, Vampire Hunter* novels, but each one has more sex and less serious plot than the last. Each novel puts Anita in more situations in which she must have sex with one or more of the several males in her adventurous life. Hamilton writes great sex, if you like metaphysical fantasy, which I do. It's explicit and raw and beautiful all at once. Is it porn?

On the literary side, Jane Smiley has a beautiful lovemaking scene in her novel *Horse Heaven*. I've given it to several friends as an example of a beautiful piece of writing, whether about sex or anything else. It too is graphic and powerful. Is it porn? Is it adult entertainment? Or, because it is literary, is it erotica and is that less smutty than porn, more respectable to be seen reading?

My column Sex Drive is not explicit, either pornographically or erotically. But I don't hold back, either. If I think readers need to know where I'm coming from, why I know what I know or feel what I feel, I tell them. It's not about exhibitionism, it's about credibility. And I take a "we're all adults here" stance, even though I know not everyone who reads Wired News is eighteen.

I concluded that "adult" is merely a code word for "sex," and in that case, yes, Sex Drive very much falls into the adult realm. And there's absolutely nothing wrong with that. We don't diss food writers for writing about food, and we don't diss fashion writers for writing about fashion. (Well, okay, sometimes we do, but not with the same scorn reserved for porn.) If food and clothing are two biological needs—and I would defend clothing as a biological, not just a social, human need—why wouldn't we afford the same respect to sex?

I think our perception of porn and adult entertainment is built on notions about the business and its players that may not always be true, especially now that women have moved up and revolutionized parts of the industry that used to belong solely to men.

The only way that perception will change is if the realities behind it change—and we let people know about it. That's part of what Sex Drive can do, and it's part of what every woman in this anthology is doing.

We're rewriting "adult" into more mature content and business models, and I don't mean as in "for mature audiences only." I mean in terms of how we approach sexual content, whether in writing, in performing, in distributing, in experiencing, or in any other capacity.

I don't know why more people aren't writing about technology and sex together in a positive light. I know of only a handful. Annalee Newitz has a wonderful column, Techsploitation, syndicated through AlterNet.org. Jonno and the Fleshbot.com team look at porn through geek eyes. And sometimes you'll run across an essay by a counselor talking about how cybersex has helped clients heal sexual problems.

But when you consider just how much technology we have that centers around sex—from Viagra to teledildonics to portable porn for your mobile device—it's amazing to me that sex-tech is not a common phrase, or that women's magazines rarely stray beyond the safe, ubiquitous vibrator when offering advice about sexual aids.

The mainstream media seems to focus on the fear. I've seen so much written about Internet infidelity, pedophiles using chat rooms to lure kids out to piers, CEOs and priests with porn on their hard drives. I don't pretend it's not happening. People do bad stuff with sex-tech.

Yet we have so many ways in which technology enhances our relationships. That's where I go with Sex Drive. I like to focus on the individual even if I'm writing about society-wide implications. Here's how I use a particular technology, or here's how so-and-so uses it. And here's how you can use it, too.

I like making associations that I don't see other writers making. All my life I have been told that I see things from an unusual angle, and I try to let that perspective guide me. I also feel tremendous pressure to be brilliant every single time, even though I know that's not possible. Sometimes informative has to be enough. Informative and funny. And insightful.

I am not an advice columnist. I just want to get people thinking, paying attention, and talking about these things. My role is to make the connections, to start the conversation and to provide a safe community where we can have that conversation.

I don't have all the answers. But I sure as hell can raise the questions.

JAYME WAXMAN

. . . ON HELPING DEBUNK THE PERVERT MYTH SURROUNDING PORN THROUGH MAINSTREAM MEDIA.

YOU DON'T CHOOSE SEX, IT *chooses you.*

I am not a survivor of sexual abuse. I don't have many sordid skeletons in the closet. I haven't been raped or molested, I don't have father abandonment issues, and I wasn't picked on for my sexual preferences, even if at a young age I didn't understand what they were. There isn't a reason I chose to become involved in the sex industry, other than that it's the only place I've ever truly belonged. That's what's sort of strange about this industry. When you work on the inside, the potential is limitless. When you see it from the outside, you've limited your potential. For many people, sex will never be good enough.

Even today we are taught to think of sex as bad, as perverse, as something that we shouldn't be doing for fun, unless of course we want to procreate. Some of us are taught to think that sex should only happen between a man and his wife, and not between two lovers, two friends, or even random strangers. Some of us grow up believing that sex is dirty and degrading, and when it's not done in the confines of one's bedroom it's morally wrong. I don't come from a world that thinks like that. I come from a place where sex is loving, consensual, experimental, fun, and sometimes plain raw.

I didn't find a job in sex because I oozed some sort of sexual pheromones, although there's something strange about working in sex that makes you start giving off an "other" vibe. I didn't grow up with the religious foundations that sex was wrong. I wasn't chastised for having sex—although my mother most definitely wasn't happy when she found out that I had sex before college, let alone marriage. I wasn't told I was disgusting, used, or unwanted as a result of my sexual encounters. And as I got more comfortable talking about sex, people got more personal, more open, and more comfortable talking with me about it as well. Not so ironically, I've had a lot more dating opportunities since this all started. Yeah, I know, when you're comfortable talking about sex, you're usually comfortable doing it, and men . . . well, men just know.

I'm a Jewish girl who grew up in the middle of Long Island. It doesn't get less exotic than that. I've been reading porn since I was a little girl, sitting on the toilet in my parent's bathroom, flipping through my father's supposedly hidden *Playboys*. I loved to look at naked ladies, at how their bodies glistened. I'd stare at their pussies, because I felt that if those pussies could talk, if they could verbally communicate, they'd share stories about life in the big clitty. Those pussies looked like they knew how to live. The women in the magazine turned me on, but no more and no less than the boys at my school did. I secretly wanted to pose in *Playboy* when I grew up. The thought of other people getting excited when they looked at my naked body was as satisfying to me as the thought of looking at them. I never imagined I would become part of the industry that made this happen.

Porn made the VCR a household word.

But people have been making sex long before they were making VCRs.

I like sex. I like sex a lot. That doesn't make me a pervert. Sex doesn't create perverts, or naturally attract them to a particular line of work. Working in sex may attract perverts to you, but that's because there are perverts everywhere. We all have our moments.

Sex is a funny thing. It's like eating, sleeping or breathing, a part of basic body maintenance and functioning. Sex is something human beings are supposed to be having. Alone, in groups, or on camera, we're supposed do it how and when we want to.

Porn doesn't make perverts. You won't become a pervert from watching a guy or two fuck a girl in ways you wish you'd get fucked. Porn can't make you do anything, even if, at times, porn has been made to seem like it can. Porn isn't the reason men like to watch certain kinds of sex, or the reason women can only get off in certain ways. Porn doesn't make men abusive, or bad; genetics, society and culture are responsible for that. Porn shows that there are different strokes for different folks. Porn is a natural extension of who we are as human beings. Porn is about sex, sex that someone is hoping you'll pay to watch.

My stumbling into the world of sex was hardly an accident. From my first moments at eYada.com, one of the premier talk radio sites on the Internet, to becoming the sex advice columnist for a magazine devoted to female sex drive, this was a door I was destined to open. I had been working a seemingly fulfilling job as a talk radio producer for a big "liberal" name in political media, and he treated me well. But Internet radio sounded exciting, and when the job was offered to me, eYada.com became my home, and the place where I got to explore.

The show I produced was all about sex. Night after night of talking to sexperts teaches you about becoming one yourself. Except that I hate the term sexpert, because it implies that I know more than you on a subject that anyone can learn about. I like to use the term sexplorer. For me sex is all about the ways in which people relate, and I'm continually fascinated by human relations.

The first night that I worked on Internet radio, the host was more than a bit perturbed. He had come in to work without expecting that his male producer was about to leave. I was his replacement, and Bob, the host, wanted to make sure I could handle myself in any situation, so he brought me into the studio, turned on my microphone, and began asking all sorts of personal questions. "When did you first masturbate?" "How old were you when you had your first sexual experiences?" "What about intercourse?" While I knew I didn't have to answer anything, something inside me knew that I did.

I shared stories that had been bottled up for years. I opened closets and aired my dirty laundry. I started to understand my sexual experiences, and how they all led to this place, this space, this next step. My coworkers wouldn't look at me the same way the next day. They didn't want to know about my experimentation with women or my favorite position. As I continued to speak about sex, I actually felt myself evolving. I describe my transition the same way my pediatrician talked about my breasts on the eve of my puberty. I blossomed, I budded, I grew, and it was liberating.

The radio job came to an end in 2001. I began working at a sex toy shop when I was twenty-six. It was my second job in sex. While I had years of experience talking to sexologists and doctors, my experience with real people, the paying customers of sex, was only beginning. The most important lesson I've learned is trite, perhaps, but true nonetheless. Don't judge a book by its cover because you can't. It's that simple. There's no way to tell what a person likes sexually by what a person looks like physically. In over four years of working at Toys in Babeland, a well-known adult shop in New York City, I can still say that the guy with the leather vest and an arm full of tattoos might be more afraid of the nipple clamps than the suburban, middle-class husband. You can't base someone's orientation, behavior, or identity on how they present themselves. None of us knows what's going on behind closed doors, unless, of course, we're invited in.

In other words, you can't tell a pervert from a nonpervert.

I got my own radio show around this time. I love radio. It allows me to be a faceless, bodiless vessel of information. Radio is the smartest of the communications media and it forces us to use our imagination, which means we use our brain—our most powerful sex organ. We paint our own pictures, and that's what I did on my own show, "Aural Fixation," which ran on the short-lived Web site wsexradio.com. I loved the double entendre and my listeners loved hearing me talk about sex. As with my *Playgirl* advice column, people always asked questions that began with *Is it normal,* when I don't know what normal is anyway. Nobody is exactly like anyone else. We all have our quirks, our turn-ons, turn-offs, fetishes. We are all obsessive-compulsive or have attention deficit disorder, at least to a certain degree. While my boyfriend might not like dressing up in women's clothing, it's okay that yours does. So who's normal?

I eventually went back to the "normal" world of mainstream radio, but it was only because I was offered the chance to produce for a really famous female comic. It was there that I realized where I had to be, and after she successfully managed to piss off the management, they successfully managed to aid in her departure. I remember one night, she brought me on air and we talked about popular fads in the sex industry. I told her about "Bend Over Boyfriend" and how women were consistently coming into Babeland to buy things they could put up their boyfriends butts. The next day I got called into the program director's office. Apparently I had pissed off a listener somewhere in the Midwest and now I was on probation. If I "offended" anyone they would seek my immediate departure. Some of the other producers couldn't believe I still had a job. After all, I had gone on national radio, with an international celebrity, and had told men to take it

up the ass. I was devastated. Not because management repri-
manded me, but because they thought they had to in the first
place.

That's when a friend saw an ad for a job at *Playgirl*. I became
Playgirl's sex advice columnist. By this time I had gone back to
school for my master's in Human Sexuality Education, and I
called the column Sex.Ed.

What exactly does a master's in Human Sexuality Education
entail? I get asked this question a lot. It's definitely a bizarre
degree, but the only graduate degree I could ever see myself
earning. The program was designed with a heavy emphasis on
communication and learning through group experience. There
were no perverts in my classes, at least not the students I met. In
fact, I was surprised at just how regular some of these professionals really were. Teachers, nurses, ministers, these were the
people that I sat next to on a weekly basis. I was the one who
talked about porn. I was the one who would rattle their academic
minds.

The hardest class I ever sat through was when my professor,
who also happened to be a therapist, invited one of his clients to
speak. The client was a pedophile and his story both horrified
and amazed me. It was one of the first times I had to deal with
not being comfortable about sex, and at the same time, feel sym-
pathy and compassion for the man I saw in front of me. I drove
home that night with tears in my eyes. I couldn't understand how
this man who had done something so abhorrent could still feel
human. It was one of the first times sex made me uneasy. It
wouldn't be the last.

I started having sex at sixteen, and I've been sexually active
ever since. I don't remember talking to most of my friends about
sex until I was in my twenties. I don't remember much about sex
outside of the sexual experiences I was having up until that
point. Sure, after I lost my virginity they all wanted to know how

it felt, or what to do, but we would only talk about things in an "advice" kind of way. Maybe that's why it's natural that I became a sex advice columnist. I was always busy telling someone something about sex.

I get all kinds of questions at *Playgirl*. From husbands who want to wear their wives clothes to women in search of their G-spot, there's nothing that can shock or disgust me. There's no question I won't try to answer either, not even questions about sex in the family. I remember one in particular from a man whose fantasy was to watch his wife have sex with his brothers. I thought that keeping it all in the family might be a better fantasy than reality, but I'm not the one who will make the final decision. We all make our own decisions when it comes to sex. Maybe that's what makes us all perverts. Maybe we all defy definition in some way, even if it's never been admitted to another human being. We all know that deep down inside, and maybe not so deep down, we all have our fantasies. Sometimes, I'm merely here to listen.

Sometimes I'm here for more.

I don't remember watching porn until I was in my mid-twenties. Working in porn came through working in radio. I became very good friends with a former adult star turned director. She offered to show me what life could be like on the flip side of the camera. Obviously not everyone is comfortable with "the industry," and that's the way it is. One of my best friends still won't let me talk to her about some of the things I'm doing. And as I learned more and more about the porn industry, I understood why. Porn needs more strong women. There are those great few who have paved the way for others to share in their glory, but still, for the most part, porn was and is ruled by men.

My first job on a porn set was assistant to a top female director. I stayed by her side and tried to hold back my anxiety on our first day of production. I had never been on a set where sex wasn't only supposed to happen, it was the reason we were all there. The girls, the porn stars, they walked into a room and everything would shift. People took notice. Their confidence and their exuberance were the types of things I wanted to take away from the experience. This, I thought, was the way having sex should make everybody feel. Of course, to be fair, things aren't perfect in the industry either. I noticed more drinking than on a normal shoot, I noticed how skinny and "porn perfect" these ladies looked, and yes, how sexual energy changes a scene. But all of this, all the positive and negative experiences, are par for the course. The truth is that you can't help make change until you accept something for what it is. Porn is porn.

I was nervous about the first time I would actually see sex. I remember the director spending a few minutes talking to all the actors, mentally preparing them for what was about to happen. None of the men had acted in a high-budget sex production before, and with the exception of one, none of them had ever had sex on camera for anything outside personal pleasure. It didn't help that the first scene we were shooting was the largest scene in the movie; a group sex scene that consisted of one girl and four guys in a warehouse in Brooklyn. There were toys and lube and one seasoned professional porn star who knew how to get into the minds and cocks of each of her costars. She was laughing and silly, and she just loved sex. Things heated up and I did too. I tried to control myself, to look around at the fifteen or so other faces in the room with us. *Were they getting turned on too?*

I've had my issues with porn. I remember crying and cursing down Bourbon Street in New Orleans at two in the morning on a hot July night, while I was actively "casting" for a movie. I remember wishing I could be anywhere else at that time, and how I hated the producer for where he had sent me. I remember thinking maybe I'd never do this again, but now I realize I just wouldn't do it again with him. Of course there's bad porn out there, and of course there are bad people making porn. But that's why I feel the need to stick around.

It's silly to deny that most young boys and girls get their sex advice from porn, because if you really think about it, most of us did. It's accessible, it's taboo, it's sex that they can see in their parents' bathroom, in the privacy of their bedroom. Porn is sex education, whether you like it or not, and I am a sex educator. Most of us have learned something from porn, so let's make porn we can learn from.

Does that make me a pervert? If I got asked that question in my *Playgirl* column I'd immediately respond, no, of course not. Well, unless of course you want to be called a pervert. Haven't you heard that while sticks and stones can break your bones, names will never harm you? So, what's in a name? It's all about how you define yourself, and not how the dictionary defines you.

So, me? You can call me a pervert. You can call me a sex educator, a producer, a writer, or blogger. You can call me smart, stupid, sassy, or sexy, but just remember to call me a girl who wants to be in this industry, a girl who couldn't see herself anywhere else. And now, watch where I go.

LISA MASSARO

. . . ON BEING THE MANAGING EDITOR OF ONE OF THE WORLD'S MOST RECOGNIZABLE PORN MAGAZINES.

MY BACKGROUND—BOTH PERSONAL AND social—never prepared me for a career in the adult industry; in fact, I believe that my upbringing and education would have done anything *but* get me involved with pornography.

I was brought up in a close-knit family of Italian heritage. My parents have been married for over fifty years. I was raised Catholic and attended parochial school for eight years. I was an A student, a "good girl" who attended college to pursue a major in wildlife management—that is, until a curriculum heavy in science and organic chemistry forced me to rethink my career path. The one thing I knew was that I loved to read and I embraced the written word, so I changed my major to English, figuring I could do something in the publishing field.

After a few years of bouncing from working in customer service to cooking for a whitewater rafting company, I settled back in Connecticut and got a position as an editorial assistant in a small publishing company that specialized in trade magazines for Latin America and Asia. I learned the basics of magazine production, typesetting, and editing. From there I moved to an analytic instruments and computer publication, then an aviation engineering journal, despising my jobs and the dry, uninteresting, technical subjects with which they dealt.

Luckily, I had a girlfriend who temped for an agency that was looking to place someone as an editorial and production assistant for a company that published an adult magazine called *Club*. They'd been having difficulty finding someone for the job because the applicants interested in the position weren't qualified, and those who were qualified to do the job weren't interested due to the subject matter. I had never heard of the magazine and had never even seen the inside of an adult publication, but I didn't care. I hated my job and wanted a change. I also figured that at least with an adult magazine, I'd know what all the words meant. I had no idea how wrong I was, but after a fifteen-minute interview I was hired and I've never really looked back. Twenty years later, I'm still here.

My family knows what I do; they have from the start. They tease me about my trips to the strip clubs and are curious about the trade shows. They tell me when they see an adult personality in the news and we chat about what happens at a photo shoot. I like to think that, through my involvement in the adult industry, they are a little more understanding and accepting of this business. My boyfriend thinks I have the best job in the world, and I had to stop him from bragging about it to perfect strangers everywhere we went.

When I first started with the magazine, I worked on associated companies as well: a mail-order adult toy company and a monthly soft-core video line for Playboy cable TV. I did a little bit of everything for everyone, which is how I received my introduction to sex toys and videos—both new to me. As both my experience and my abilities grew, I took on more and more responsibility and chose to focus entirely on handling the editorial content of the magazines. Ours is a unique situation because the senior editors and art departments are three thousand miles away in London, while the adult industry as a whole is three thousand miles in the other direction—California. I am the linchpin between the two. I am now the U.S. editorial manager and, all U.S.-based editorial comes through my office to be forwarded for the editors' consideration. I'm still multitasking; a few of the things I handle are the photo shoots; the custodian of records ID responsibilities; our review processes with our attorney and Canadian liaison; on-set reports of video productions; and the models.

Club has always been known for having spectacular contract "girls"; my first were Marilyn Chambers and Seka. Once they're under contract, the girls become a part of the *Club* "family" and I adopt them as my own and truly care about them. Over the years, I've been lucky enough to work with Ginger Lynn, Jenna Jameson, Janine, Tera Patrick, and Gina Lynn, to name a few. I promise all my girls three things: I will not make a promise I can't keep; I will not bullshit you; and I will never make you do anything you don't want to do. I do my best to keep those promises. While I can't say there have never been problems, I do believe there has always been mutual respect. I do what I can to keep both the girls and the company happy, and it seems to work. I resent the generalizations that mainstream society applies to the adult models and actresses, that they're all sexually abused, they're all drug addicts, they're all ignorant flakes, etc. They are all women and they have all made a choice to work in the adult industry, but beyond that, they're all individual personalities.

We publish three monthly titles: *Club, Club International* and *Club Confidential,* and I have seen the magazine content change over the years. In 1985 there was no genital-to-genital contact; we had to have that millimeter of space between any two models. Though our magazines have never been the first to push the envelope, we've progressed with the rest of the field to hardcore pictorials showing full penetration, however our titles do not include cumshots. I accept that we are providing adult entertainment, but I admit that I have seen things over the years that have shocked and disgusted me. When that happens, I have to take a mental step back and remind myself that "to each his own" and everyone has an opinion on what they consider appealing or titillating. I've met businessmen with more unusual tastes than bikers, and housewives who are kinkier than strippers. I've been sent photographs from readers that are too bizarre or hardcore to publish, and I've received diatribes from "Christians" who feel a need to "save" me.

This is a business. I work in an office and am surrounded more by paper than by naked women; we don't do photo shoots down the hall or have orgies in the conference room. I work on a computer, negotiate deals and contracts, do interviews, edit articles, respond to reader mail, and file. We have production schedules and editorial schedules and advertising schedules. The only models in my office are in photos; the only sex in my office is on film. It's always interesting to see how people react when they find out what I do, and I'm usually circumspect when first asked about my job.

First: "I work for a publishing company."

Next: "I'm an editor."

Then: "We publish magazines."

And: "They're men's magazines."

Finally: "Yes, it's porn."

Boom! The reaction. They're always surprised because I don't look as if I'd work in the adult industry, though I'm not sure what that means or how they think I should look. They're always curious and have lots of questions whether or not they're fans. But if they are fans, they now feel they can admit it to me what they would otherwise keep secret so as not to be judged by others. Some people want my job; others think I should be flogged for distributing filth. I've has both political and religious discussions about pornography; I've had to defend myself to social reformers who tell me that adult magazines cause people to become sexually aberrant and commit sex crimes. For me it comes down to this: we publish a magazine that is available to adults 18 or older. If you don't like it, don't buy it. We don't stand on street corners giving it out for free and we don't force anyone to look at it. This is a voyeuristic society, and that's a fact, so why should it be surprising that some people like to watch others having sex? Sex is a good thing. People like to have sex and they like to read about it and see it. We learn by reading, seeing, and experiencing in all areas of life.

Our society is hypocritical when it comes to sex. The mainstream media uses sex to sell products and attract viewers; runway models expose themselves through high couture; celebrities flaunt their numerous sex partners—excuse me, "love matches." Television evangelists sleep with whores, anti-porn politicians have secret sex lives, but they're all "really sorry." Drug companies advertise products to increase your sex drive, but we don't want to promote condom use and sex education.

I grew up without sexual guidelines; I had absolutely no sexual education at all to speak of other than the fundamentals of biology. I have learned a lot in these past years at *Club,* and I'm not referring to different sex positions, and I'm not saying I use all this information in my personal life. But all knowledge is power and I am more empowered by what I know, and more able to make my own choices because of it. I have been more willing to experiment sexually because of what I have seen and learned. I know better how to give and get pleasure, and that the female orgasm is not that elusive. I have learned a whole new vocabulary: an ATM will never be just a cash machine to me. I believe sex toys are not a joke but a supplemental tool for a healthy sex life. I am appalled that oral and/or anal sex could actually be against the law in some U.S. states; how dare we presume to govern the specifics of a consensual natural act? I believe that everyone is entitled to their own opinions, but those beliefs should not be forced upon others.

I have had the opportunity through my job to travel and to meet people from all walks of life, from hookers to high society. And some of the nicest people I've met, and some I'm proud to consider my friends, work in the adult industry. There's a bond between us, perhaps because we are involved in a business that is scorned, and that sets us all apart as "black sheep." But for whatever reason one has, the people I encounter are usually friendly and open, kind and generous, and nonjudgmental. It's not a perfect little utopia, but more like a large, dysfunctional family that knows how to play well together. Photographers and porn stars, directors, company execs, stylists and cameramen, writers, salesmen, agents, graphic artists, craft services, and receptionists—we are a microcosm of society, and through our work we contribute to that society.

I stumbled into this business; it wasn't my goal, there was no plan. I was sexually naïve but open-minded. My first day at work I found a large box under my desk with a note that said, "Don't take it too seriously, remember to laugh." The box was filled with a variety of sex toys, and books like *Sexual Secrets, Good Vibrations,* and *Joys of Fantasy.* I read all the books, threw out all the toys (you never know where they've been), and I still remember to laugh. That has come in handy during the Traci Lords scandal, the Meese Commission, and other times when we've been under attack for one reason or another. Then there are the times when shit happens: we publish the wrong date on a magazine cover; the model doesn't show up for a photo shoot, store signing, or trade show; the courier loses the package with artwork for this month's issue; your computer crashes. Whatever gets thrown our way, we deal with it and continue on. That's life, in or out of the adult industry.

It's been a long, strange trip but I'm still here. And I'm still laughing.

JULI ASHTON AND TIFFANY GRANATH

Juli Ashton: My story of how I got here is surprisingly standard. I was in college and had just turned twenty-one when my boyfriend took me to a strip club to celebrate my birthday. I was very excited. It was a small-town club and the bartender there just loved me. He said, "I need a waitress and I want you working here with me." I needed a job, so I started waitressing there. All the customers would tell me, "Oh my god, you're so hot, when are you going to dance?" "Never, ever, ever am I going to dance," I'd answer.

I learned to turn my bills so that all the money was facing the same way or else I'd have to show my tits, and I vowed that I was never going to get caught. That's how I met Kylie Ireland. She was a brand-new dancer at the club. So one day I just got so sick of being a waitress. I was tired of getting a quarter for a tip, because drinks were $4.75, but these guys would put a five- or ten-dollar bill on the stage. I thought, "Are you kidding me?" So I finally put down my tray and started doing the topless thing, convinced that I would never go fully naked. But then a new club opened up in town and I thought, "Oh, what the hell, it's just a pair of panties." So I started dancing naked.

I moved to Florida with my then-husband. I was stripping at a club that had the features come in, and that's where I met Shayla LeVeaux and Victoria Paris. I hung out with them as a fan and we would have date nights. One of us would pick dinner and the other would pick the movie, and then we would switch. I read *Adult Video News* religiously so that I could pick good movies for us to watch. It was through spending time with the girls that I decided that what they were doing was a fun job. They were having a great time making great money, they were traveling, and they were good girls. They were fun—they weren't psycho or hurt in some way, so I decided, "I can do that." So I moved to Los Angeles and got into the business.

I saw a different side of the industry than most girls do. I had a manager to block me from the scum, and I went under contract pretty quickly. I met him through Shayla because he was managing her at the time. He'd given me his card and I held it in my makeup case for nearly a year before I decided to call him. So thanks to him I never did things like fifty-dollar blow job scenes—that just didn't happen for me. I saw a really nice side to this industry. Shortly after that, I got offered a gig hosting *Nightcalls* on Playboy TV, and ten years later I'm still doing that. I was offered the position at Playboy Radio two and a half years ago. I've been with the show since it first started.

Tiffany Granath: My story is a little different. I moved to Los Angeles to be a dancer. Not a stripper—I'm talking tap, jazz, ballet. I did some tours with people like The Beach Boys and Bette Midler for a while, and until then I'd never done anything naked. But during the Bette Midler tour they had this little burlesque segment during which I had to wear pasties, so that was my first bout with "nudity."

When I came back from the road I worked on random things like *Married . . . With Children* and doing bit parts in movies while I go-go danced at all the clubs at night. One of the clubs was a lesbian club. I was fully clothed, but they could tip us so it was a lot of fun. One of the girls I used to work with there was from New York, and we used to feed off each other by doing these really awful dance moves in the back room. I'd sing, she'd dance, and we'd mess everything up. Not long after that I heard about this audition where a TV show was looking for dancers. We went in that morning after making something up the night before at the Key Club. We'd been up all night. So it's eight A.M. and we're in the bathroom at the place we're auditioning at, exhausted and fried, and we're about to go in and perform for the executives, because even though they'd already finished doing the casting for it, a friend did us a favor, so they were going to see us anyway.

So we're in the bathroom trying to remember all these steps, and I said to her, "Listen, if we panic, let's just talk to each other and do our shtick." So of course we get in there and blank out, so we start into our little routine. The execs said, "What the hell are you talking about?" We told them it was just our way of trying to remember the steps, but they asked us to do it again, but louder. So there we are, dancing around making complete fools of ourselves, saying, "And a wing ding ding, and a wing ding ding, and a wing ding ding, and pop it! And lock it!" We did one show for them. That was it.

Two years later they called us up and said that they were looking for a sidekick for a new show on FX that was starting up with Bobcat Goldthwait, and did we want to shoot the pilot? Of course—we were broke, so five hundred dollars seemed good to us. We went in and did our thing, and they picked up the show. They told us they needed thirty little ditties for each show. We wound up doing a hundred and ten episodes.

In the meantime, I heard about an audition for *Nightcalls* on Playboy TV. Someone called me for it and I said I'd go, but I was really freaked out about it. I'll never forget it. There I was sitting on a couch all by myself taking phony phone calls, and I had to play along with it and get naked. It was so goofy. I did one show and then they hired someone else. But when Juli went out of town, they called me in as a ringer. But by the time Juli came back from her trip they'd decided they wanted me as her cohost.

It was interesting because we came from two different worlds. I had done Playboy videos before, like *Playboy Cheerleaders,* where I was topless with Carmen Electra, but then to go and do this show . . . and I was so freaked out. The producers asked me, "Do you want to see the girl you're working with?" I said sure, so they handed me a tape. The tape they gave me was one of her pornos. I remember watching it and thinking, "Oh my god, I'm so out of my league." I almost didn't do it. I nearly called them and said, "You know what? I can't do this." And they said, "No, no, no—we want you because you're so different!" Now somehow over the course of doing the TV and radio show, Juli's turned me out into being this wild pig and she's gotten to be a prude. So we've evened out somehow.

When I first started working here everyone was so nice. The girls were always saying, "You're so beautiful!" In mainstream you'd sit in an audition and all the girls would just stare you up and down because they saw you as a competitor, but then I came over here and everyone was so complimentary. I thought, "This is so much fun!" I could never go to a real audition again.

Juli: Being here for so long, we were aware that we were pretty much the oldest women on Playboy TV, let alone the industry in general. I'm thirty-five. There's not a lot of thirty-six-year-old porn stars that are still active. I'm not active in the traditional sense, but even on TV you just don't see that age group. Plus, TV is taxing. How do you have a baby? You can't be on a diet all the time. We were thinking, what's next? There's got to be life after. I think that's the biggest dilemma of the industry—what is life after? Even with Tiffany not even being in porn she's hit a wall in being the *Playboy* girl. She's not done it, but she's been labeled. So we knew that we were going to be done soon.

Meanwhile, the president of the company had gone to college with the XM CEO and they were talking. At the same time I had mentioned to him that Tiffany and I loved radio. We had done a million radio interviews and it just seemed like a neat "life after." We could still be together, we could have babies and not worry about how we looked on air. So they worked it out and they got Playboy radio going. But the concept behind Nightcalls Radio came from us.

Tiffany: The show does really well for them. And I think they know that we've always been responsible—we've always gone out to do interviews. So when it came down to "Who do we give it to?" it was me and Juli. I don't want to say that we went through a trial run, but even though we'd done a million things with radio, we'd never hosted our own show before. But we've seen it progress a lot. The first day we were on the air we had seven subscribers. We were so giddy that day. There was this skit on *Saturday Night Live* where the women are doing the skit about NPR, and that's what we felt like—we felt goofy. But then we started talking about our own personal lives. We'd just broken up with our boyfriends, so we were kind of bitter. But we talked a lot about that. I was on this mission—I was like, "Fuck all guys, and I'm going to go out with everybody!" So every day was just a recap of the night before.

Juli: The other part of it was us talking together in this small room with one engineer. Everyone else was behind us so we couldn't see anyone, so we really kind of forgot that we were talking to people who were listening. That's when we started saying things that most radio and public people wouldn't say on the air about their lives and their experiences.

Tiffany: I remember one day we were on this trip. Here we were being the *Playboy* girls doing this whirlwind press tour in Chicago, and on the way back on the plane, Juli had brought this Martha Stewart kit on how to make homemade valentines. I'm getting drunk, and she's sitting there with her little scissors making doilies and making really cute valentines. And I'm saying, "Dude, you're out of your fucking mind." This was when she was still with her boyfriend. So she gives him the card when we get home and he thought it was stupid and threw it across the room.

After they had broken up, we were talking about it on the air and she was having an "I miss him" moment. And I said, "What are you talking about?! What about the time that he . . ." I started listing all the horrible things he had done to her, and she started crying live on the air. That's how human our show is. We've had huge fights on the radio where we can barely speak. We've even had train-wreck scenarios where we've had too much to drink one time and we couldn't keep it together, but I think it's the human element of the show that keeps people listening. It's just us being human. And I think that people need to hear that.

Juli: Now that we have thousands of subscribers we still treat everyone the same way as we treated those first seven listeners. Instead of doing a radio show where people call in and we're like, "What do you want?" they get a lot of air time. People will be on the phone for three, five, seven, ten minutes telling their story, and I don't think a lot of other places give them that kind of voice. We encourage that. We encourage them to talk about their sex lives and ask questions.

Tiffany: But we've had porn people on the show from the very beginning. And I've never been on a set before, so this was a whole new world for me. I've only ever been on one of Juli's sets and it was at her house. So there's definitely strange things that

I've seen in this studio, like the guy who comes in here and fingers his girlfriend while he's being interviewed and then sniffs it while he's talking. He's been here a few times, and whenever he's here we say, "Oh god, the finger sniffer is here." It's so disgusting.

Juli: This industry is endlessly fascinating. I mean, how is that appropriate? Just because you're a porn star doesn't mean that he can get away with anything gross.

Tiffany: What's also funny is that even though Juli's been in the industry for so long, we recently did this commercial where the guys starring in it along with us were in these little G-strings. Juli was embarrassed just looking at them. We were supposed to check them all out and pick one, and neither one of us could look at their packages. We were giggling like ten-year-olds. That day we couldn't look at mostly naked guys, but then later on the show we had this girl come in who was learning how to female ejaculate. She had no problem being fully naked straddling the couch, and the guy who's trying to get her to squirt is eating her out and really going for it. The evidence of her ability is still on the wall behind us because as she was coming he took her ejaculate and flung it all over. And it's funny because I was watching that day and Juli was embarrassed. But my thing is if people come in here and they're so open with what they're doing, then I'm going to look at it. I've never done porn, but I've learned so much about the business.

Juli: Now we've evolved into having mainstream people accept us and come on the air with porn people, but in the beginning we were so new that we had no track record and it was impossible to get anyone but porn people in. But in addition to them we've also had dominatrixes, hookers, producers, directors, sex-related authors, doctors, relationship coaches . . .

Tiffany: And now we've had a lot of mainstream people. Mick Fleet-wood, EG Daily, Trey Parker, Nick Lachey, Jamie Kennedy, Aero-smith, Steve Guttenberg, The Ying Yang Twins, Judy Tenuta . . .

Juli: It's been fucking hilarious to mix the mainstream with the porn. Sometimes it's awkward—we tame it up a lot when our mainstream guests are in here, and we offer to give them the chance to leave before we bring in the next guest, and a lot of the time they want to stay, especially when we have this hot chick coming in. The porn stars usually dress up for us. Sitting across from Mick Fleetwood and some random porn star talking about anal sex was definitely a highlight of my life. It was just really brilliant to me.

Tiffany: Usually we're really good at cracking our guest's shell and getting them to get comfortable enough to open up. Some-times it's hard, but if we can get anything out of them we defi-nitely try. We ask them about their relationships, their sex lives, how they keep it together on the road, and then sometimes we get really dirty with them if they let us go.

But since having porn people on the show, I've become more open to things. It's not that it's necessarily made my sex life better, but I'm definitely more open to trying things. Listening to them and their stories has opened my mind up, but I have to admit that there's days that I've had a huge opinion of people and what they do. I don't know what it is, but there's some days where some-thing will just push me over the edge and I'll just gross out. I'll admit it—I've been really hateful. I've said things like, girls will get into porn because they don't have any other talent. Those are the days Juli and I get into fights on the air. But it's changed me. I really understand why people swing. I can't do it—it's totally not in my head—but I talk to people and it really works for them. I try to understand why people like pain. It's opened my mind in a great way because I don't judge anymore. I listen to people and I try to understand what makes them tick. That doesn't mean I do it all in my personal life, but yeah, now I gag myself when I brush my teeth so I can get used to the idea of deep throating. And our listeners will call in all the time and say, "I've learned so much from listening to your show." And that's really gratifying.

Juli: I think that once you become exposed to the sex industry, it's really not that big a deal. And that's the healthiest thing. There's really nowhere that you can talk about sex and porn. Not that long ago there was a story about how a guy was fired from his job for talking about masturbation at the water cooler! There's nowhere to talk about it when you're single, and if you're in a relationship with someone who's conservative, where can you go to ask questions? People want to know if their interests in these subjects are normal, and it's so incredibly normal, but people don't know that because they're not taking a chance on talking about it. I think the best part of doing the show was when we had a caller tell us that he had the best sex of his life with his wife after ten years of not— it was almost over for them. He thanked us profusely, but that's part of what we do: we preach communication.

Tiffany: That's why I feel like we're pioneers in satellite radio. I can say that with all confidence. When we go out to promote Playboy Radio we do other huge radio shows that are supposed to be the biggest there are, and people say, "You guys rock." Plus, after having the guests on here, I'll come back into the control room and guests will say, "I'll come back any time—this is the most fun I've had on radio in my whole life." I feel really good about that. That's when it's all worth it, and we wouldn't change a thing.

DANA HARRIS

. . . ON COVERING THE PORN BEAT FOR THE
HOLLYWOOD TRADES.

IF YOU'RE NOT OBNOXIOUSLY NOSY, there's really no reason to be a journalist.

There certainly isn't any money in it. Or respect; surveys rank us somewhere below used-car dealers. However, it's the only job I know of that lets you ask questions that would otherwise get you slapped. Even better: if they do slap you, they're the ones who get in trouble. Really, for a nosy person, it's a sweet deal that's hard to beat.

And ever since I was ten years old, I've been nosy about porn stars.

Nosiness brought me to porn in the first place. It was in the old attaché case under my parents' bed, which I discovered in the fifth grade while looking for Christmas wrapping paper. It was full of long-forgotten smut—an old *Penthouse* and *Hustler,* a Tijuana bible compendium, and cheap airport paperbacks with titles like *Banging Bonnie!* and *Leer of Flying.*

My discovery inspired me to discover masturbation (*Leer of Flying* made me tingly, I started pressing on the tingly spots and, well, you know the rest). However, as a shy kid who thought it daring to raise my hand for a bathroom pass, I was awed by horny stewardesses who thought nothing of using their galley breaks to fuck themselves with the heel of their pumps. Or *Hustler*'s Girl with the Bubble Gum Pussy, whose labia really did look like "someone lost his chewing gum along with his cherry." Even the matter-of-fact cartoons of Betty Boop fingering herself or Dagwood impaling Blondie on what looked like a hairy cucumber had something to teach me. I returned to the brown shag-carpeted bedroom again and again, even breaking the combination when the contents were suddenly transferred to a locked briefcase.

I was sixteen when I saw my first porn movie, at a party where I had no business being. The images of *Debbie Does Dallas* were faded and staticky, but it was like watching a slow-mo car wreck: *That penis is really sliding into her vagina.*

I have no more instinct to document my own sexuality than I do to compete in monster truck pulls. My first boyfriend begged me to let him take a naked Polaroid; as soon as the image swam to the surface, I made him burn it down to ash. But watching that fourth-generation videotape was a revelation. It was proof that, just as there weren't little singers inside the radio, real people did this.

I wanted to know more. I made my boyfriend take me to Fort Worth's only X-rated drive-in. It wasn't much of an outing; our headrests kept getting in the way and he seemed relieved when I wanted to leave early.

I found other ways to pursue my fascination. When I found out that a porn star, Jerry Butler, had written a tell-all autobiography, I pounced on it. I was a fast reader, so it only took a few visits to a bookstore finish *Raw Talent*; I was too scared to buy it. Later, when I lived in New York, I discovered *The Robin Byrd Show*, hosted by a former *Debbie Does Dallas* starlet who had transformed herself into a cable-access Oprah Winfrey for the raincoat set. "So, you've got a three-week engagement at Show World," Robin would say, leathery in her macramé bikini. "Why don't you tell us what we can we expect to see?"

By the time I went to work at the *Hollywood Reporter*, porn could sometimes serve as jerk-off material, or at least some of it did (I still can't shake Butler's description of emerging from Ginger Lynn with a lump of coal at the end of his penis), but the sex had nothing to do with why I memorized porn stars' names as if they were Latin verbs. I didn't care about the acrobatics. I wanted to know how these people went to the grocery store. Does Jamie Summers live in fear of a soccer mom chucking a yogurt at her head? I know Janine can suck off two guys at once, but does she have any friends? Did she do this on purpose?

Porn was the last thing on my mind the night my editor said, "We've got to do something about this." It was our last night in Milan, where we'd been covering a film market and it wasn't much of a leap to believe that *do something* meant *get rid of me.*

There's a reason shyness isn't known as a defining quality of Pulitzer Prize–winners and, after more than a year at the *Reporter,* I was beginning to realize that I couldn't break a story with a gallon of truth serum and a cattle prod. Every phone call to a would-be source gave me hot and cold flashes, which left me feeling as if icicles dangled from my armpits.

I was too scared to say anything, so I was relieved to hear Cathy say, "Stephen, the market's dead." Aside from an ill-advised stint as assistant to Walter Matthau's son and to a studio exec who ate nothing but oatmeal, my colleague had spent her career writing business stories for various entertainment magazines. "The stories just weren't there. You can't expect us to make things up."

Stephen was unmoved. He didn't look intimidating—a former child actor, he once served as a stand-in for a pre-Monkees Davy Jones—but he was wholly capable of firing me in a foreign country. "No, but I do expect us to provide a good read. You make the mistake of focusing solely on the deals. We never write about the personalities surrounding these markets, and in Cannes, that's going to change."

Cathy and I looked at each other. Unless lying was considered a personality trait, sales agents didn't have personalities.

"We've never written about the monks who make the honey on that island outside Cannes. And the people who rent the yachts every year—who are they? What are they like? A few more ideas, and have one in every issue of the Cannes daily."

"Who's going to write all these, then?" Cathy asked.

"Dana can do it," Stephen said. "You and I can focus on the business stories."

I put down my fork. Cannes was six months away, but I'd already lost my appetite.

"You should be writing these down," he said. "Oh, and what about the porn stars in the basement? I've always wondered about those."

"What porn stars?" I asked. "What basement?"

"They're in the Palais, the big convention center. All the mainstream companies are on the top floors and then you have the porn people underground. Follow them around, see what they're like."

Once we were safely back at our hotel, Cathy railed, "Porn stars! What's he on about? You don't have to do it, you know."

"No, but I'd better," I said, working to disguise my mounting glee. "You know how he is."

Later, Joy King, vice president of Wicked Pictures, drove me down a dark highway I'd never heard of to an exit I'd never remember, turning on a residential street whose residents certainly wouldn't appreciate the thought of a porn movie being shot on their block. We were visiting the set of Jenna Jameson's comeback movie, *Hell on Heels,* and I was there to take notes. If anyone asked me, "How could you?" I could say, in all honesty, that it was my job.

The truth was that I'd never been so happy to work on a story in my life, and even the industry's most mundane aspects brought me delight. They had contract stars, just like studios did back in the 1950s! Wicked had a foreign-sales agent, one who was every bit as dull as his mainstream counterparts!

Even better was what the story brought me back at the office. If not exactly respect, my coworkers looked at me with a new curiosity. Until now, I was the paper's least interesting film reporter, one who wasn't given to raging at publicists and whose name appeared infrequently on the front page. But as word spread about my porn assignment, my mostly male colleagues would find a moment to ask how it was going and what I'd discovered so far. It was as close as I was ever going to get to being asked about my trip to Kosovo. I'd watch their eyes shine as I told them that it was a strange and challenging piece, feeling every bit like Br'er Rabbit all the while: *Please don't throw me in the briar patch.*

"Try to be quiet," Joy whispered. "I think we're rolling."

The set was an old stone church, its stained-glass windows lit with an intensity that suggested Jesus was paying a quick visit. I followed Joy's footsteps, tiptoeing through a tangle of black cords and milk crates and averting my eyes from crew members. I'm a reporter, I thought. I'm here to report. I'm not here to stare.

I stared.

There's a part of your brain that's used for sorting things out and putting them in their place, the no-nonsense nanny of the cerebral cortex. But when I saw Jenna Jameson standing five feet in front of me, wearing nothing but knee-high platform boots and a breast-baring satin corset as she slid an oversized silver bullet in and out of her vagina, my Mary Poppins packed up her carpet bag and split.

The director called "Cut," and Jenna handed her dildo to a production assistant, but Nikki Tyler wasn't finished. "Hang on," said. "I've got a good one." And with that, she hocked a loogie onto Sydnee Steele's spit-shiny crotch and went back to work.

I tried to break down the scene into more familiar elements. There was a PA, but he served as the dildo wiper. There was a director, one who never took his eyes from the playback screen, but Joy said something about how he and Jenna no longer spoke to each other, even though they were still married. Even the craft services table, with its paper plates of assorted Cheetos, eluded me. Wasn't that a risky foodstuff, considering the circumstances? If you forgot to wash the orange off your fingers, it seemed like it might sting. I felt like a drunk who closes one eye while seeing double, and it didn't work any better in these circumstances.

On the way back, Joy apologized that there wasn't much of a chance to talk with Jenna. She promised to set up something later in the week. She did, but an interview scheduled for 8 P.M. at the Sportmen's Lodge became ten o'clock at the Spearmint Rhino. "I'm sorry, but it's been all this drama," Joy said. "Jenna was with Nikki and then she got engaged to Jay. Now she's back with Nikki, but she's kind of still dating Jay. Anyway, she'll meet you there."

Jenna was going to the strip club in Van Nuys to watch her girlfriend. I immediately began to drop the factoid into as many office conversations as possible, but I was glad to have my fiancé, Doug, by my side when we arrived at a deserted stretch of Oxnard Street. Spearmint Rhino was supposed to be a high-end strip club, but it looked like an oversized concrete bunker.

Inside, I gave my business card to the cashier and explained why we were there. He asked for our IDs and said, "That'll be $40."

I'd been to a strip club before, but it was the kind where the dancers competed with the football games on big-screen TVs. Here, the only light source seemed to be the stage, but it was a Tuesday night and Jenna wasn't hard to find. She was standing at the bar with a man who I presumed was Jay. He was handsome, but his face looked freshly sharpened, with long blond hair held back in a tight ponytail. They were holding hands, but the expression on their faces suggested it wasn't so much a gesture of affection as a way to make sure no one got slapped.

She let go of his hand to shake mine. "Let's go to Nikki's dressing room," she said. "It's quieter." Nikki was shucking her schoolgirl's uniform, surrounded by smoke that smelled like the inside of a new refrigerator. We wove our way through the tables and past the stage.

Backstage consisted of a short hallway with a pay phone. There was also a dancers' dressing room, a men's room, and a door marked with a large star, one that Jenna knocked on before opening. Inside was a tiled bathroom, large enough to meet city handicap codes. Jay leaned against the sink, Doug sat on the toilet, I sat on the floor and Jenna perched herself on top of what looked like a plastic tackle box, close enough to hold Jay's hand.

"It's impossible to have normal relationships," Jenna said. There was a knock at the door. Jenna leaned over to open it and Nikki came inside, wearing a G-string and a white oxford cloth shirt knotted at the waist.

"I need my blow dryer," she said. "Did I look okay out there?"

"Yeah, honey, you looked really good," Jenna said. Nikki disappeared.

Ten minutes later, Jenna told me that she expected to be in porn for only another year or so. "You can't do this forever. I want to get rich enough so I can stop working, get married, and have lots of babies." Another knock and Nikki reappeared, the G-string gone, the shirt unbuttoned and untied.

"I think I forgot my other shoes." I watched her do a deep knee bend, never teetering on her white platform heels, her shaved vagina just inches from the floor. "Did you see that? Did it look good?"

"Sure, babe," Jenna said, "You were great."

The article appeared on the front page of the *Hollywood Reporter*'s Cannes daily. I'd never gotten so much attention for anything I'd published in my life. Yes, I met Jenna Jameson. Being on a porn set feels like being on a low-budget film shoot, only with a lot less clothing. They have weird relationships, but porn stars themselves are kind of normal. Really.

And I meant it. I liked these people. I liked Jenna, who praised Joy's marketing skills by saying, "She could sell a vibrator to a nun." I liked Joy, who was as sharp as anyone I'd met on the upper levels of the Palais. I liked the idea that there was a strange but friendly underworld where sex could be broken down into positions and pop shots on a set list.

And, even though reporters are never supposed to think such things, I was worried about what they thought of the story. I wrote about the strip club dressing room. I mentioned that porn stars are always known as "girls." I used the nun quote.

"It was awesome!" Joy said when she called later that day. "The girls loved it. Can you come out with us tonight?"

For most people, the city of Cannes translates to a strip of hotels and restaurants that, if they didn't face the Riviera, looks exactly like Beverly Hills. However, Joy asked me to meet them at an address that fell some ten streets behind the Croisette. I walked up just as a limousine drove down the cobblestone street and stopped at the club's front door. It was dark, but there was no mistaking the passengers as the platform-heeled silhouettes emerged from the car.

"Hey, you guys remember Dana," Joy said. "She was the one who wrote that great article."

Missy, Jenna, Serenity, and Stephanie waved or nodded before turning their attention to the flashbulb-wielding photographers who were waiting for them.

"Come on," Joy said and we were swept inside the club; velvet ropes were pushed aside and we were seated in a private corner where the porn stars might be approached but never annoyed. Bottles of vodka were presented; trays of puff-pastry hors d'oeuvres were delivered.

The girls tip-tipped to the dance floor. They bumped-and-ground into each other, a dirty version of the locomotion. Jenna and Stephanie went to the DJ booth and began another dance, this one involving flashes of tit, tongues, and disappearing hands. Joy replaced Jenna, but neither Stephanie nor the crowd seemed to mind.

I didn't know where to look so I tried to make conversation with Missy, a girl under contract at Wicked with her husband, Mickey G. She hadn't gone down to the dance floor. She wasn't drinking. In fact, she wasn't doing anything. She looked miserable in her corset and blue jean miniskirt. Mickey, however, was full of ideas.

"Yeah, that was a great article. It's so rare when people try to see us as we really are, you know? It's, like, they think we're all having orgies all the time and, really, it's just work." Cameras flashed behind his head as Christy Lake, a freelance porn actress, raised her T-shirt for the photographers.

Joy reappeared. "Come on guys, come dance with us."

"Yeah," Mickey said. "Come on."

So I followed Mickey and Joy to the dance floor. Joy disappeared with Stephanie, leaving me with Mickey.

I started dancing. Mickey started dancing.

Then Mickey started grinding.

I kept dancing, but took two steps to the left. Mickey took two steps the left

Two steps to the right. Mickey took his two steps, and then another straight for me. I took one step back. We'd probably still be fox-trotting if I hadn't begged off at this point, claiming thirst.

"Hey, you're a really good dancer," he said, white teeth gleaming behind what now seemed like a vaguely satanic goatee. "We should get together when we're back in L.A."

"Ah huh huh ha ha," I said. I did my best not to run back to my drink. I was happy to see Joy back at our table, but she told me the only reason she didn't dance with us was Stephanie wouldn't let her.

"Yeah, I've been hanging with Stephanie, you know, and she's just so clingy and it's starting to drive me nuts. I mean, I wanted to dance with you guys and she just wouldn't let me." My face must have twisted at this point because she said, "Oh, now that I've told you I'm bi, you probably won't dance with me."

The drink hadn't helped. I tried to think of something to say, but standing in front of me was Joy's assistant, a plain and somewhat doughy girl, her eyes closed. Mickey ran his dusky hands around her head, tilted to expose a white neck, down to her breasts. His wife displayed a heretofore unknown enthusiasm as she crouched on the floor and stroked the girl's legs under her skirt, flapping the edges as if she was creating a cool breeze.

It was at that point that I decided to call it a night. I ran all the way back to my hotel, where I called Doug and told him I'd had enough. "They were like vampires," I said. "It was like because I wrote an article, they thought I might be one of them."

Three years later, I was sitting in the office of World Modeling, the world's largest porn star agency.

"Oh hi, Romeo. Wherefore art thou? Uh-huh. I see. Well, for which shoot was it?" Jim South flipped through Polaroids, barely looking at them before he went on to the next. "Okay. Which girl was it?" He put down the Polaroids. "You showed a girl your weenie and you don't remember her name? Romeo! How am I going to get you paid if you . . ." He picked up the pictures again, looked at them and then put them down. "Okay, you think her name might have been 'Night.' Is that 'Night' with an 'N' or 'Knight' with a 'K'?" First name or last name? She was white. Now we're getting somewhere. Romeo, do you know how many 'Nights' there are in this business? Okay. You think it was 'Night Sky.' All right, I'll see what I can do. Give my love to Suzy. Hello, World Modeling?"

I wasn't quite sure what I was doing there, but Jim didn't seem to mind me sitting on his ancient polyester couch while I figured it out. I wasn't there to write an article; I'd left *Hollywood Reporter* for *Variety*, but I covered Warner Bros. and Sony, neither of which showed much inclination to expand into porn. However, I'd asked my boss, Peter, for permission to spend Friday mornings in the office of Jim South's World Modeling, saying that I wanted to do research for a book. Peter agreed, which was generous, since my pitch couldn't have been very good.

A girl with long black hair walked into the office. She wore a plaid miniskirt and five-inch white platform sandals with white ankle socks. Barefoot, she wouldn't have cleared five feet.

She sat next to me with her legs splayed, clutching her panties. "Do you guys have any ice packs?" Her voice was as clear and tiny as Minnie Mouse.

Jim kept talking. "Okay, let me get this straight. You're going to get pregnant and . . . no, you are pregnant. How far along are you? Your due date. When the baby comes."

I saw a tattoo etched on her inner wrist. It looked like some kind of Chinese calligraphy.

"That's really pretty," I said. "Does it mean anything?"

"Pain and suffering," she chirped. "It's not a dom thing. I was just having a bad day, I guess. I figured it was better than slitting my wrists." She giggled. "Jim, do you guys have any icepacks? My pussy's sore." She asked the question as if pussy ice packs might be a standard in any first aid kit, next to the Band-Aids and Tylenol.

"Hon, I can't help you right now," Jim said to the phone. "I do sometimes book those shoots, but they like the girl to be showing and if I remember correctly, there isn't much to see at three months. Call me again in another three, OK? 'Bye now. Well, hello Miss Cherokee. I was just talking about you with Jill Kelly. She wants you for a girl-girl on the twenty-seventh."

Cherokee flipped through her datebook. "Is she nice?"

"Yeah, she's real nice."

"If she's not nice, I'm not doing anything. Wait, I can't do the twenty-seventh. I have Mr. Marcus then."

Jim let his hands fall on his desk. "When did you book him?"

"He called me last week."

"Honey, I've told you this before, if someone calls you, you have to let me know. Otherwise, I can't book you and I don't get paid." Jim looked at me. "I keep telling the girls this and they never remember. World Modeling? Oh, busier than a one-legged man in an ass-kicking contest. Karen? Oh, you mean Cherokee." Jim shot her a dirty look. "She's a really, really pretty girl from Ohio. She's been booked solid ever since she got here. I booked her from an e-mail with a bad picture and even then she had eight jobs waiting for her. What day?"

Cherokee shook her head. "Whoever it is, I'm not canceling Mr. Marcus. After this much work, I have to have a black guy to reward myself."

"Let me call you back." Jim hung up the phone. "Honey, you're not Karen. You're Cherokee. Now, you have to learn to say, 'No, I just can't do this.' You have to have them call me. You'll burn out. Tell them you're saving yourself."

"I'm saving myself." She giggled.

Jim shook his head. "Can I get you back to business? I've got you a job for Friday. It's sex, but just stills. He usually pays six hundred dollars for stills, which is excellent."

Cherokee frowned and clutched her crotch again. "My pussy can't take that much pounding. I need an icepack."

"You booked yourself with Mr. Marcus," he said, "and you're worried about pounding?"

Peter likes to see his reporters as characters in his personal comic strip, one that's more *Doonesbury* than *Brenda Starr.* And he loved the idea that one of his female reporters volunteered—no, asked for permission, her own idea—to spend time in the strange and murky world of porn and came back with stories of amusement rather than condemnation. He loved my Valley forays and began to ask if there wasn't something here worth covering for *Variety.*

So I wrote about Jenna, now with Vivid Entertainment, shilling for Pony sportswear. I wrote about the supposedly recession-proof porn studios, which were consolidating like their mainstream brethren. I quoted Cherokee in an article that followed the HIV-positive diagnosis of the porn star Darren James. I wrote about how the government was looking to clamp down on porn just as Brian Grazer was producing *Inside Deep Throat*, and I covered the Adult Entertainment Expo in Las Vegas—all for *Variety*'s front page.

My friends and family were used to seeing me take career detours that sent me from corporate shill to sautéing lobster mushrooms to reviewing restaurants to interviewing. They might say, "I don't know how you do it" when I came back with stories of how I went back to the kitchen with my arm in a sling or received death threats from angry restaurant owners or yelled at agents to calm down, seeing as I hadn't even written the damn thing yet, but they'd never be any less than thrilled to see me happy in my work.

Porn was different.

"This isn't all you're writing about now, is it?" my mom said, holding a copy of *Variety* at arm's length.

"I don't know, maybe it's because I'm pregnant," my sister said, her hands draped over her own five-month belly.

"All of those people lead messed-up lives," my dad said. "The next time you see Ron Jeremy, do you think you might get his autograph?"

"But that's evil." This came from Lisa, a high school friend I hadn't spoken to in nearly a decade. I called her on a whim while in the office late one night and told her about Jim South's office, with its posters for forgotten porn movies, and Cherokee's tiny voice, using the squeak of *icepack?* as a punchline.

I tried to explain that porn made me feel brave and invisible all at once. If no one says anything about the girl who's using nail scissors to trim her tampon string, no one's going to notice the girl who keeps scribbling in her notebook. But she didn't think it was funny, or even interesting; it was as if she was forced to watch me hang a mobile made of pentagrams and inverted crosses over a baby's crib.

Later, I told myself to consider the source. A devoted mom of four—one from the boyfriend who bolted when she was three months' pregnant, two from her husband, and an adopted child with significant mental handicaps—Lisa was also an air force wife who had recovered her Catholicism. No wonder my strange tales sounded so . . . strange. Still, I couldn't shake the sense that she'd said what everyone else wanted to say.

Recently, Variety sent me to cover the annual lobbying efforts of the Free Speech Coalition, the porn industry's lobbying arm, in Sacramento. I had a great time.

"If they throw the word 'hardcore' at you, that word has no legal definition," said Jeffrey Douglas, a First Amendment attorney and FSC board member who coached the lobbyists on how to deal with potentially hostile politicians. "Tell them you don't know what it means."

Sitting next to me was Wicked Pictures' contract star Stormy Daniels, who rolled her eyes and muttered, "Hardcore means, 'Don't block the light.' "

I came home and wrote another article, one that described how well the porn people were received by both Democrats and Republicans and how they had hired a federal lobbyist as they prepared for a brave step: making their case in Washington, where Attorney General Alberto Gonzales had virtually promised to shoot them on sight. I e-mailed a copy to the FSC's head lobbyist, Kat Sunlove, with a brief note of thanks.

The next day, AVN.com published another article, about my article. Citing it as "another example of mainstream journalism still not quite Getting It," it quoted Kat as saying, "The whole thing smacks a little of sexism, since all she speaks of about me is my age, a suggestion about my looks, and my sexual background," adding, "I feel it's just inaccurate to characterize me that way."

"That way" referred to my description of her as a sixty-year-old former dominatrix. I'd also cited her as deserving much of the credit for FSC's success and as a longtime political activist, one whose work stretched back to Los Angeles mayor Tom Bradley.

My first instinct was to write Kat and explain that she'd misunderstood, but what stopped me was how she'd bristled at being called a dominatrix. Did she really think that her former life as a sex worker had nothing to do with channeling her political energies into an organization devoted to defending the rights of the porn industry? If the porn industry wants to be accepted by the mainstream, I harrumphed to myself, it might help if they accepted themselves first.

And at the same time, it's hard to blame her because no matter how many porn stars write best-selling autobiographies, porn will never be mainstream.

It doesn't matter how may times the E! Channel runs Jenna's *True Hollywood Story*. Or that at this year's *AVN* Awards, patrons at the Venetian formed an impromptu receiving line, one that stretched all the way from the casino to the ballroom, cheering and toasting the porn stars in formal wear. "Oh, I think I recognize that one," says a real estate agent who came to Vegas with her girlfriends from Ohio. "I think we have one of her tapes."

None of it matters because if that porn star moved next door to her, she wouldn't haul out the Welcome Wagon. She'd plant a For Sale sign in her own yard.

Just as our great-great-grandparents might have sneaked over to the carnival to see the Bearded Lady, HBO subscribers tune in to watch Jessica Drake say she can't imagine how anyone can live without having a husband and a girlfriend. A carny couldn't sell a single peek at the Bearded Lady with a pitch about how she's a really nice person whose hobbies include needlepoint and bridge. Audiences are drawn by the promise of a shadow world, where the wild things are. Once they've crossed over, however, you're just as likely to see the hirsute gal sitting in a chair, eating an apple.

For myself, I like Joy, and Cherokee, and Jenna. I like Sarah Blake, who covered herself with a ski jacket as she walked from her room at the Venetian to the Expo show floor. "I wish people wouldn't bring their kids into casinos," she said. I like Stormy Daniels, a Wicked contract girl who gives strip-club bouncers a picture of her mom with instructions to keep her out. "Believe me," she said, "there's nothing more disturbing than standing buck-ass naked and looking between your legs to see your mom standing at the edge of the stage holding a dollar bill."

They're why I still like writing about porn. I don't want these people to be invisible—or worse, want them to wish they were.

EROTIC ENVISONERS

THE WOMEN WHO ENABLE OUR VIEWING HABITS

TRISTAN TAORMINO

. . . . ON CROSSING THE LINE TO CREATE FEMINIST PORN.

IN 1997, I WROTE A book called *The Ultimate Guide to Anal Sex for Women*. It was a taboo subject I am very passionate about, and no other book like it existed, so I decided to write one myself. I began teaching workshops around the country based on the book, and an amazing mix of people showed up: straight, gay, bi, trans, men, women, single, couples, old, young, from every walk of life. Lots of them asked me, "When are you going to make a video?"

I had always been a fan of adult movies, and I liked the idea of making a how-to video based on my book, but most of the instructional videos I'd seen were, well, pretty boring. I wanted to make an educational anal sex video that not only taught viewers *how* to do it, but that was so sexy and hot, it also inspired them *to* do it. I wanted to combine the heat and excitement of a full-on fuck film with the foreplay, technique, and information of a strong instructional.

Much like any aspiring filmmaker, I had two options: go independent or pitch it to a mainstream company.

My idea of independent would be that I would beg, borrow, and run up my credit cards, ask my friends and their friends to work for little or nothing, and somehow get it made. But then, how would I get it out there? On my own, I could sell it to my readers, fans, and workshops participants. I could get it in sex-positive stores like Toys in Babeland and Good Vibrations, but that was like preaching to the converted. I wanted to reach as many people as possible, so mainstream distribution was a must.

Beginning in 1998, I pitched the idea to several top companies in the adult industry, who all turned me down. When I described the video as both "educational" and "for women," the way porn people responded, I might as well have been speaking a foreign language. I was a writer, an outsider in their world, pitching an idea that defied well-established, easily marketable genres. They didn't know what to make of me.

One of the people who turned me down was legendary porn mogul John "Buttman" Stagliano. John is the head of Evil Angel Video and creator of the wildly successful *Buttman* video series. I first discovered John as a fan when I saw a *Buttman* video. John created the character of Buttman, a man obsessed with women's asses. He likes to get women to show him their asses, play with their asses, put things in their own asses, and let him put things in their asses.

One of the arguments made against porn is that it is produced by and for straight men, and therefore can't possibly appeal to women. My identification with Buttman's point of view directly contradicted this assertion. I want women to show me their asses, play with their asses, put things in their own asses, and let me put things in their asses. I could totally relate to Buttman! But after our first meeting, John seemed less than interested.

Several months later, seemingly out of the blue, I got a phone call at home. I remember that I was sitting on my couch, laptop glowing in front of me, typing up a freelance article, when I answered the phone. He identified himself, and I wanted to scream, "Oh my God! Buttman is calling me!" but instead I listened to what he had to say, and we set up a meeting.

Besides our common lust for derrieres, another reason that John appealed to me was that he is credited as the father of "gonzo" video. Gonzo is a genre of adult video where the camera is acknowledged in the film; call it documentary-style porn or reality porn. Spontaneity, realness, and hot, raw sex are emphasized over stylized plots, sets, and other elements of big-budget productions. I think that if porn stars are good at something, then we should just highlight that thing—giving them elaborate dialogue, sets, props, and costumes only distracts from their talent: delivering a scorching sexual performance.

After several meetings, John agreed to fund the project. Like so many experiences in my life, it was everything I expected, and more, and less.

Let's talk about the more—the positive part of my first porn experience. Casting was a crucial part of the process. Lots of actors can give what industry people call a "strong anal performance," and don't get me wrong, I wanted plenty of strong anal performances. But I also wanted people who actually loved anal sex and who were really into the project. If someone I spoke to said, "Sure, I'll do your movie, I'm not doing anything else that day," that was not the performer for me. I wanted open and honest porn stars who truly loved anal sex and were ready to articulate the reasons why on camera, not to mention demonstrate their experiences from start to finish. I think I ended up with an impressive group of people, including a real-life couple, a porn legend, and several newcomers who went on to become award winners and studio contract stars.

And then there was the learning curve. The first day on the set, there I was—I'd never made a movie, never taken a film class, never read a book on how to make a film, never even picked up a video camera before. Imagine cramming an entire lesson on porn production into seven days. Imagine if you knew little or nothing about filmmaking, and your first directing gig is along-side Steven Spielberg. And that's who John Stagliano is in the world of porn. It was incredible! First of all, I got to watch people have sex all day. I know there are plenty of people who work in various sectors of the sex industry who find sex to be redundant, boring, and utterly uninteresting. Call me old-fashioned, but watching folks fuck right in front of me turns me on. They also stun me (they get turned on, switch positions, and get right to it), inspire me (they're uninhibited, expressive, beautiful to watch) and impress me (they come practically on command). I observed and learned something from each and every cast member, from Ruby's hesitation to Nina Hartley's wisdom to Chandler's open-ness. The powerful dynamic between Nacho Vidal and his then-girlfriend Jazmine, Sydnee Steele's clarity about her desires, the honesty of Chloe and Kyle's communication, the confidence of Inari Vachs, the enthusiasm of Jewel Valmont (now known as Ava Vincent), the sincerity of Tony Tedechi—they all touched me in a real way.

I was determined to challenge not only sex education video conventions, but those of traditional hardcore films, to include more realistic portrayals of sex. For me, that meant filming it all: sex toys, lube, and plenty of foreplay. One of the reasons that you don't see more vibrators in video, especially with male—female couples during intercourse, is that the vibrator often covers what the camera can't take its eyes off: the pussy. And some vibrators can be so loud that it sounds like there's a blender in the back-ground. Visual and sound challenges be damned: I wanted per-formers to use vibrators if vibrators were going to turn them on and enhance their experience and thus their performance. It's important for viewers to know that vibrators, as well as lots of other sex toys, should not be intimidating or off limits, but are a fun, healthy part of partner sex. Likewise, it was especially important that scenes of performers using lube for anal penetration did not end up on the cutting room floor as they often do because they are messy, awkward, or noneventful. Sometimes sex is messy, awkward, or noneventful. I also filmed extensive foreplay scenes (which also often get cut out of the final product) in order to show people that all kinds of stimulation can be sexy. And I included moments where performers communicated with each other about what they liked and what they wanted, even if that meant slowing things down in order to properly warm up for penetration. After all, no one should go from zero to sixty in five seconds flat.

I decided before the shoot that I wasn't going to have any facial cum shots. I felt that it had become a cliché in porno, to say nothing of being a stereotype of the male-centered world of adult film. It's the one moment onscreen when most women look bored, turned off, or downright miserable. Don't get me wrong— having a guy come on your face can be spontaneous, fun, and a total turn-on for plenty of women, but in videos I've never been impressed with this typical "pop shot." When I directed my performers that there were to be "no facials," they expressed surprise, even shock, but they went along with it, reluctantly in some cases, as did Buttman.

Speaking of Buttman, since his money was funding the project, I had to make some compromises. Amazingly, he let me call a great many of the shots, but he also had plenty of input. John's loyal audience is primarily straight men who like a hot anal sex flick; I knew going into it that I wanted to make a video that not only taught people (especially women) about anal sex but actually inspired them to do it, while simultaneously adhering to what sells tapes—the jerk-off factor.

So while I fought for no facials and won, each scene with a guy culminates in an external orgasm, i.e., "The Money Shot," a staple in porn videos that I personally think can be redundant, unnecessary, and even disruptive to the flow of action. Buttman gave me no facials; I let the money shots remain.

The biggest issue we tangled over was the use of condoms. John relies on industry-standardized HIV and STD testing to ensure that performers are disease-free and can have sex without protection. Plus, he doesn't like to see condoms in porn. One insider warned me, "John doesn't do movies with condoms. He'll never, ever make a picture with a single condom." We disagreed on this point, because while all performers did arrive on my set with negative HIV tests, I still thought it was important to show people using condoms. In fact, my movie was the first released by his company to include condoms in all the scenes but one, and that one was between a real-life couple, which was established on camera. I also managed to introduce latex gloves as a safer sex method in several of the scenes, including one between two women and one threesome.

The biggest surprise to me was that the world of adult movies was entirely more complex than I anticipated. Or perhaps than I wanted it to be. I went into the experience as a cheerleader for porn, and I got a reality check. I hand-picked my performers, and wanted them all to be shining examples of the best and brightest of the industry. But it turned out that, like the industry itself, they were full of contradictions. I was frustrated and ultimately depressed that one actress drank on my set, and it definitely affected her performance. One performer was very guarded, an impenetrable (and protective?) shield around her no matter how she got fucked. Some were flaky, others professional, some excited, others just doing their jobs. It became a lesson as my cast represented a microcosm of the adult industry.

There are women who love sex and women who hate sex; women with low self-esteem and women with strong self-images; women addicted to plastic surgery and women with less than perfect bodies who like themselves just the way they are. I have met women who are sexually feisty, in control of their bodies, lives, and careers; but there are also women who don't feel they have a lot of work options, who feel compelled to look a certain way to succeed, who are motivated more by money than anything else. In the course of producing my movie, I got a glimpse of all sides.

Lots of people ask me why I decided to be in the movie. That's right, the rumors are true: after spending six scenes dishing out tips and techniques, I surrender to my entire cast, who show me what they've learned in an anal orgy where they each get to have their way with me. I was the subject of a ten-person, all-gender, all-anal gang bang. It was important for me to be in the video to show not only that porn stars can enjoy anal sex, but that any woman can. I think lots of women are intimidated by porn stars, and believe either that their performances are fake or that they can do things ordinary people can't do merely because they are "professionals." I needed to show those women and others that the girl next door, which I am for all intents and purposes, can have just as fabulous a time. Plus, as a director/producer, I knew I had a unique hook: a respected writer who's never performed on film would make her debut in a ten-person anal orgy . . . well, *that* should get the movie some attention.

I got to call the shots in my debut. As the director, I created a safe way to be fucked by a group of ten people I'd never had sex with before—I told them what to do to me and how to do it, then I momentarily surrendered and just let them all do what they do best. As I read the long list of detailed instructions to them, John asked me on camera, "Did you go to Vassar or something?" He meant to make a joke about my approach to the entire scene, which he clearly recognized as feminist. He thought I approached my sexual surrender to a group of seasoned professionals the same way I'd organize a pep rally. In many ways, it was my pep rally: I wanted every performer to be as excited as possible, and for viewers to feel their—and my—enthusiasm. Everyone on the set teased me: "Sure, we'll do exactly what you say . . ." (wink, wink). In the end, if you listen to my direction (which I included as part of the behind-the-scenes footage at the end of the video), and then watch how the scene goes, they do, in fact, follow my instructions almost to the letter. And, for me, that was an important element in creating the ultimate feminist gang bang. Even John got in on the action, when I surprised him (and everyone) at the end of the scene, inviting him to put his fingers in my ass. Was it wild and extreme in the eyes of many? Sure. But it was my vision for the movie and a fantasy as well. I am entitled to my fantasies, as everyone else is to theirs.

As feminism has taught us, the personal is political, and I believe my unique story can have broader implications for sex, porn, and feminism. I graduated Phi Beta Kappa with high honors from a top university. I've worked in the not-for-profit sector and the publishing industry, and even had an ultra-corporate marketing position with a dot-com company. I'm a published writer, I've got income and skills. I'm in therapy, consider myself (and am considered by others) to be psychologically sound. I'm self-aware, I'm not self-destructive. I do not drink, smoke, or use drugs. All this, and I *chose* to do porn.

Anti-porn advocates want everyone to believe that pornographers are predatory, seedy people who pluck Midwestern girls from bus stations and force them to do things they don't want to do. The media loves to cover stories of victimization, but seldom do we see performers who are activists, educators, or astute businesswomen firmly in control of their career choices. Linda Lovelace and Traci Lords get more airtime than Juli Ashton and Nina Hartley. My experiences on the set of adult productions and dealing with people in the industry do not reflect the supposed horrors that anti-porn advocates want us to believe. Ultimately, porn is both incredibly diverse and undeniably subjective, so it's impossible to make any blanket statements about it. Like all other forms of media, from the grassroots independent to the mainstream, it is neither all good or all bad. Is there porn I find boring, stereotypical, not sexy, even degrading and offensive? Yes. Bad porn cares less about everyone involved, reduces people to their body parts, is devoid of emotional connection or mutual pleasure. When pornography represents women as helpless, dehumanized receptacles for male fantasy and orgasm, that's degrading. But not all porn does that.

So what the heck is feminist pornography? For me, it means that the process of making it is fair and ethical. There is absolute consent and no coercion of any kind. The work environment is safe, everyone wants to be there, and respect is essential. Women and men are given choices: they choose who they will have sex with, they choose the positions they want to be in, they choose the toys they play with, all based on what feels good to them, all based on their actual sexuality, not a fabricated script. The movie is a collaboration between director and performer, with the actors' input and their ideas about how they want to be represented. This puts a new spin on the notion of objectification—What happens when the so-called powerless object willingly and enthusiastically participates in the creation of his or her own image? I think it is possible to create sexual images without stripping away someone's entire identity.

Feminist porn is porn that empowers women and men: it gives them information and ideas about sex. It teaches. It inspires fantasy and adventure. It validates viewers when they see themselves or a part of their sexuality represented. It presents sex as joyful, fun, safe, and satisfying. It counteracts the other messages we get from society: sex is shameful, naughty, dirty, scary, dangerous, or it's the domain of men, where theirs are the only desires and fantasies that get fulfilled.

And yes, it arouses, but even if that's all it does, that's a good thing. Our sexuality is part of who we are, and pleasure has value.

While my two videos may seem to be pebbles in a sea of titles, I do think I've made an impact. The first video received praise from industry veterans and publications and won three awards. The average video title sells about four to six thousand copies. My two videos have sold almost fifty thousand copies and are available all over the world. I didn't want to make a traditional sex ed video that was all talk and anatomical diagrams. I wanted a little more SEX and a little less ED. I knew that including plenty of hot sex would automatically put my videos into the realm of hardcore films, but that was okay with me. The truth is that a lot of people who would never rent, buy, or watch a so-called educational flick got to see this film, and got more than they bargained for. They bought it for the entertainment and arousal factor, but in the process, according to the extensive feedback I get, they also learned something. Which was exactly my plan.

Porn is a ten-billion-billion-dollar industry, and growing. It's here to stay. I was exposed to porn made by and for women, and I saw that there could be alternatives. I did not forge this path I'm on; that was done two decades ago by pioneers like Nina Hartley, Annie Sprinkle, Betty Dodson, Carol Queen, Debi Sundahl, and others who have all created women-centered, sex-positive porn. Are feminists a minority in the adult industry? Absolutely. But if we ignore or dismiss this prevalent, powerful medium, I think we walk away from a significant opportunity. The process of making porn can be not only consensual, it can be safe, professional, political, empowering, and fun. As a feminist, I consciously choose to engage this supposed "enemy of women" and to challenge the status quo of a historically male-dominated industry. Instead of using my energy and resources to silence others' voices and visions by boycotting or campaigning against porn, I choose to *add* my voice and vision to the mix.

I recently spoke on a panel at a university with others in different parts of the sex industry. In response to a question, one panelist, a writer and performance artist, said that her work was entertainment, and she had no delusions that with it she could change the world. I turned to her, then back to the audience, and uttered my immediate response without a pause: I do believe I can change the world. One feminist porn video at a time.

HOLLY RANDALL

. . . ON FOLLOWING IN HER MOTHER'S FOOTSTEPS TO BECOME AN EROTIC PHOTOGRAPHER.

I KNEW WHERE THE KEY was. That's the thing about adults—they think kids are so naïve, when in fact they are more perceptive than you can imagine. This was the blanket of assurance my parents wrapped around themselves—if they kept the porn in the office (which was the guest house, by the way) under lock and key, their darling little girl would be shielded from their world of smut. Yeah, right.

So once the front door clicked shut, I listened to my parents' retreating footsteps, and the chime on the gate as they left the house. Gotta give them a few minutes unless they come back—forgot something, you know. And then it's . . . dash to the key's hiding place, dart to the office, and looking around fearfully I clicked the key in the lock. I crept into the room cautiously, even though I knew there was no one in today—it was a Saturday, after all. I walked toward the bathroom and opened that magical door that revealed a little closet, with installed shelves. And on those shelves were stacks and stacks of porno magazines. Aaah, heaven. I always pulled magazines from the center or bottom of the pile, so that my parents wouldn't notice the most recent ones missing. But I was sure to mark exactly where the magazines were, as if my parents kept notes on the order of the carelessly stacked magazines. A careless thief always gets caught, after all. Furtively, I stole back to my room with my precious cargo. It was porn time. And I was eight years old.

When people ask me (and they ask me this all the time) when I "found out" my parents worked in porn, they always seem surprised that it was never hidden from me. My mother, Suze, is a famed erotic photographer (and sometimes director) for all the top mens magazines, while my dad, Humphry, helped her run the business. Granted, we didn't sit around the television set watching mommy's latest smut flick, but they never lied about it. Normality is relative, and to me my parents had a perfectly legitimate job. Just one I wasn't allowed to look at.

What is so incredibly ironic about this situation is that my mother's motto has always been, "Rules are meant to be broken." Well, evidently by breaking into my parents' office, I was simply following my mother's instructions. I still vividly remember one of the first layouts I ever saw from my pilfered stash. It was a girl/girl/boy threesome in *Penthouse*—a softcore layout, because it was the time before hardcore was published in magazines. The basic scenario was a man asleep on the couch, while two women creep into his house and essentially take advantage of him. At first he resists, but of course the vixens overcome the poor man, and they all engage in a hot and heavy three-way. For me, it was a fitting introduction to porn, because casting the women in the position of power was a situation I was all too familiar with. It was appropriate because my mother is such a powerful female figure, one who had to overcome the male-driven opposition she faced early on in her career. This photo shoot, though not done by my mother, was an illustration of the male/female power structure that I had grown up with.

At dinnertime, my mother and father would often talk about work. Of course I didn't understand most of it, but I do recall someone named Larry Flynt being brought up fairly often.

Apparently my brother and I used to go swim in his pool as kids, and once my brother purposely stood by the edge of the pool and pissed right into it. Larry got upset, but his wife at the time, Althea, dismissed it as kids being kids. Through those hazy memories of the Flynts, Larry may have actually been my introduction into parody. There was a photo taken of him, looking like a homeless person in a wheelchair, holding out a tin cup for change. When I asked my mother who that was, she explained that it was Larry Flynt.

"But Mommy, don't you work for Larry? Is he poor?"

"No, sweetheart, he's a very rich man—it's a joke."

I wrinkled my nose. "I don't get it. What's so funny about it? He looks sad. Does he need our help?"

My mother laughed. "No, silly. It's called a parody. It's depicting someone as the opposite of who they are."

I still didn't get it. And I remember thinking about that picture for years, until I finally understood the joke. You see, you have to have a sense of humor when you work in porn, otherwise it just swallows you up. Laughter is the key to distancing yourself from the act.

As I grew older, I had to cautiously mask my parents' profession, which made me very good at being vague. Skipping around the topic, changing the subject— all these things I do now as defense mechanisms when I want to shut people out. Hiding a part of my life with the world could prove very difficult at times, but it taught me to be able to hide myself in personal relationships.

One of the most lurid examples of this was an essay I had to write in the fourth grade. I sat at my desk, doodling unicorns in the margins of my notebook, when the teacher began giving out the assignment.

"This week's essay topic will be . . ." *Damn, the head was too big for the body*, I mused as I ascertained my poorly drawn unicorn, ". . . what your mother does for a living. See if you can spend a day with her on the job. You will be excused from class on that day."

I literally dropped my pencil as my head snapped up, looking at the teacher with a woeful expression. "Don't worry," she said soothingly, misinterpreting my apprehension, "even if your mother is a homemaker, she still has a job. Find out what she does on a day-to-day basis." And then with a smile and a pat on my head, she continued to stroll down the aisle of desks, but I didn't hear what else she was saying. This was just one assignment I *couldn't* do. And what was I going to do, approach the teacher and tell her?

"Excuse me, Mrs. Patty, but I have a question about the essay. You see, my mom is a pornographer, so I was wondering that if I go on set and take notes, would you have a preference to a girl/girl scene over a boy/girl scene?" Wonder how she would have taken that one.

Defeated, I trudged home with my dreaded assignment. I waved it in front of my father accusingly, as if he was forcing me to lie at school. After his initial chuckle, my dad sat down with me and helped me write a paper on the very few mainstream jobs my mother had taken, and filled in the rest of the gaps with "model portfolio work." Ha. You should see these portfolios.

The paper came back a few days later, and I thankfully had received an A. That's my favorite thing about English—writing allows you to bullshit your way through almost anything. And I accomplished that at a very early age.

As I grew up, I too fell in love with photography; it began as a voracious devouring of all the fashion magazines my mother brought home, to my first darkroom classes at twelve, to attending Brooks Institute of Photography by the time I was nineteen years old. Brooks was a very technically oriented school that focused mainly on portrait, wedding, architecture, and still life photography—essentially, subjects that failed to interest me. I have always said that I will not photograph things that do not move, for I thrive on the animation of the human spirit. And in looking back on my earliest work as it began to spring up in middle school, it's quite obvious to me that it began as a precarious teetering on the brink of sexual tension, which has plummeted into the chasm of explicitness my photography embodies now. But to me it has seemed a natural progression, not the kind of reeling fall into the world of pornography that so many experience. Years of exposure that gradually began from a young age padded my fall.

After a year and a half of schooling, I began to feel that perhaps Brooks Institute was not the right environment for me. I must admit I have never been a techie—and so the detailed attention we had to pay to lighting ratios and the zone system bored me. My strength has always been the ability to communicate with the model, and to know how to play a girl up to show her best angle. But this restlessness turned to total aversion from the campus when I witnessed the butchering of a fellow classmate's graduation show. Mr. Brooks is a very conservative man who disapproved of images with any pornographic leanings, which to him apparently included artistic and abstract nudes. This student's show was a series of very *un*pornographic, abstract nudes. When he led his family down the school hall to where his show was hung on the wall, he encountered what I can only define as a massacre of his work—Mr. Brooks had taken pieces of white tape and placed them over the nipples of the models. I was horrified. And that very night I packed my bags.

I left Brooks Institute for Los Angeles, to rejoin my family and help my parents run their suddenly booming Web site, Suze.net. How the money flew in those early days of Internet porn! My father called me with promises of an apartment in Malibu and a Ferrari, and though I laughed at the lasso of riches he tried to rope me in with, I thought at least perhaps I could get a shiny new Tahoe and the guesthouse at my parents' last house in West Los Angeles. In the end, I only got the guesthouse, and a much bigger paycheck than the one I had been collecting at Samys Camera during my schooling at Brooks Institute.

But the money wasn't really what interested me. I had never realized the level of fame my mother had achieved until I began working by her side. As a teenager and a young college student, I did not hang around people who knew who Suze Randall was. Sure enough they looked at adult magazines, but what frat boy actually pays attention to who the photographer was? Certainly no one at my school.

It really began to sink in at the adult conventions we began to sporadically attend: Erotica LA, Glamourcon, and of course the AVN show in Las Vegas. Fans would stop and yell my mother's name, asking for a picture or just to express their admiration. I would stand next to my mother and watch these strange men, wringing their hands as sweat glistened along the hairline, stammering words like "legend" and the repeated phrase of "I love your work." My mother would graciously thank them and sweep me to her side, introducing me as her daughter, like some kind of prized possession. Shoulders would hunch forward anxiously and intent eyes would peer at me, as if trying to see into the soul of a child who was raised by a pornographer. And it was (and still is) the same question: "What is it like to be the daughter of Suze Randall?"

If I could issue some blanket statement that would satisfy this question, it would save me a lot of time trying to explain what it was like to grow up in the environment that I did. But I cannot offer any stereotypical account of my childhood, I cannot offer the expected answer that would satisfy people's preconceived notions about the way my mother raised me. My mother is a dichotomy of opposing ideals—on the one hand she is extremely generous and maternal, yet she can also be very aggressive and competitive. She can turn from dumping a glass of water on my date's head because he won't dance at a party, to sending him home with soup and leftovers like she's feeding some kind of starving artist. She can go from sweet-talking a producer into letting her shoot their contract stars, to fighting with magazine editors and losing their business. Ultimately, my mother is both feared and respected, loved and hated. There is no middle ground with Suze—you either adore her or you despise her, for ultimately she is impossible to ignore.

So now that my mother has established herself in the adult world, and many know what to expect from her, curiosity always abounds about the child. It's a pattern we see in Hollywood, in sports—basically in any situation where children choose the same career path as their parents. I always thought I was mostly like my father, but as I grow older I sometimes hear my mother's voice echoed in my own. Though my demeanor in general is much calmer, I've definitely inherited my mother's wild streak, which anyone who has been to a party with me will confirm. I'm also very competitive like my mother, and I have her deep sympathetic streak, which embarrassingly enough makes me cry at sappy commercials. Yet of course our differences are quite noticeable—my dark moods are quiet and brooding, whereas hers are snappish and irritable. I always sweet-talk my way into getting what I want, while she mostly fights to get what she wants. My mother's blunt honesty that can sometimes border on tactlessness has caused me to become so careful about what I say to people that they often can't gauge what I really think of them. I really do believe this all stems from the protective shield I had to surround myself with growing up—the buffer I had to put between my social life and my family life.

But all bets were off when I chose to make this my career. Though the day of my first photo shoot was with my good friend, Aimee Sweet, I was petrified. It was actually a combined effort—

Thomas Rifter and I both shot a couple of sets each on her that day. It was the first time for both of us, and so as to not risk a shoot day gone horribly wrong, we shot in conjunction with a shoot my mother did on a new girl from Amsterdam. Rifter and I shot on the sidelines, and to look back and realize how clueless we were makes me laugh. Yes, the lighting on that first shoot wasn't perfect, and perhaps the poses were a bit off, but there was a youthful quality to those photographs. It was as if inexperience infused something into that shoot—not a feeling of desperation, but an honest attempt to try really hard to prove myself. And when those pictures came back, Aimee backlit, with her gorgeous red hair and wonderfully freckled pale skin (not to mention the amazing body!), I was in love. And it was then I understood why my photography—from the age of twelve when I began studying it—was always infused with sexuality. It was something that had lived in me all my life.

One unexpected effect of working in the adult industry is that I believe it has made me a more tolerant person. Though I was raised in a very liberal family—one that believes in such things as the legalization of prostitution, drugs, and euthanasia—I think my job has also played an instrumental role in my general attitude. Unlike the fashion world, where every model is stick thin and frighteningly tall, porn embraces women of many different shapes and sizes. In fashion, one is selling the clothes, and therefore the woman is more of a walking mannequin, an animated clothes rack. In porn, the focus is on the woman herself—her performance, her sexuality, and her uniqueness. I have shot very skinny girls with almost no breasts, and voluptuous women with ample busts and hips. Through many years of shooting nudes, I have learned how to shoot a woman at her individual best angles, and how to use the camera to trick the eye. I have seen these girls come in at 8 A.M. with no makeup on, looking like a train wreck. After two hours of hair and makeup, they are completely transformed. Ultimately I work to produce a fantasy, which means that I am constantly trying to trick reality. And wrapped up in a career that thrives on illusion and pretense, I must admit it is hard to remember what reality is anymore. But I think that was a fate I signed up for when I began my life as a photographer, not necessarily when I began life as a pornographer.

I cannot say that the little girl who used to have a little pink playhouse and dreamed about unicorns and princes meant to choose the road that I have. But I don't know anyone whose life turned out exactly the way they planned it. Destiny refuses us the simple path of traveling through life without the adversities that confront us, and the adversities that shape us. I do not regret a single moment of having chosen my atypical occupation, though I cannot say I would recommend it for everyone. But for me, it has been a kind of bizarre personal victory—the little girl who stole the office key has now finally become the woman who has earned it.

TERA PATRICK

. . . ON BECOMING AND BEING A PORN STAR.

WHEN I STUMBLED INTO JIM South's office in late 1999 I had butterflies in the pit of my stomach, my adrenaline was making me dizzy, and I thought I was going to either throw up or hurl myself from the window. This was the place every father dreads his little girl ending up in. I was about to commit the sexual sin that can't be taken back. I was crossing the somewhat blurred line of what our society finds acceptable. It's what some of us in the business call taking the "porno plunge." Little did I know I would end up as president of my own multimillion-dollar porn empire not five years later.

This is not the story of every girl in the business; it is mine. I'm one of the lucky ones. My name is Tera Patrick, and I am a porn star.

My story is one of coming of age and learning lessons, mostly the hard way. My story has to do with recognizing where your true power lies. For me, the power was my looks. Since the beginning of time, men have been making money off women's beauty, women's sexuality, and the power both possess. From the beginning of my life, nearly every man has wanted something from me—my body, my face, my tits, my ass—to possess me in some way. Lots of men got a piece of me along the way. Some-where on this timeline I took the power back, and took myself from the back of the bus to the driver's seat of a Ferrari. The road is hard, long, and seems never-endingly uphill, where your only escape is to leap to your doom over the nonexistent guardrail of self-worth. Sometimes the hopelessness of the business is centered around the fact that for many of us, there is no real long-term goal. That's pretty depressing to look at in print, but it's true in most cases. How often do we hear about a porn performer working his or her way through law school on a porno salary, or segueing into a huge Hollywood career? Well, maybe Tony Danza, but that has yet to be confirmed as more than a rumor.

So, this is how it goes: you show up at some house in the Valley, walk past some really shitty half-eaten catering, pass some burnt-out, indifferent crew guys who help you feel like an intruder. You shake a few hands, unsure of who you're about to fuck that afternoon, try to get through the scene without getting cum in your eye or your hair, pick up your check, and go home to wash up. But some things can't be washed off with soap and water. There is a cleanliness that comes from within that, more often than not, becomes emotionally soiled from doing porn. My pussy might have been sore, but it was my emotions that took the worst pounding. It's hard to not feel like a whore when you fuck for money.

Sometimes it feels as though even if the sex is outrageous and you experience multiple earth-shattering orgasms. Every time you have sex on camera you give a little piece of your soul away. I had been shooting less than a year and—although I was instantly famous and held the desire of virtually every man (and woman, in some cases)—I knew something was missing. Everyone wanted a piece of me, and no matter which way I turned I was getting fucked. Most times there were some nice guys like Randy West who were straight shooters—no strings attached. Sex performance on film for pay, a nice lunch, plus common courtesy and respect. This was something you didn't see every day. Then there were nameless, maladjusted assholes who choked me unconscious while having sex with me, and never paid me.

I was able to avoid the real bottom feeders, about whom I've heard the most horrifyingly degrading stories, which sound like nothing more than torture or abuse. There's no union like the Screen Actors Guild for sex workers, to protect girls from malicious creeps whose only shot at a second of false self-esteem is to hold a girl's orifices open with speculums, defecating in her throat while having a dozen different guys rape her bleeding ass. The business is so obvious and painful sometimes, like homeless people in the street begging for change. Everybody wants to help, but it's not really anyone's problem. Porn chicks get whacked out on drugs, defect to prostitution, go mental, run away and change their names. Some even die or commit suicide. But who really cares? New girls fall off the bus every day and land in all the wrong places. I was very inspired by something I read in a book: *The Four Agreements* by Don Miguel Ruíz. It had to do with coexisting harmoniously with your surroundings and finding true inner peace. I decided that if I couldn't heal myself spiritually, I was going to make damn sure that I could buy my soul back.

How did I get here? I was an army brat who moved around more times than I can remember. While I was a student at my third high school, I was discovered in San Francisco while attending the world renowned Barbizon Modeling School. I wasn't even fourteen by the time I was living in Japan, Europe, or wherever the job was, modeling in fashion shows, print and fashion campaigns, and even billboards in some cases. But I didn't want to be Kate Moss or Heidi Klum. I loved Betty Page and Jayne Mansfield. I idolized sexy, voluptuous women who weren't going to apologize for their sexuality by looking emaciated and androgynous. These women seemed powerful and liberated, appearing to bathe themselves in some sort of love potion that held the men of the world spell-bound. They were adored by presidents and workingmen alike. I wanted what they had. I wanted to be a pinup girl, a centerfold, the dirty thought in the back of every man's mind. I didn't want to be the forgotten housewife in the apron making dinner in the sub-urbs. I wanted jet planes, diamonds, and excitement. I wanted the impossible dream: to be a sex symbol. To rise above the humdrum existence handed out to so may women like the K-rations my dad was given in the army. I wanted spontaneity in an overcalculated world where married couples plan fifteen minutes for sex on every other Wednesday. There was no lovemaking in my home as a kid. There was fistfighting.

After years of living out of a suitcase in model apartments and photographer's flats in Paris, London, or Capetown, I decided to take my turn at academia and do something noble and construc-tive with my life. My dad was in the military as a doctor. Although I hated him and all the awful things he put my sister and me through, I loved medicine. It was a sort of problem solving with scientific answers. In the medical journals I pored through at night were remedies for all the ills of the world. Maybe I thought I could fix my own pain. Maybe I was just burying my head in books like an ostrich buries his head in the sand, to shut out the ominous, impending doom. My life was the equivalent of pain most of the time. Either way, I saw that other people needed help, and I was going to give it to them. It would at least take my mind off my own problems. The only question was, who was going to save me?

After earning one and a half college degrees from Boise State and the University of California at Santa Barbara, I had a full-time job as a nurse and was going to school at night. After one long, hard, sobering day during which a patient flung a bedpan full of shit and hit me in the face, I sat and thought long and hard about my life decisions. I decided that there must be something better out there. Coincidentally, in a twist of fate, my Candy Striper girl-friends were going out to a *Playboy* casting call. I had never gone with them to any of these things, but this time I said what the hell. In the blink of an eye I was whisked from my casting call to studios and was shot by *Playboy, Penthouse, Hustler,* and practically every men's magazine there was. Everybody loved me, everybody paid me, bought me gifts, and tried to date me. I had a big smile on my face—I had arrived. I never looked back. But I wondered, where do I go from here? I lived at Suze Randall's home for a while, and when she wasn't busy hitting on me she was getting me published in every magazine imaginable. In retrospect, she probably paid for that house off the pictures she shot of me, but no matter. I was going to be a star if it killed me! Especially because I could smell that bedpan in the back of my mind every day!

Like a college athlete looking to go to the pros to make the big bucks, the natural progression after nude modeling is hardcore porn. A lot of girls hang on the fringe of the adult business and stick to nude modeling and simulated sex. These girls build Web sites and hustle their asses off, shooting for free and trade to try to hang on to their Web site members and beg for parts in B-movies. Lots of those girls are broke as a joke. I didn't know what I wanted, but I did know I didn't want to struggle. I was no stranger to hard work, but I wasn't in this to get famous. We are all ho's on this bus—everyone is giving up something for something else. A Midwestern housewife may give up her ass to a fat balding man who repulses her because he lets her keep her JC Penney charge card to buy all the costume jewelry she wants. Women date players, rock stars, athletes, executives, and millionaires, looking the other way at their indiscretions because they live in a multimillion-dollar mansion and can shop at Barney's or Fred Segal without an open line of credit. So when I entered the business I decided that I'm no better and no worse than anyone. I called all my own shots. I decided who I slept with and how. And if I didn't like the situation, I walked.

I didn't want to marry some guy I didn't love. I came from a dysfunctional and abusive family, which didn't help me in the relationship department, and I was damned if I was going to spend my life with some lame, boring asshole because I didn't have my own money. This is the land of milk and honey, and I was going to use my honey to get a piece of this pie. I began to work freelance in the business and soon became one of the most sought after girls in adult entertainment. Before my first full year in the industry I had won about every conceivable award I could have, including the coveted *AVN* award for Best New Starlet and the Hot D'Or award for Best New Starlet, plus Best New American Actress at the Cannes Film Festival. I had my own apartment, a little car that I owned, and some nice clothes and shoes, but I had nothing saved. I kept thinking, is this all there is? A lot of girls I knew were escorting and making a lot of money going off to New York, but the idea of being alone with a man in that capacity scared me to death. I felt safe with the camera man, director, and the rest of the crew that was either staring at me salivating or looking the other way because they were so desensitized to sex. I knew none of them really gave a shit about me, since I was just another porn chick. I just hoped they wouldn't let me get hurt too seriously.

I had made about twenty-five movies, traveled all over the world, and shot in Mexico, Costa Rica, and St. Martin, but mostly in the San Fernando Valley. My family had no idea what I was doing, and to be completely honest, it felt good to be defiant. Something I set out to do to make a little cash on the side, however, had grown into an out-of-control, three-headed monster! One head was the money, as I was making more than I ever had in my life. The second was the fame and recognition. It was a scummy pond, but in just one year I felt I had somehow risen to the top of it. It felt good to belong somewhere, and even better to be adored. I had fans who sent tons of mail. I was beautiful, sexy, and I was free! This was empowering beyond belief. The third and final head of this behemoth was my drive to succeed—my drive to do my personal best. You must be asking yourself, "What in the world was she looking to achieve? To fuck the best?" Honestly, I actually had no idea at that point. All I knew is that people were rallying around me to congratulate me, offering me contracts, money, gifts, and trying to date or buy me. Literally.

I knew deep inside that somewhere there was a way for me to parlay this momentum I had into something beyond my wildest imagination. I was now a *Penthouse* Pet, Pet of the Year, on the cover of *Playboy,* and pretty much had an open road ahead of me. I was going to write my own ticket—I just had no idea how to do it. Every time I cried myself to sleep and thought about quitting, I thought about that bedpan. It served as a powerful incentive to keep going.

Most girls who gained a certain amount of popularity angled to become a contract girl for a major company like Vivid or Wicked (who I actually met with and didn't sign with). At this point in my life I was drinking heavily, and—under the influence of about five gin and tonics and a few joints—I signed possibly one of the worst white slavery contracts in the history of the earth. I had no attorney and basically signed my life away to some people who were out to rob me blind. What did I know or care? This was standard practice in the industry. I lived on the covers of both mainstream and adult magazines. I hosted a show on Playboy TV and became the industry's sweetheart. I was the good girl of porn. While so many girls were doing more and more extreme things—like gang bangs, double penetrations, double anal, 65-guy anal cream pies—I was outselling them all with my sensual "vanilla" brand of sex. Guys were coming to get my autograph on their Tera Patrick portrait tattoos. I had back-to-back-to-back number one bestselling movies.

There was only one problem.

I wasn't getting paid.

I was standing on top of the world in a sense, but instead of dollars, I had only a few cents . . . which made me question if I had any sense at all. I felt stupid, embarrassed and ashamed. I always felt I could live with myself and the names people called me behind my back (and to my face, in some cases) as long as I knew I was in charge of my own life. I had set out to make some money, not to get famous! Financially, I had been duped, and I decided I was leaving the business after just over two years. I think back to how the excitement of my very first scene quickly turned into an awful feeling that I had made some kind of mistake. This was worse. I had learned all the tricks in the book: how to give a hands-free blowjob because it looked better on camera, how to point my toes to make myself look graceful during sex, how to position my body so that the camera could capture my big, natural boobs swaying to the motion of the scene, how to make sure the camera could see my face even though it was shooting from underneath a guy's balls. I was a performer, an overnight sensation. Men wanted to be with me and women wanted to be like me. I was the girl who made porn okay. Couples loved me. If only I had loved myself half as much as my fans did.

I had dated a few guys in the industry. They all asked me out, but somehow I turned down all the really nice guys and only dated the creeps. One time, a guy I was dating was all freaked out on meth and broke my wrist. I dated some rock stars, celebrities, you name it. I never loved any of them. They were mostly people to party with, have sex with, or share my bed with so I wouldn't have to sleep alone. Sometimes I just needed someone to call to pretend I was normal. I even dated some nerdy guys who would do anything I would say because no matter how successful I became, I felt as though after what I had chosen for my career, what man was ever going to love me? Ever? That's how I felt until

I was watching the HBO series *Oz* one night with a guy I was dating. I saw this tattooed, superhard, sexy man sitting naked on the floor of a jail cell. And I thought to myself, "That's the guy I'm going to marry."

I called HBO and couldn't track him down. A mutual friend who was also a spectacular photographer, Anneli Adolfson, told me that his name was Evan Seinfeld, he was in a Brooklyn, New York–based hardcore metal punk band called Biohazard, and he was an old friend of hers. She told me she would introduce us, but to absolutely avoid anything serious with him whatsoever, since he was a womanizing pig, known for his sexual exploits on the road. He called me over the summer and we were both instantly in love over the phone. Due to his intensive filming, recording, and parenting schedules, we were unable to meet until September 4, 2002. We didn't leave the house for four days. The sex was the best I ever had, and the companionship was even better! The fact that we were relegated to speaking on the phone for three months forced us both to really get to know each other. We were both used to instant sexual gratification, and I really think that the way we met dug deep roots for our relationship to grow strong.

We moved in together that day and haven't been apart for more than a few hours since. We got engaged on Halloween at the Delano Hotel in Miami. Evan FedExed a huge diamond ring to our room. The FedEx guy interrupted us in the middle of sex, and I tried to get Evan to ignore the door! I ended up crying the happiest tears of my life. It wasn't a conventional relationship by most people's standards, but it was my romance and my love story. He was my Prince Charming, even if he did look like some sort of skinhead convict. We were married in January at the Adult Entertainment Expo, accompanied by Evan's friends from the Hell's Angels and a few of my friends from the adult industry. Alexis Amore was there and so was Mercedez, Keith Gordon from

Bizarre Video, and Jason and Raff Rayes from Viper Grafx. The guest list was definitely an eclectic mix, and while Elvis sang "Viva Las Vegas," I looked through joyous, tear-filled eyes at the man who was going to be my lover, my partner, my best friend and my champion. Then, over his shoulder, I noticed that a few hookers had crashed our wedding. I let them stay and be in the pictures because I recognized that I was hope for them—I was happy. And, of course, we're all ho's on this bus anyway.

Evan and I went on tour with his band all over Europe for two months. They were headlining a traveling festival called the Resistance tour, which was full of these super-agro political hardcore bands like Biohazard, Agnostic Front, Hatebreed, and Discipline. I was the only girl on the bus most of the time, but everyone made me feel so welcome—kind of like a big family. It was so exciting! There was a big downer when we got back to reality, however. Calling back to my lawyers in Los Angeles every day, it was brought to my attention that my deal may not have been aboveboard. When I attempted to get a copy of my original contract, the company I was working with decided to shut off my cell phone, repossessed my car, and had me followed. I signed with this company because the president was a woman, but once again, just like my mother who savagely beat me until I was taken away by child protective services (that's another story), a woman had betrayed me. She violated my trust and preyed on my longing for a mother figure. She fucked me for real, in ways that hurt so bad I could never describe them with words. To make matters worse, not only wouldn't they cooperate with me wanting to go out on my own, but they filed a full-blown lawsuit against me that claimed they owned my name, and began a poison-the-well campaign to attempt to blacklist me from the industry. I cried for months. I had done this all for nothing. Everything I had worked so hard for was going down the drain. I was so angry that I was having uncontrollable violent outbursts. I was so depressed that

I would lie in bed for days on end, yet something inside me told me not to give up. Evan was incredibly supportive, telling me that I was a warrior princess and had to fight for what was rightfully mine regardless of the outcome. It was better to fight and lose than to roll over and lie down for someone.

I had broken my contract with my former company and didn't own any pictures of myself—or anything, for that matter. This is par for the course. Other people get rich off your blood and sweat. They don't have the guts it takes to do what I did. I was out of the business and happy. After I had traveled with the band for about a year, and lived in New York, discovering real shopping and Italian food, Evan bought a camera and a video camera and began shooting me every day in Europe, around New York . . . pretty much anywhere I could get naked! He began to encourage me to start my own company. I was scared, but I knew that my destiny was to write my own ticket. Evan helped me by paying his album advance straight to our litigators. I began to feature dance, even though I had never stripped onstage in my life, to help pay my astronomical legal fees. I took one lesson from Lisa Ann at the Spearmint Rhino in Van Nuys and headed out onto the exotic dancer circuit. The price of freedom is high, but worth every penny. With the help of the Lee Network, I became the highest-paid feature dancer in the history of the strip club world.

This became a superfun bonding ritual between Evan and me, with the two of us taking turns touring the world with the other one coming along for support. And even though the money went to lawyers, we knew we were fighting the good fight, and not only for myself. This legal battle was bigger than me. I was the little guy, fighting dirty, wannabe corporate pornographers without a conscience. I represented every girl who ever got a raw deal and couldn't afford to fight back. The drama of the case was followed closely by the entire adult industry, but very few people stepped forward on my behalf. I was being sued over the right to use my own name. I was in jeopardy of having my name stolen from me and never being able to work again, not only in the adult business, but in any business at all. If I had been a mainstream actor, none of this would ever have happened. Fortunately, the judge on my case couldn't care less that I had done porn. He acted like I should get whatever comes to me, even if I was being sued over egos and money, with my identity at stake. It was astounding to me that of all people to support me, the courts were going to come to my aid and help me find some justice. The thing I remember the most from that time was crying so much I thought my nose was going to be permanently red from rubbing it with Kleenex.

The judges in the state court were perplexed, as injunctions were filed against me and people were afraid to work with me. My former company felt that if they exhausted my resources, I would come crawling back. I think they decided that if they couldn't have me, nobody would. Eventually, with some clever legal maneuvers, I finally became free from the awful contract I had signed and learned some valuable lessons: don't believe everything you see and hear, sometimes wolves are cloaked in sheep's clothing, and don't leave home without a great attorney.

After that, I was free to start my own company. We began compiling content and building a Web site with fellow porn entrepreneur superstar Jenna Jameson, which is how ClubTera.com was born. I formed my own production company, Teravision, and signed an exclusive deal to become a prestigious Vivid Girl. It was really Steve Hirsch, the owner of Vivid Video, who came to my aid as consultant, confidant, and contractual genius. In conjunction with the best young attorney in L.A.—and the best looking— David Beitchman, who worked my case through deaths of his family members and law partners dying in motorcycle accidents, from my bankruptcy to my ex-parte injunction hearings where people tried to prevent me from using my own name, and my husband, I regained my freedom and got a new lease on life!

But the whirlwind was just beginning. I re-signed my deal with Susan Colvin of California Exotic Novelties to rebuild my adult sex toy line, which had been extremely successful before, but now I was really getting involved! Now I was cutting deals and getting myself paid! I figured out how much money I should have earned at this point in my career and it made me sick. I had been beyond flat broke, but now I was free! For the first time in my life I was truly happy.

One of Evan's high school buddies, Dan Davis, was the editor of *Genesis* magazine. We were introduced, and within a week I became the publisher of the magazine and began writing a monthly column titled "Teravision." The magazine took new shape and began growing exponentially! Then my good friend Wankus gave me my own radio show on KSEX Radio, where I share my lusty secrets with porn fans and horny housewives. I began to realize my true potential in the marketplace and began licensing my name to everything lucrative that I felt was a good match, from online stores to erection pills. You name it, I've been branding it! The epicenter of my brave new world, ClubTera.com and TeraPatrickStore.com, continued to gain momentum, and I could barely keep track of it all. I was now in complete control and looking at the world through different eyes.

With my husband acting as my manager, literally keeping the industry creeps off my back, I was hungry in a whole new way. Hungry to make my bank account equal to my fame. Hungry to fuck my husband on film and work with great directors, like Paul Thomas and Chi Chi LaRue. But most of all, hungry for my first taste of pussy! Up until this point in my life I had only ever had sex with men. I was always curious, but because I had a horrible mother I was always afraid of women, and found comfort in the arms of men. Boy, was I missing out! I remember on the set of "Tera,

Tera, Tera" in early 2003, I spent a week not getting any sleep, lying awake thinking, "What am I going to do when I get down there!???" My first scene with a guy was definitely nerve-wracking, but not because of the sex. I kept envisioning people I grew up with renting the video and jacking off to it. This time it was completely different. It was like having rough sex with my husband—I was terrified and completely turned on at the same time!

But I had nothing to worry about, because Savannah Samson and Chi Chi LaRue turned me out. Evan was giving me tips on pussy eating, Chi Chi was screaming directions, but I went blank. I became like Freddie Mercury—I could have sex with anyone, man or woman, as long as they turned me on. I threw Savannah back and dove in. We gave each other the kind of orgasms that make your hands and feet numb, and make your legs shake for an hour. I never knew it could be that good until I did my first three-way scene, where I was getting fucked super hard and having my pussy eaten all at the same time. I was reborn. Sex was all brand-new to me and the possibilities were endless!

But even more important, I have recently launched my adult talent agency and model management company, The Tera Patrick Agency, in hopes of helping girls avoid the pitfalls of the business and not end up hating themselves so much that drugs, booze, or even suicide are the only ways out. It's been way too long that Larry Flynt and a dozen older guys from back East have been making all the money in this business, and none of them have even fucked on film. So what is every pimp's nightmare? One of his ho's wising up that she has absolutely no use for him, and stepping out of line. That's why they call it the pimping game, because it's a mind game for the pimps—or in this case, porn producers—to convince the girls who are the product that they will be nothing without them, to keep them down and broke so they can continue to profit from them.

Not anymore.

Today I'm making real estate investments and shooting my own Teravision movies. As I type this, I'm on an airplane heading home from London, where I just shot for *FHM* magazine and did in-store appearances representing Vivid Europe. My first Teravision feature, *Reign of Tera,* is the number one–selling adult movie in America right now. I have my own offices and amazing staff. I own luxury cars and take vacations to exotic places. I don't owe a penny to anyone. All of my ventures are booming, and best of all, I am happily married. I'm working out and doing Pilates, and I'm in the best physical shape of my life. I've even put my little dog Chopper in my movie! I have nothing to complain about.

But I'm not trying to make a list of my material accomplishments to sound shallow. Actually, these are just by-products of my success. I hold my head high every day. I have fans, both men and women, who adore me. I have connected myself with them in so many ways. If people don't like what I do, they don't have to buy it. If people have nothing better to do than protest porn, they need to take a look at the deeper issues. In my opinion, porn isn't the problem. I think tobacco and alcohol are way more detrimental to society, especially to children. Oh, I forgot—the government imposes levies on those things, so I guess until they figure out a way to make a porno tax, the witch hunt is on. America needs to relax and get laid. Period.

I don't really expect people to understand me, what I do, and the personal strength I derive from it. What epitomizes how I feel is that I really don't care what people think. People judge everything. Human beings have prejudices. Even the most self-righteous, politically correct Dudley Do-Rights may not like black cars because they get dirty too fast. As someone who is judged every day for what I do and who and what people think I am, I say when you point your finger at me, remember that three point back. The difference between you and me is that I don't care if you think you are better than I am. As you judge all of us in the adult industry from your cubicle or your sofa glued to the TV watching bad shows, ask yourself this: Are you loved? Are you free? Who do you answer to? What do you stand for? Anything at all?

If a man figured out a way to make millions by getting laid all the time, he would be a genius. But as a woman, I'm branded a whore. But I love what I do. I enjoy sex! I make sexy movies that you call dirty. Do you work for corporate America? I say you are the whore! But guess what? I still don't think that makes me any better than you, because as I've said before, we're all ho's on this bus.

So, yes, I do wear a scarlet letter. Three, actually—XXX—but they're diamond-studded.

MASON

WHEN I WAS TEN YEARS old I watched porn for the first time. My mom and I were cleaning the house one Saturday night. She was in the kitchen washing dishes and I was in her room vacuuming. With my concentration on the task at hand waning, I began to randomly switch channels on her TV. Suddenly, there were naked people on the television screen doing things to each other I had never seen before. I was so horrified that I pulled the bed sheets over my eyes and turned the volume down so the vacuum would drown out the noise—because, of course, in spite of my shock and confusion, I wanted to watch as much as I could without my mom discovering what I was up to.

I was always curious growing up. I remember roller-skating to local convenience stores to read *Oui* and *Hustler*. I used to hide the smut rags inside kids' magazines so if anyone walked past they could only see the outside cover of *Tiger Beat*. I was banned from my fair share of stores doing this. Honestly, it became a real pain in the ass having to walk farther and farther away from my house to get my daily fix of apple Jolly Ranchers.

I attended college and earned a degree in political science. I'd taken the LSAT in the pursuit of a career in law, but soon realized that deep down, in spite of my deeply held convictions to confront injustice and fight for those who couldn't fight for themselves, I didn't feel the prospect of being confined to the day-to-day rigors of a courtroom would allow my spirit to flourish. On some level I yearned to break free of societal norms.

While for most it starts out as an accident, I actively sought out the porn industry. I always had a love-hate relationship with pornography. While I was drawn to it out of a sexual curiosity, I had significant ethical reservations. I felt that it was wrong and harmful to women. As part of my degree, I had taken some courses in feminism, and it was there that I began to question my own habituated ideological orthodoxy. I started to consider that the issues I had with pornography were simply reflections of the way society treats women generally. I started to feel that all of the guilt I felt when viewing porn was predicated on my own discomfort with being a sexual woman. Why did I feel so much shame after watching others have sex?

I decided the only way to come to terms with my sexuality, and resolve my questioning of pornography, was to get personally involved in the adult entertainment industry. I knew it would help me in my quest to better understand my sex, and wrestle my mind free from the preconceived societal notions of femininity I'd been subjected to.

After my graduation in 1999 I began to strategize my future. I did lots of homework, researching old copies of the industry trade publication *Adult Video News,* and reading thoroughly every smut magazine I could get my hands on. I familiarized myself with all of the key industry players: the contemporary talent, directors, and companies that were successful. I started watching videos from Shane's World and Ed Powers, slowly progressing into more hardcore territory with the likes of Elegant Angel and Anabolic.

I knew I would have to work my way up the industry ladder. I always retained the humility and respect to recognize that I had an awful lot to learn, and I think this gave me an enormous advantage. In my quest to further immerse myself in the intricate details that comprised the industry, I traveled to the Erotica L.A. convention. It was here that I met Rodney Moore.

I approached Rodney at the booth where he was signing, and we began to talk about my passion and eagerness to get involved and learn the tools of the trade. I soon discovered that, coincidentally, Rodney's cameraperson had left him just two weeks before the convention. I think he recognized my raw desire to improve myself, combined with my capabilities as an individual, so he offered me the chance to work for him. I was absolutely stunned by my good fortune. There was a confluence of events that seemed to be fatefully leading me forward in the pursuit of the career I craved.

I was so excited by the opportunity that I purchased a video camera and began to train in preparation for my tutorship. I rented prostitutes and shot a close friend of mine having sex with them. I'd practice my shots and the technical aspects I'd amateurishly discerned from my personal porn viewing. But I soon found myself drawn more to the deeper levels of human sexuality than to the basic aesthetics. If you look back at those tapes—and I have kept then all—there's a real intimacy to the interviews and the exchanges with me behind the camera. I was fascinated by who these women were as sexual beings. And through my interactions with them, I learned a lot about their history, and in turn about myself.

I officially became Rodney's cameraperson, and within a few months, he taught me how to edit his movies. After a year with Rodney I had gained enough confidence to continue moving forward. I began interning for another director, Andre Madness, and I closely studied his impressive technical expertise. It was hard work and a difficult period, but it was a crucial part of my professional evolution. I remember one day shooting a blow-bang (one woman/multiple men oral scene) with Andre overseeing the action from in front of a monitor. Confident I could handle all eventualities, Andre left me in control and tended to some other responsibilities. When he returned to the set, the blow-bang had transformed itself into a full-fledged gang bang, with the star of the scene insatiably embracing every cock inside her hole, one by one. Andre was stunned. That day, I realized I had a gift for bringing out real sexual feelings from women. For some reason, my presence behind the camera made everything less of a performance and more of a real human experience for them.

As I began to gain this sense of my own identity, I decided I was ready to undertake my dream—the prospect of directing, the ambition I'd harbored from the beginning. Andre Madness made a call on my behalf to Patrick Collins, the owner of Elegant Angel.

My meeting with Patrick was a pivotal moment that defined the shape of my career. As I sat down in front of his desk, I swear I was peering up at Pippi Longstocking's dad. He's a huge man with an extraordinary presence. He's also a legend in the industry, and one of the godfathers of gonzo porn. I tried to look as professional as possible. I had collated thirty pages of notes the previous night on the different ideas I had for revolutionizing porn. I was ready and willing to employ all of my recently acquired knowledge from Rodney and Andre. It all came down to this.

I sat down across from him, and he asked, "What do you want to do?"

"I really like blow job movies," I told him. "But I'd like to transform them into something a little different from what's out there. I am very confident I can direct a great movie for you, sir."

He responded enthusiastically, "You know what I want you to do? I want you to reach out in front of that camera and I want you to suck all those dicks off, yourself! I want you to show those women what it's like!"

I literally sank down in my chair. All of that hard work for two years, and it came down to: *I'm a fucking object. Nobody is going to take me seriously. I gave up law school and put everything behind me to follow my dream. And here's this asshole treating me like a fucking piece of meat.*

In a very soft yet firm voice I told him, "You know what? I don't think that's my place. That's not something I can do. I would be doing your productions a disservice."

"Okay, then," he said. "How many movies do you want to direct for us?"

I couldn't believe it. I had tears in my eyes. I came into this industry believing that all of the men were perverts and misogynists who wouldn't treat women as equals. And Patrick was proving me wrong.

We went back and forth for weeks trying to find the right director name. I wanted it to be generic, and non–gender-specific. My intention wasn't to be a female director, but to be a damn good porn director, period. I chose the name Mason because it was sexually ambiguous. Even more, it had a male connotation to it. There are still many people to this day who think Mason is a man.

Before I got into the industry, one of the people I was sexually drawn to was Jamie Gillis. My boyfriend at the time had one of Jamie's movies and I found the psychodramatic dynamic he captured compelling. There is one scene in particular with Alexandra Silk that remains to this day my all time favorite. It was something I always tried to recreate in my personal life, but it never dawned on me that I could incorporate it into my movies. When you get the opportunity to start directing, you don't necessarily have the luxury of deep self-reflection. You take what you can, because you're excited to get your shot. The first movie I directed, *Lady Fellatio,* while remaining innovative, authentic, and well received critically, didn't really mirror my sexuality at all.

Patrick and I had a long meeting in which I explained that I didn't feel sexually invested in the scenes I'd been shooting. I wanted the freedom to explore my sexual curiosities, and my passion for the kind of aggressive psychological exchanges I had witnessed between Jamie Gillis and Alexandra Silk. The end result of our deliberations was the *Dirty Trixxx* series, the movies I would become notoriously defined by.

Dirty Trixxx, volume one, was the second movie I had shot, and it was unlike anything I had created before. I shot a scene where Michele Raven was slapped around, choked out and dunked in a toilet bowl. I had a girl riding a horse with a dildo inside her. I had another locked in a dog cage.

Working for Rodney Moore was just a job. It was an observational experience: watching and learning. Shooting scenes that were formulated from my own sexual fantasies was a completely different experience. It felt like I was a part of the scene. The scenarios, dynamics, and relationships I had with these women were an *explanation* of my sexuality. More than documenting, I was spiritually and sexually evolving. It was amidst this perpetual flow of adrenaline, excitement, and creativity that I knew I'd found myself for the first time in my life.

In the subsequent months, I encountered a great deal of public criticism. My movies were decried as degrading to women. Some argued I was simply a male construct, single-handedly crafted by Patrick Collins himself. I attempted to explain in interviews, online forums, and in a column I wrote monthly that the women I carefully selected to appear in my movies were, like me, passionately into this kind of sex. The sex was meant to be degrading, because that's what we, together, found sexually exhilarating. I fervently asserted that there shouldn't be any restraint or shame in our ability to explore and experience those intrinsic desires.

I found the entire critical dialogue personally challenging but vitally important to the way women were viewed in the industry. It's important to state that what I shoot comprises about 1 percent of who I am—those sexual desires should not completely define me as a person. The same should be said for the women I shoot. My idea of a good time is going for a ten-mile run or rummaging through flea markets for that perfect find for my house. I love going on hikes with my dog and carefully tending my rose garden. And yet, within the context of the industry, I'm 100 percent defined by the type of scenes that I shoot. Yes, it's degrading, and yes, these women like to be dominated, but it's one aspect of our sexuality, and an even smaller part of who we are as human beings. To be honest, it's a big part of my sexuality, but I also enjoy being made love to tenderly and awakened with soft kisses. But why should our sex be limited to that?

While the first volume of the *Dirty Trixxx* series had been a speculative sexual quest, *Dirty Trixxx 2* was the sexual awakening I had always yearned for. It was the most intense and aggressive movie I had ever shot. The locations were stunning and diverse. I'd made dramatic technical improvements to my shooting style. The sex was hard, passionate, psychological, and very, very rough.

Alexandra Quinn gave me one of the performances of her career. I met and used for the first time the male performer Manuel Ferrara, who soon became an instrumental partner in helping me realize my sexual visions. And of course, I captured Ashley More getting fucked with a bar stool. I knew that my desires, my sexual conflicts, and the psychological dynamic between Alexandra Silk and Jamie Gillis that I'd found so haunting had finally blossomed into my own distinctive directing style. For the first time I really knew who Mason was. During the shooting of *Dirty Trixxx 2* I also met my muse, inspiration, and close friend Julie Night.

In the beginning, I always thought that women in porn felt

ashamed and embarrassed to be having sex on camera. To be quite honest, I felt sorry for them. I had this notion of evil forces coercing them into doing things against their will. When I entered the industry, I expected to find a collection of scared, intimidated victims.

Julie Night is no victim. She's a highly educated, witty, independent, beautiful human being. She's also an unabashed, self-proclaimed, "cock junkie whore"—which for many, is difficult to connect. She likes to fist-fuck her face while she masturbates. She likes to service men and make them cum. She craves sex and adores her job. Julie's three-way with Manuel Ferrara and Steve Holmes was the most talked-about scene in *Dirty Trixxx 2*. She was dragged across the room by her hair, spat on, slapped, her nipples were squeezed with pliers, she licked airplane propellers, was penetrated with a screw driver, and took two of the biggest men in porn up her ass, *simultaneously*. During the scene she screamed so loud in ecstasy that the roof of the airplane hangar we were shooting in reverberated as if we were having an earth-quake. To this day, Julie tells me it was the one of the most grat-ifying sexual experiences of her life.

Alexandra Quinn's scene began with a projector reel of a scene I'd shot of her before, from *Lady Fellatio 2*. She played with her cunt uncontrollably as she watched herself lick a load of cum off an oil-stained piece of asphalt on the projection screen. Manuel's dark shadow forebodingly emerged on the screen and began what would be a dark exploration of her sexual feelings of guilt and shame.

During part of the scene, I felt compelled to intervene because even I'd grown uncomfortable with the level of emotional inten-sity. Manuel asked Alexandra to bark like a dog, then threw a dildo across the room, shouting, "Fetch." I don't know why I responded the way I did—in retrospect the act was relatively tame—but within the context of the rising levels of aggression and domination, I felt unsure of what Alexandra was experiencing. The funny thing is, when I let Alexandra know my concerns, she laughed and said, "This is nothing, honey. It's great, don't worry." During editing, Patrick and I discussed the raw footage of me lowering the camera and asking Alexandra if she was okay. I've always believed that women don't need elaborate demonstrations of their autonomy and consent. I remember I saw a "couples' " movie where a woman being fucked aggressively by five guys spontaneously said, "Stop!" and all of the participants, responding like robots, let go of her in unison. It was apparently the director's intention to make it absolutely clear that the woman retained power over the experience she was involved in. I found it so insulting. Why do we find it so hard to believe that a woman has control over her sexuality? Why is it required to explicitly demonstrate that a woman is sexually powerful over what she chooses to engage in?

I fought very hard to keep her explicit statement out of the final edit. But in the end, I acceded to Patrick's wishes to preserve it. For the first time, I felt like I had sold out.

When the movie was released it created a huge uproar. While it was broadly acclaimed, there were also very passionate levels of criticism. At the time I felt hurt and misunderstood. People thought I hated the female sex, and I found that to be infuriating. To me, these grown women had made choices, informed by a sophisticated sense of their own sexuality, and they were being publicly reduced to victims. The last time I checked, we had power over our cunts, and I wasn't going to let anyone get in the way of that.

The common denominator in my movies was always authenticity and passion. Passion can take a variety of forms. It's all about being driven by your emotions. You can express your feelings of lust and desire through a slap, a kiss, or an intense embrace. It isn't simply about capturing extreme sexual acts. In some of the most aggressive scenes I've shot you will find kissing and tender moments, because a deep, authentic chemistry has been established between performers, because they're sharing something so honest and real.

I had developed such close relationships with the performers in my movies. Women like Alexandra Quinn, Julie Night, and Michele Raven had become my inspiration. The courage and self-confidence they had to express themselves as filthy, depraved whores was something I found astonishing in a society that is still so challenged by the most basic female sexual expressions.

People bring a lot of their own biases when they view porn. When I first watched videos I couldn't understand why these women would behave like total "sluts." "How could she do that to herself?" I often thought. So I can comprehend the negative reactions to slapping, spitting, and choking. But I know these women. They're normal human beings, no different from you or I. They shouldn't be defined exclusively by their sexuality just because they're brave enough to embrace who they are and what they feel. They're autonomous, complex individuals, and once that is grasped, it should be recognized that they retain the power to make informed choices about what turns them on. They are not victims.

It was during this time that I began to make public appearances wearing a burka—something that has became indelibly associated with my career. For me the burka symbolized the caging of women and their sexuality. It was an ironic statement, something I felt reflected what I stood for and what my movies represented. A lot of people missed the point. I think the impact it made helped to quickly elucidate my cause in the minds of many, but in the end I think it trivialized everything. More people thought it was about shrouding my identity rather than making a principled stand.

The *Adult Video News* awards show in Las Vegas that year was memorable for many different reasons. I won two awards and made an appearance onstage at the ceremony. The support I received from friends and family was very special. My mom attended the show by my side. It made me value how fortunate I'd been, never having to confront the stigma of working in porn, because everyone in my life was so open-minded and under-standing. I had never felt so much joy in my life. I finally felt I belonged.

Unfortunately, all was not well. Clues to the changes that were about to take place at Elegant Angel were beginning to surface. At the convention I felt that the family we had fostered together over the previous twelve months was about to break apart. When I returned to Los Angeles, the internal politics of Elegant Angel came together as I had expected and I was forced to leave. There was a direct personality clash with someone who I felt had not represented himself honestly, and who I felt would damage Patrick and his company. I cared so much about what we had all accomplished together that I couldn't keep quiet and watch it all fall apart. So, Patrick and I parted ways.

My stay at Elegant Angel was incredibly intense, both profes-sionally and emotionally. I grew to love and respect Patrick as a father figure. I found him to be a beautiful human being who understood women and their desires. He, likewise, had a gift for bringing out the truth in the women in his productions. He showed me how to peel away the shame often associated with being a sexual woman. He taught me how to accept women for who they are and accept their sexuality for what it is. I will be for-ever indebted to Patrick for allowing me to find my sex through the productions I made at his company. I simply wish we could have parted on better terms.

I was very fortunate to land at Platinum X Pictures after Ele-gant. The first movie I shot for PXP was *Sexual Disorder*. It was an elaborate ode to the wonderment of Julie Night. I tried to challenge myself and be more ambitious. I incorporated a story line, delved deeper into the visual aspects of my directing, and constructed powerful imagery, all the while trying intently to capture the emotional and human depth of Julie. But, to be honest, *Sexual Disorder* was a failure. There is a purity to celebrating whoredom; it can't be manufactured. With *Sexual Disorder*, I lost sight of that.

However, something very positive evolved from that production. I met an incredible woman named Katrina Kraven. I didn't realize that Katrina's spirit would drive my future productions. Her scene in *Sexual Disorder* completely transformed my perspective on porn. What she shared with Manuel Ferrara and Denis Marti wasn't the type of sex I'd been accustomed to shooting. There was very little slapping, hair pulling, or violent sexual exchanges. It was all about the passion, soul, and honesty that she let run free. There were tears in her eyes as Manuel held her in his giant arms, plowing away beneath her. It was a completely new experience for me.

When I spoke to her after the scene, as she nervously tried to recall what she enjoyed most, I realized she had been just as courageous as any other woman I had shot. She had shared so much of *herself*. It occurred to me that if I was going to change peoples' minds I had to stop being so militant. I had to understand that while my sex was right for me, it wasn't necessarily right for everyone. Changing people's perceptions of woman was, after all, my motivation. I wanted to open up a different perspective and show people that women weren't just one way, that we all have different sexual identities. It was important to get my philosophy out there, and I realized I couldn't accomplish this by taking such a confrontational stance. *Riot Sluts*, the movie I made following *Sexual Disorder*, while still aggressive and very intense was more diverse. I shot my first girl/girl scene (something I never thought I was capable of doing). There was romance, and a real emphasis placed on kissing and emotion. I worked very closely with all the women to develop scenarios based on *their* fantasies, *not mine,* while making sure they worked with men or women that they found sexually attractive. The reaction to *Riot Sluts* was incredibly positive; I was finally able to get my point across.

In early 2005 the opportunity arose to work for *Hustler* and Larry Flynt Productions. I was thrilled to be involved with such a high-profile porn brand name. Kat Slater, a vibrant female force in the industry and head of production at *Hustler,* brought me into the company and guaranteed me the creative freedom I'd been afforded in the past. Being at a company that seemed to be overflowing with a more artistic, substantial approach to pornography, with the likes of Jack the Zipper and Eon Mckai directing, was a prospect I couldn't refuse after the ever-narrowing marketing philosophy of Platinum X Pictures.

In the span of a month, my world was turned upside down. From signing my best contract ever and beginning to shoot my first movie for *Hustler,* a corporate reshuffle took place. The direction of the company was redirected, and I was called in for a meeting at the *Hustler* building in Beverly Hills.

In that meeting two men in suits I'd never met before, and who'd never seen any of my movies, took turns lecturing me about why the videos I produce are morally wrong and degrading to women. I was shocked and upset, and I made it clear that these weren't circumstances in which I could continue to work.

Even now, after all of the changes that I've witnessed in the industry, and the ever-growing self-confidence of the females who work in it, there remains a pervasive notion of women as frail, weak, and mindless individuals who need to be protected from themselves. While being a woman has never hindered my career opportunities or advancement in this industry, standing up for an image of womanhood that contradicts societal prescriptions of femininity is still something that even in the world of pornography is a constant struggle.

I'm personally and spiritually at a place where I'm liberated. Porn has been therapy for me. It has validated my desires and helped me accept them. Porn has allowed me to develop a more complex image of womanhood, one that isn't exclusively defined by but fully embraces the spirit of women who are proud and unashamed of their sex. I have a lot of brave, beautiful women to thank for my transformation. I can honestly say, I found myself through porn.

STORMY DANIELS

I DON'T REMEMBER THE TITLE, where I was when I saw it, or what I was wearing, but I'll never forget the first time I saw porn. I was about sixteen when my boyfriend, who was eighteen at the time, rented it for us to watch while we were having sex. It was a Vivid movie starring Chasey Lain. It was amazing. And from then on I was hooked.

I didn't have a lot growing up. My family was basically poor. I would look at the magazines and think, "Oh, look at those girls, they're all so beautiful." I don't know what it was about them, but I remember being very young and thinking that that's what I wanted to be, that kind of *Playboy* girl. I always thought it was cool. I never really understood what the big deal about sex was. It made no sense to me why it was bad, or why some people thought it was bad, Everybody has sex. If we didn't have sex, none of us would be here.

I'm from Baton Rouge, Louisiana. I was raised by my mom, a single mother after she and my father split when I was four. I wasn't abused, I was just left to my own devices a lot, which is why I'm so creative. I'm an only child and I grew up in a not so nice neighborhood—not that I was beaten or anything like that, but it wasn't the best place to grow up. I spent a lot of time alone because my mom had to work all the time. I didn't have anyone to play with, and she didn't have a lot of money to buy me cool toys or send me to day care. I took care of myself from a very young age. It also made me a bit of a loner—I don't think a lot of people know how to take me. I've been told so often by people that they thought I was such a bitch because I'd never talk, but it's just because I was observing. I had to figure out how to do things my own way.

When I was seventeen, I moved out on my own. I was still going to school and I figured out that stripping was a great way to make money and continue to attend school. A lot of strippers will use that theory, but the thing is, I never wanted to go to college. I started dancing and I didn't know anything about feature entertainers, how you got to be in magazines or in movies, I just knew that I was very interested in being a part of that. I came to work one day at the Gold Club in Baton Rouge, where they had feature entertainers every week. They didn't have porn stars— they didn't usually hire that level of entertainer. But when I was eighteen I saw this feature named Cameo who went onstage in costumes and a entire show worked out. She commanded more respect from the crowd than the others. I remember watching her and thinking, "That's what I want to do."

The following week we hosted Devon Michaels. She and I talked and she told me about how I had to get in magazines. So after some time went by I decided that that was what I wanted to do. People said, "Yeah, right, Stormy, whatever. It's not going to happen." I got a boob job when I was twenty. It took me about two years to perfect my dancing and work up my courage. I finally called a photographer in Atlanta named Don Sparks, who shot my very first couple of layouts . . . which he never paid me for. I didn't know I was supposed to get paid until I moved to L.A., but at least he got me in a lot of magazines.

From there I contacted an agent and said, "Look, I've been in all this print work and I can dance." I was booked as a feature dancer and wound up doing two solid years on the road, forty to forty-two weeks total. I basically lived in my truck. It's pretty funny, because my roadie would joke that I could smell a porn shop. Sometimes when we'd be driving and I'd be asleep in the passenger seat, I'd suddenly wake up and say, "Pull over! Pull over!" I'd make him stop and buy me porn so I could watch it on my laptop in the car.

Although adult film was something I always knew I wanted to do, I didn't know how to get started. I was the highest level of feature dancer there was, and yet I was still just the magazine girl. I had pretty much topped out on rates, and I worked for an agency that didn't book porn girls so they couldn't help me. At one point I sent my pictures to the infamous porn talent agency World Modeling but I never heard back, so I was pretty discouraged. I thought, "I'm not pretty enough." At all. Today he regrets that, but at that point I was ready to give up.

About six months later Devon called me up. She said, "I'm going to L.A. to do a couple of girl/girl scenes. What are you doing?" I told her I was off that week, so she invited me to go with her. I had never been to California and I didn't go there with the intention of doing a movie. But she said, "Just come out to hang out with me. I've got a room and a rental car, just pay for an airline ticket." So I did. Then a couple of days later she said, "Listen, I have a scene today for Wicked, and then tomorrow I have another one for Sin City. They haven't booked the other girl. Do you want to do one?" I said, "Okay, why not?" She called Wicked and asked if it was okay for her to bring her little friend to the set, and they said it was fine.

So there I was on the set. It was for a Brad Armstrong movie. Mark Kernes from *AVN* was there, and he took a couple of pictures of me that wound up being the shots they used for my fresh-off-the-bus profile that ran later in the magazine when I officially entered the industry. I wound up being an extra in that movie—I wasn't even in the scene, I was just in the background. I started talking with Brad, who said, "You're really pretty. Have you ever done anything?" It was kind of encouraging after what had happened with World Modeling. The very next day I did my first scene. It was with Sin City and Michael Raven was the director. From there we wound up going out for dinner with Brad, and Michael said, "I could get you more work if you wanted." Five days later Devon got on a plane and went home. I never left.

I was such a huge porn fan that when Brad told me things about his movies I knew already what he was talking about because I'd seen them. I don't know what it was that made me such a huge fan, I really don't. I just really enjoyed it and thought that the girls were beautiful. I watched mostly couples porn. Honestly speaking, I didn't even know what gonzo was until I'd been in the business for a while. I've become a big fan of it. Back then, however, I didn't even know it existed. I was a Vivid and a Wicked fan. Mostly Wicked, because I liked Jenna Jameson and story-driven movies. You could look at all the videotapes and DVDs I owned and 90 percent of them were Wicked, so it made sense that I ended up there. That's why I held out so long for the Wicked contract—I wanted it so bad because I knew the most about their product.

But more than that, I knew when I was a kid that I wanted to be a director. We didn't have TV when I was growing up, and I used to read a lot. I started writing really young. I had notebooks upon notebooks filled with short stories. I wrote at such a young age that I was writing stories about my stuffed animals. When I started going to high school I became editor of the paper and I took a lot of creative writing classes. So fast forward to when I finally land my Wicked contract. As everyone knows, I was dating Brad at the time and he writes his own scripts. He's a very talented writer. I remember sitting there watching him write one night, and I said, "You know, I can write."

"Can you?" he asked.

"Yeah," I said. "I want to write a script."

He didn't exactly laugh in my face, but he smiled as if to say, "Okay, Stormy, whatever," and went back to work.

And that's when I decided that writing was my next goal. It wasn't a woman power thing, I just felt that I could offer a different perspective for people watching these movies. I remember watching these movies and knowing exactly what movies I'd put in the VCR, which ones I'd turn off, and exactly which movies I'd watch more than once. Here's the difference between men and women who watch porn: a man can watch a porn and get off, but when a woman watches a porn she wants to know why they're having sex. It's not a bad thing—I'm the same way, and I now make movies that I like watching because I feel that I had an insight, having been a fan. Women want to see that those people have a connection. It's okay for them to have really dirty sex and do all these nasty things, but we want to know why.

I wrote a script with absolutely no intention of directing it because I'd only been under contract for six months. It was called *Kink*. It was a suspense thriller starring Devinn Lane as an undercover cop trying to find a killer who's murdering these beautiful women and leaving them in the positions they're photographed in. Brad read it and said, "You wrote this!?" When I told him yes, he asked, "Can you do another one?" Which I took as a nice way of saying "Fluke!" I wound up writing a lot of scripts for Wicked that first year.

When the time came for me to renegotiate my second year, I decided I wanted to direct, and of course I got it all over again: "Sure, Stormy, whatever." The main reason I wanted to direct is because when I write a script I see it vividly in my head. I see exactly who is in which part, exactly how it should be shot—everything. And although our company has some of the best directors in the business, it's still only their interpretation of what I wrote. I immersed myself in that side of the business. I went to the set with Brad every day that he directed. Even if I wasn't in the movie I'd sit for hours in front of the monitors, and I'd be thinking, "If I were shooting this, I'd be doing this, or I'd be doing that." So finally, I told Steve Orenstein, the owner of Wicked Pictures, that I wanted to direct a movie. He didn't laugh at me, bless him! I don't think most companies would let a girl who'd only been in the business for a year direct anything, let alone a feature. But Steve asked, "Do you think you can do this?" And I said yes. I wanted to try at least one movie to see if I could do it exactly the way I'd envisioned it in my head. I was both his newest and youngest contract star at the time, but he said if that's what I wanted to do I could do it. But first I had to give him a script.

The first movie I directed was *One Night in Vegas*. The experience was nerve-wracking because suddenly everything was on me. It's not that I didn't know what I was doing and how I wanted to do it, but I was still learning the technical side of things. I made sure I surrounded myself with the best crew that I wanted, but still, that just opened up another door: how were they going to look at me, seeing as I'm the stereotypical blonde porn star with blue eyes, big boobs, and big hair? Never mind that I'd only been in the business a short time and had just won Best New Starlet at that year's *AVN* Awards. How were people going to react to me giving them orders? I had people working for me on that set who had shot my very first scene. So factor in all that with my choosing to direct a comedy with a fellow contract star, and you could see how I'd be worried about getting respect. Not only was I responsible for all those people, the location, and the equipment, I was responsible for Steve Orenstein's money. But I knew exactly what I wanted to do with it.

I didn't sleep for a week before the shoot. I'd lie in bed and think about camera angles. I spent a lot of time organizing the shooting schedule, and I had a hand in everything. So the morning of the shoot, there was no getting up and out of bed—I was already out of bed and in somewhat of a panic. I'm a bit of a list writer, and the older I get the worse it becomes. Nothing makes me happier than scratching things off my list. That day I had so many lists that if I had been tying strings around my fingers I wouldn't have been able to bend them. Luckily, we shot the movie at my house, so I wandered around the house with my camcorder looking through the lens, getting a feel for things. Then everyone started showing up, girls started to appear and went into makeup, and I had that fear: "What if nobody listens to me and it becomes total anarchy?" I don't want to say I was second-guessing myself, but it would be pretty stupid to say that I wasn't nervous. It was a huge undertaking.

About halfway through the first day, I was asked, "Okay, what do you want to do next? Where's our next setup? Where do you want lighting?" I had people getting ready for sex, people in makeup, people practicing dialogue in the back yard, and I stood at the top of my staircase and thought, "All of these people are here because of me." I had that same feeling in the most recent movie I directed. There was a huge bar scene. Everyone was in the movie, I had a ton of extras, and I remember standing at the top of a staircase and I saw an angle I wanted a cameraman to get. I called out, "Okay, everyone quiet down! This is what we're going to do!" Everyone instantly got quiet and looked up at me. And I thought, *This is it, this is where I belong. I wrote this and these people are here because of me, and this is coming to life because of me. And people are going to go home and watch this and have sex with their husbands because what I directed turned them on, or the story that I wrote, or the sex is so hot that guys are going to go home and masturbate*. It was very fulfilling. I called, "Action!" and the whole bar scene just came to life. I watched it on the monitor and that's when I knew I'm going to be here for a long time. I'm going to be the old woman in the wheelchair yelling, "Fuck her harder! Hold my teeth. Let me show you how this is done!"

I directed *One Night in Vegas* in July 2004 and even I was surprised by how well it turned out, but the true test was the reviews, and they exceeded my expectations. Everyone sat up and took notice in a whole new way. I definitely surprised people. And—I'll admit it—part of me felt vindicated because of those who said that porn stars shouldn't direct. But most of all, I was happy that I didn't let Steve down.

When it came time to work out my deal after my second year, it was carved in stone—I was now a performer, a contract writer and director, and the first girl in the industry to ever have such a deal. It feels amazing. Porn years and stripper years are like dog years—you've got to have a plan, and what you're doing today is because of the foundation you set. This is something I tell new girls all the time. I'm smart enough that I could go to college and do whatever I want, but there isn't anything in the world I'd rather be doing than this. I've found where I belong; I've found my calling. I knew that this is what I wanted to do and I went after it. I'm very ambitious and very driven. In fact, I'd use the word calculating. People think it's a bad word, but I've remained very much in control of what I do, who I do it with, and how I do it, and I haven't let other people take control. I own my Web site. I trademarked my name. With my toy line, I test out all the toys and my picture only goes on the ones I like. I write my own movies, not only the ones I direct, but most of those that I've starred in as well. If I want to be a cowgirl, goddammit, I'm going to write a movie where I'm a cowgirl. I've been very careful not to give up control.

The adult business is run by men, but it's women that sell the tapes. And I'm not trying to sound sexist, but I want my part. For those who think that women are held down here, I think they're pretty ignorant. However, I also don't feel like those feelings should be limited to the adult industry. I think it's like that in every aspect of every business. I wouldn't call myself a feminist, but there are things that I'm good at that my boyfriend or my husband isn't as good at. But it shouldn't matter if I'm a man or a woman. I understand that I have to prove myself, but I'm also going to say, "Ha! Take that!" at the same time. I'll do it, Devinn Lane will do it, Bridgette Kerkove is proving you don't have to be a man to shoot intense gonzo . . . this isn't just a man's world anymore. The more that female directors step up and do their thing, the more of us will have the opportunity to follow suit.

I just directed my second movie, which was a lot bigger than any I'd done before but I'm a lot more confident now. I've developed certain formulas that I follow that I feel really make a difference. And it's not just the things I do with the actual making of the movie. It doesn't matter who it is—my actors, my PAs, my hair and makeup person, even the extras—but I explain exactly what I want, how I want it, and I give them a reason. On the last movie we shot I had set a goal for being done at 10:30 that night, and we were done at 10:29 because I was so specific about my needs. Most directors don't do that. And I've done mainstream movies. I was just in *The 40-Year-Old Virgin* with Steve Carrell. Directors will tell you where your mark is, don't step out of your light, and these are your lines, but that's it. I try to explain why and go into great detail. I'd rather overexplain things than have to shoot things over and over again. As a result, I've gotten some great performances out of people who have never done it before.

My goal is to be known as one of the best directors in the business. Not one of the best *female* directors in the business. Why? I really hate to say this, but I feel that people expect less of the women in this business. So I don't want to hear, "Oh, there's Brad Armstrong and Michael Raven and Nic Andrews, and then Stormy Daniels is the best female director." Why can't I be in the group with the other guys? I don't want people to lower their standards and expect less from me because I'm a girl.

I still go on set with other directors and take notes on things they do that I'd like and incorporate them into what I do. For example, Brad Armstrong is a great storyteller. If you watch one of his movies, you find a whole story. You don't see the clichés. Michael Raven is an outstanding cinematographer. He will spend hours waiting to get the sun in just the right spot so it'll hit a diamond in the right way, and it's just stunning. And then there's Jonathan Morgan, who is just hysterical. He's so funny and he's not afraid to try things that might be silly or stupid. He's adventurous. But I also like Nic Andrews and Andrew Blake.

So now when I write and direct, there are two things I keep in mind: one, I will probably never venture into the straight gonzo stuff. I like it and I'm a fan of it, but features, couples, and women-oriented porn is my thing. And two, if there was no sex in this movie at all, could you still watch it? Likewise, if I took out all the dialogue, would the sex scenes be hot enough to make it sell? Everyone always asks how I'm going to set myself apart. They say, "What is Stormy Daniels going to do that's different from what everyone else has done?" So I want my sex scenes to be as beautiful as Andrew Blake's, but as hot and nasty as Jules Jordan's or Pat Myne's, and the story needs to be as solid as Nic Andrews's or Brad Armstrong's. Because I believe there's no reason why I can't do it all.

JACKIE STRANO

... ON MAKING PORN THAT'S TITILLATING, EDUCATIONAL,
AND FEMINIST.

I CAME OUT OF THE closet in the early '80s at the peak of
the Reagan and Bush Sr. just say no/sex will kill you/Russia is
the evil empire/we-have-enough-bombs-to-destroy-the-world-
over-a-million-times era. Rock Hudson kissed Crystal Carrington
on *Dynasty* and sent everyone but Elizabeth Taylor running
away screaming after coming out with the news that he was
dying of AIDS. We hadn't had 9/11 yet, but there was definitely
a general malaise blanketing the country. In the meantime, in
San Francisco, Debbie Sundahl and Nan Kinney started a magazine called *On Our Backs* with Susie Bright at the helm as
editor. It was a real-life lesbian sex magazine produced with
stripper money, with the subscriptions sold to dykes and men
who wanted to see real dykes having real dyke sex and read
writing about real dyke sex. For me, it marked a new beginning.

I remember the thrill of going to clubs like Faster Pussycat and
Female Trouble with latex gloves in my pocket because you had
to be prepared and able to have safe sex or you wouldn't be
having sex at all. Dykes were very careful about not spreading
cooties because, you know, as girls we've all been indoctrinated
from day one about our "down there" being the equivalent to
some foreign germ incubator. Thank God my mother told me

that douching was totally unnecessary when you had good hygiene. But like good Girl Scouts leaving for a camping trip, besides cab money and cigarettes, you always checked for clean gloves before leaving the house. Some nights I would feel even more adventurous and pack a dildo to be ready for anything or any femme.

At the time I worked for political groups and not-for-profits, went to demonstrations, canvassed door to door for the environment, wrote and performed songs against "them" and "the man," and poured my guts into drunken poetry at open mics across the "Gay Mecca." Fast forward to meeting the love of my life and the Queen of all my dreams, Shar Rednour. And just like the song says, "sky rockets in flight . . ." True forces of nature became one burning desire to birth a porn company to show what real dykes *look* like having sex. With that one single goal in mind, I went to work at a dot-com company for six months at the height of the Internet hype, and with some cashed-in stock options, Shar and I started our company. With less than $10,000 and a leap of faith, we launched SIR Productions. What does it stand for? Sex, indulgence, and rock 'n' roll. No bank loans, no trust funds, just a do-it-yourself attitude and a willingness to forgo some creature comforts for a while.

We were artists. So while some of our friends got to go on extravagant vacations or buy new cars, we were pouring our blood, sweat, and tears into an idea that might just work and afford us free creative time as well. Both of us are from working-class and immigrant backgrounds, so the thought of working hard and working for ourselves was very easy to wrap our minds around, even it meant that I couldn't always buy my beloved the latest color from the MAC counter or take my girl out for fancy meals. We know how to have fun with no money—if you know what I mean!—and luckily I'm a kick-ass cook. Shar and I worked out of our small apartment and joked that as long as we had a computer, a phone, and a fax machine, we could rule the world!

I had deliberated about leaving my job and the security it provided in those early days. I definitely had some anxiety about it for a few moments, but jobs are made for quitting. I'm a creator, not a quality assurance manager. Working a computer job had led me to start smoking again, so Shar informed me that it was time to quit and, not to worry, she would still love me even if we lived in a van down by the river . . . which did actually happen to us, but that's another story.

Our vision for SIR Productions was to change the way people have sex for the better in addition to showing hot butch/femme dyke sex and how it's truly relentless in its lust and screen-melting chemistry. We started our company with the launch of the *Bend Over Boyfriend* series because we knew the world was hungry for boys' butts to bend over and take it like real men. We needed to raise capital for the movies and we knew that showing how men can truly love their asses to be played with would be lucrative.

When we were casting *Bend Over Boyfriend 1,* we had to look high and low and beg and plead to find some couples. In fact, we had to pair up a dyke and a gay boy who were into the thrill of it, because we needed more couples. Of course, we knew the dyke would be able to wield the dildo perfectly and that our gay boy was an expert at taking it. Their scene was hot and fun and they became good friends afterward. Meanwhile, if you don't know her, Dr. Carol Queen is the sweetheart of sex. Listening to her gently discussing boy butt sex in *B.O.B. 1* and then seeing her with a leather strap on giving it hard to her man is just too good for words!

We also learned a whole lot we didn't know about male sexuality and the spirituality of the sexes. I remember one performer in particular confiding to me how he worried about looking too fat on camera. In true locker-room fashion I asked him how much he could bench press, and after being impressed with his answer, I told him that a butch dyke like me would think of him as thick and that was a sexy thing, because being able to pick up your lover is hot—especially while you are fucking her. He felt great, and after being fed orange slices and misted with cold water, he was up and running again and ready to please. I felt a twisted sort of maternal pride as we cheered him on to the final conclusion where after "performing" he gets his turn with his legs in the air. I admit that the irony of starting a movie company on the backs of men's butts always amused me. As we filmed men having full-body orgasms without ejaculating and coming while being penetrated, fully feeling what it means to allow someone inside them, I felt compassion and empathy take over where more of an objective separatist mentality had existed before.

When it came time to cast *Bend Over Boyfriend 2*—which boasts Chloe in her first-ever strap-on role—we were actually getting inundated by folks who wanted to sign up. That's how much of a phenomenon it was! We knew we had hit on some kind of simmering, pervy pop culture vibe—I will never forget the episode of *The Sopranos* when Janice and her boyfriend talk about her doing him up the butt, and I can't help but think we had something to do with that!—which exploded when we started reading about our movies in Dan Savage's pieces, Susie Bright's articles, and Tristan Taormino's columns. Our favorite media hit was when folks were debating what to call the act of penetrating your boyfriend. "Bobbing" was one suggestion, but "pegging" won out, much to our chagrin. It's interesting, because I guess some men find it easier to deal with a woman's name instead of a man's name as they're wrapping their legs around their woman.

Soon after *B.O.B. 1* and *2* we started our little labor of love, *Hard Love* and *How to Fuck in High Heels*. That's right, two movies on one tape. We literally put our asses where our art was and put ourselves onscreen. This was our chance to show what dykes look like—or at least, the fringe of the fringe—and though it was very San Francisco-centric, we knew we had hit a nerve as one queer film festival after another contacted us and played our movies to packed and often sold-out crowds. Dykes around the world were hungry for some images that weren't just coming-out stories where young girls lick chocolate off each other.

In the meantime, the *AVN* awards nominations were announced, and lo and behold, we were nominated for Best All-Girl Feature. That's right—not specifically lesbian, just all-girl . . . as in more gay-for-pay pussies for your dollar. Shar and I high-fived over the fact that the Los Angeles porn establishment had given us the nod. But not only were we nominated, we won! There we were in all our pierced and tattooed, high butch/femme drag finest when Ginger Lynn announced our movies as the winner in Las Vegas in January 2001.

We did it. And not only had we done it, it was done on our terms. We were true to ourselves, and we had taken a top prize in the industry . . . the industry we weren't really a part of to begin with. We were very flattered. The best part was having Chloe, Jeanna Fine, Nina Hartley, and Midori congratulate us. Shar and I worship them for their beauty, their brains, their talent, their sweetness, and of course their sexiness. My favorite part of the evening was at the end of the ceremonies when all the producers walked to the back table to pick up the awards. I was the only woman in a sea of older white men in tuxedos with cigars, waiting for my award to be handed to me. These guys had their starlets flanking them, and so did I. Driving out of Las Vegas on a starry desert night in our Chevy van with our *AVN* award in hand made Shar and me feel like true California dreamers. Our hometown paper, the *San Francisco Bay Guardian,* proclaimed us Boogie Dykes and had us on the cover to celebrate our win.

Our company has always been a labor of love. The world is a much better place when men learn how to have multiple orgasms and get penetrated and women learn how to ejaculate. Balancing power is a good thing for this planet, and playing with power is a sexy thing when it comes to fantasy and role playing. For all the feminists who confronted me for my dildo play, claiming that all I really wanted was to be a man, please know that I still bleed and have cramps every month. Though I have white privilege in this country, I still know in my body what it means to be a second-class citizen, and my "manhood" snaps on and off and gets to be put in a drawer after I make my lover come. For all the straight folks who have no idea what the hell I'm talking about, please rent—or better yet, buy—one of our movies. To keep this labor of love going, we live frugally and with sheer tenacity, and by the grace of some kick-ass women who have lent us money, we have kept the images of true sex coming. Slowly but surely we have accumulated the tools of the trade (an Apple G4, Sony camera, Final Cut Pro, and Studio Pro Production Suite for authoring, sound, etc.). We don't outsource anymore. And now we're totally consumed with our latest endeavor: *Healing Sex*.

Healing Sex is our first nongraphic foray into sex education movies. A docudrama starring the Somatic practitioner, author, and social justice activist Staci Haines, *Healing Sex* compassionately and realistically depicts men and women on their path to recovery from past abuse and trauma. It was made for people who are struggling with their partner to have a truly blessed, intimate life with healing and pleasure. As a producer I'm proud of it, but even more, as a human being I'm earnest in my commitment to get this movie known. This is the movie I talk to everyone about when they ask what I do for a living. I'm proud of our sex movies and I know they're a cut above a lot of the crap that's out there, but *Healing Sex* is more than just something to entertain and educate. It's literally about saving people's lives.

As a company, Shar and I are committed to putting images out there that you can't find anywhere else, and with *Healing Sex* we've succeeded once again. Where else are you going to see a man of color admit painfully to his wife that he was abused as a child? Where else are you going to see what it actually looks like when a lover mentally checks out during sex? *Healing Sex* is a natural progression for our company as we took a few steps backward to educate before we entertain again. With Staci, we've created a bridge between the sex world and the therapist/academic world, and we hope that—especially with the advent of the media frenzy around Michael Jackson, Catholic priests, and movies like *The Woodsman* and *Mystic River*—there will be a place for the antidote: an answer to, "Okay, now how do I get to have a normal sex life?"

With SIR Productions, we make the assumption that you deserve to have a great sex life and a truly, intimately satisfying one. And because of our dedication to that, we haven't gotten straight jobs yet!

SHANE

I STARTED IN PORN BY accident. When I was eighteen a girl-friend of mine was going to a modeling agency and asked me if I wanted to go with her, so I said sure. On the way there she said, "By the way, sometimes they do seminude and nude pictures. Are you okay with that?"

"I don't know, I've never thought about it," I told her.

Lo and behold, we pull up at World Modeling, the agency notorious for launching many a porn career. I remember walking in and seeing all the pictures of women with big boobs, and I immediately felt inadequate for being eighteen and having what I like to call avocados. I wasn't comfortable with my body at all. I took one look around and told my girlfriend, "I'll wait for you down in the car." But Jim South stopped me.

"Where are you going?" he asked.

"I'm going to go wait for her down in the car," I told him.

"Are you eighteen?"

I nodded.

"Well, then stay," he said.

"No, I can't do this."

"Yeah, you can."

I looked at my boobs. "No, no I can't."

He told me that I most certainly could, and if he got me work, would I do it? At the time I wasn't sure—the thought had never crossed my mind. But sure enough, he got me work, and that's how I started to do nude modeling.

Not long after that I met a director named Ed Powers who talked me into going on camera. From his standpoint, I was already doing naked pictures, so being on camera wasn't that much different, right? First he talked me into just talking to him on camera nude for one fee, then he'd offer me more to do just a little bit more, and by the time the day was over I was sitting on a couch between him and Jamie Gillis while they masturbated, which I'd never seen a man do before. When they came I just about hit the roof. It scared the crap out of me—I thought it was probably the grossest thing I'd ever seen. And that was my experience with porn until years later, when I met Seymore Butts.

I was working as a dancer when I met Seymore. I was still doing nude modeling too, actually. I did it for about six months solid until my first layout was published. It's funny, because taking the pictures was one thing, but I never actually thought that they'd be published. Then one day a friend showed up at my door with one of the magazines I'd been published in, wanting me to sign it. I immediately hightailed it out of town where nobody knew me. I left for about a year and then came back to start dancing, which I did for three years. When I first met Seymore he didn't tell me what he did for a living. He wasn't honest with me about what he was doing until the day he was actually shooting at his house, where I also lived. At that point he had no choice but to break it to me. "Oh, by the way, I kind of shoot porn and I'm shooting here today. I've gotta run out and get some videotape, so if anyone shows up just tell them I'll be right back."

All I said was, "Oh. My. God. Are you kidding me?!"

Of course someone showed up, and I didn't know what to say to *those people*. I'd never been around the porn industry, so I had no idea how to act. I opened the door to see this pretty black girl standing there, and all I could mutter was, "Uhh . . . uhm . . . Seymore's not here."

She said, "Okay, I'm going to go get my stuff from the car."

Her name was Toy and she was doing a scene with TT Boy, but she didn't know that at the time. She asked me on her way into the house, "By the way, do you know who I'm doing today?"

I said, "What? No! Don't you?!" I was shocked that people would show up to work and not know who they were screwing.

TT Boy showed up not long after and I watched them work. I remember they were in this swing and I was shocked, but I was also soaking it all up like a sponge. I wasn't being judgmental. It was kind of interesting. I hung out and watched like a fly on the wall. The more Seymore shot, the more I was around, watching everything, playing the observer.

I wound up agreeing to do a shoot for *Hustler* that sent me down to Mexico, so I decided to bring a video camera and shoot my own little movie for him. I shot a solo masturbation scene. I noticed when Seymore shot that he never shot his face—I called it "Seymore Style"—and that's exactly how I shot my masturbation movie for him. Not long after that I took a vacation up north to see my dad. One of my girlfriends knew I was dating Seymore Butts and she said, "I want to do a movie!" So I shot a scene with her too. I was just having fun with the camera, experimenting with it and seeing how comfortable I was. I was making it for my boyfriend—not the public—and I didn't show my face, and that was my way of showing my acceptance of what he did. I wanted him to know that it didn't bother me. But even then, I had no intention of making this my job. It wasn't something that I was going to choose as my career.

Then Seymore was approached by a group of young guys who had the idea to make an interactive CD-ROM. It had never been done before and he really wanted to do it, but it was going to be really expensive because you have to pay girls in the industry by the scene. A scene is like a pop—when the guy comes—so every time a guy pops that's considered a scene, and with an interactive CD-ROM you had to pick where you popped. So if the user had four choices of where he wanted the scene to end, essentially you'd have to shoot four scenes to make that happen. He asked me if I would do it. He said I could wear sunglasses and it would just be me and him. So I said okay. We were in this sling and he was trying to shoot us and I remember him stopping and looking at me, saying, "Can you, you know, make some sort of noise or something?"

"Like what?" I asked.

I wasn't into the whole acting thing, and I was still shy, believe it or not. Still to this day I'm not all that verbal—I'm not the "talk dirty" girl. At any rate I tried, but I wasn't pulling it off very well, so he sent me to the bar to have a few drinks. If I were a guy I would never have lasted in this industry, because it probably took me a good five scenes to start getting a bit more comfortable with being in front of the camera. But once I found my comfort level, I was just all over it. I don't know what it was that helped me find that comfort, but maybe it was because I didn't really get the chance to experiment much before that.

The first time I ever had sex with a girl was on camera, and I remember telling Seymore, "I don't know what the hell I'm doing! How am I supposed to do this? I don't know how to have sex with a girl!" But after I did that and a couple more, I felt like I knew what I was doing. And not only that, but all the people in the industry liked me, and that made me feel better—like I was accepted. So I started having fun with it.

After the CD-ROM came out, Seymore put the scenes that I had shot for him in some of his movies, and people got really curious about who I was. I was never expecting that and neither was Seymore, so it just kind of snowballed from there.

It was great for a while then everything started getting really ugly. Seymore had a different job when I first met him. He was only doing porn part time when we first got together. So as the relationship progressed he quit that job and got into porn full force, and this industry is not the easiest to survive in. He had both business and family issues going on, and he just started getting meaner, and meaner, and meaner. We didn't have a joint bank account. He didn't pay me for any of the work that I did. I kept waiting for the good guy to come back, but it became apparent that it just wasn't going to happen that way. I moved out and he freaked out, but only because of work issues between us. I was the cash cow. He asked me if I would sign a contract and continue to work for him, and like an idiot I said yes. But before I signed that contract I took a vacation for a couple of weeks to let my head clear. I decided that would be the dumbest thing for me to do because I was still in love with him. How could I work with him and watch him work with other people while he was still taking advantage of me? There was no way I was going to let that happen.

So I came back from vacation and I told him I was sorry, but I wasn't going to work with him. He lost it. He said, "Well, what do you think you're going to do?" I panicked. I don't know how to explain it, but I always felt like I owed him an explanation. So I just pulled something out of my ass. "I don't know, maybe I'll do my own line," I told him.

I was halfway kidding, but then he laughed at me. Right in my face. And he told me I'd never be able to do it. "Geez, thanks," I said. "I really wasn't sure what I was going to do, but now that you've told me that, I *am* going to do my own line."

It just so happened that my friend Yvonne and I had a bachelor party company that we'd had for years and I'd met some really nice people through that who'd actually agreed to front me the money to go out, start my own company, and just do it. It was cool because I'd always wanted to do my own line, but Seymore never wanted me to because then I would become more empowered. But now I was in charge. I decided to call the line Shane's World, which was actually a suggestion from a fan. When I went looking for distribution, everyone was really nice to me because they knew what an ass Seymore was and how he had nearly destroyed me. Paul Fishbein, the publisher of *AVN,* suggested a few people to me that I should have interviews with, and the very first person I met with was Bob Treemont from Odyssey. I didn't even meet with anyone else—I knew that's where I wanted my home to be.

So then I had to actually shoot something. The thing that I noticed that people liked about my movies was that I always played myself. I never did any acting roles, and that seemed to work well with me. So I wanted to do a line where all the talent could just be themselves and not have to play any characters, because everyone always makes fun of what shitty actors we are anyway. I thought it would be interesting.

It was a nightmare.

I was a total freakin' wreck. Before I left Seymore I was smart and made copies of all his contracts, address books . . . I copied everything I could find so I could study it. I kind of knew what I was doing, but back then Seymore wasn't the person you wanted to be learning from because he wasn't organized, he didn't do budgets, and he lived month to month. And I'd never really had my own company before. I started by doing the casting and figured out where we were going. I told everyone we were going to go on a trip and just tool around on dune buggies and motorcycles. And they'd say, "What should I bring for wardrobe?"

"Whatever you'd normally wear to go riding on dune buggies and motorcycles," I told them. "I don't think you're going to need any stiletto heels or anything like that."

"Okay, so who's the makeup artist?" they'd ask.

"No, no, no," I'd have to say. "There's no makeup artist. You're it. This is reality. We're shooting you as you. You're not going to play any roles, you're just going to be yourself. We're going to go on a trip, have a good time, party, and leave the cameras running all the time."

Everyone was totally cool with the idea, but everything that could go wrong with the shoot certainly did, because I didn't think things through.

On the very first shoot I had cast Sid Deuce and I thought it was going to be trouble. When our motor home got stuck and we had to push it to get it unstuck, she would yell, "Squished bugs! Ew!" Even when we arrived at our destination she was calling out, "Garçon!" looking for someone to help her with her bags. We had no hookups, and we couldn't shower—we had to drive fifteen minutes down the road and pay in quarters to take one of those public showers. Everyone was stuck eating my cooking. A canopy came open while we were driving on the freeway and hit a truck. We found a dehydrated person who had passed out in the bushes and we thought he was dead. So when we got home I thought, Everyone's going to tell people what a nightmare I was to work for and I'm never going to work in this town again. But they didn't. They were totally sweet. Even Sid! It's a good thing I brought enough weed and alcohol to keep everyone happy.

I really learned from that first experience. I learned that I had to think things through more. I hadn't planned for showers and accommodations—my cameraman slept on the dashboard. Me, my dog, and Tom Byron slept in the back of my Bronco. We so roughed it, man. It was grand! But the sex was awesome. Recently my husband was making a trailer for me and I asked him to put in a sex scene with Yvonne and Caressa Savage from Shane's World volume one because it's my favorite girl/girl scene ever. Even aside from what I've shot, it's my favorite girl/girl scene that I've ever *seen*. They were on a dune buggy that you could see for miles and miles, but there's nobody around, just sand hills, and they were so into it, just totally going crazy and having fun. It was like we went on a vacation and just taped the whole thing. I stuck to that way of shooting, but I decided to rent houses because it was easier to deal with. I can't believe I still kept going after that.

We were always doing crazy stuff when we were shooting. Most of my crazy stuff was with Yvonne. We blew delivery men and service people. I don't think that footage ever made it into a tape because we didn't have model releases on them. With one guy we were at a hotel and we called room service. "We want chocolate-covered strawberries," we told him.

"We don't have any," he said.

"Find us some and we'll blow you," we said.

I swear that guy was at our door in fifteen minutes with those strawberries.

We videotaped it. I remember Ruby and I gave the blow job and Yvonne videotaped it, except everything she taped was out of focus so I couldn't use any of it. And then there was another time when we were at the Sagebrush Cantina and we ran into Alex Sanders. We were going to go home and have some fun, but before we left we had to eat something, and we decided to do it topless. So we waited for my car in valet topless, we got into my convertible topless, we drove to Taco Bell, ordered food, went through the drive-through . . . all topless. We had it all on video, but I was driving and Yvonne was videotaping, but again, she didn't have any of it in focus. Shooting wasn't her strong suit. So there's crazy stuff that happens on all of my shoots, but most all of it makes it into my videos. I love when shit goes wrong. Maybe not at the time, but in editing I'm grateful because it makes for a funnier movie. Because it *is* reality. I know everyone calls it gonzo, but I call it reality porn. And it *is* real.

Reality really struck my movies when the industry had its first really big AIDS scare. That's when I made the decision to do condoms-only. A lot of companies went condoms-only, but I'm the only one who stuck to it. There was once a big meeting for all the producers in the industry and I told everyone, "I'm shooting condoms-only. If you think it's going to hurt my dollars, my distributor is sitting here next to me. You can call him any time you want and ask about my numbers. Ask him what my numbers were doing and what they're doing now. My books are open to everyone." And you know what? My numbers went up. My fan mail was astronomical. I have the most amazing, supportive fans. It didn't hurt my dollar at all. And I can sleep peacefully at night.

The split between me and the brand I created is a very lengthy and complicated story. I made eighteen volumes of the Shane's World line and five Slumber Parties. I really wanted to have children, but I'm not as fortunate as most people in that department, which is why I decided to take so much time off from work. My husband and I tried adopting and that fell through. At the time I thought that never in a million years would a court let a porn producer adopt a child. (I later found out that wasn't true.) We were with a fertility specialist for a few years before I actually got pregnant. I wanted to be a mom and it took everything I had to do that. To make a long story short, I agreed to license the name of Shane's World, and so now every month I get a check that's a percentage of the profits from the line. However the one thing I can't stand about the deal is having my name associated with something I have no control over, and I hate the fact that they're preying on college kids for their movies. I would never go after college students. They're at school, they're trying to make something of their lives, and shooting one movie while they're at school will stick with them their entire lives. They have no idea. It'll never go away.

Now that I've had two babies and both of them are going to school, I've decided it's time to go back to work. When they were younger I didn't want to be the working mom who only saw them when she came home from work to put them to bed, I wanted to hang out with them all day long. Thankfully, this industry has allowed me to do that.

I've started a new line called Shane.TV. I felt some trepidation about coming back—I still do. Last summer was when I decided to return, and since then I've been working on the Web site and have shot only one movie because my number one job is still being a mom. And that job keeps me really busy. I'm going to be shooting more now that the Web site is done.

I don't watch porn. The stuff that I know about today is all stuff that I hear about when I do interviews and people ask me what I think about current trends in the industry. Regardless, my style will not change. I still preach safe sex. I will not make movies that are degrading to women. And I just want everyone to have a good time. They don't have to be squirting shit up to the ceiling, they don't have to have three cocks in their ass, they don't have to have someone spit in their mouth, they just have to have fun sex. If someone needs the three-cocks-in-the-butt thing to get off, they can go watch someone else's porn. I'm not going to change the way I shoot just to make an extra buck.

Even though I have strict rules in terms of how I run my productions, girls that are coming into the industry are usually eighteen to twenty-three, and I have to admit I feel like I'm corrupting them. Because since I'm not having sex in front of the camera anymore and I'm not doing it with them, I feel like a predator in a way. Plus, I have a daughter, so I'm really battling this internally. I'm super moody with this issue—sometimes I'm cool with it, other times I'm not. But all in all, I think that, granted, I've had my problems in this industry, but I've also met wonderful people, I've traveled to so many places, I've made great money and I've had super fun. I have to remember that these girls can have that too. I just have to remember that the industry isn't going to screw all of them up and get them all hooked on drugs, and cast them aside in the gutter. And it's better that they work for me than for some of the other companies that are out there, because I'm condoms-only, I look out for the girls, and I don't ask anyone to do anything they don't want to do or that I wouldn't do myself.

Although I don't think anything bad about porn now, I told my husband the other day that I was going to invent a new line called Prude Porn. "I know it sounds awful," I told him, "but it's going to be fun. There's just not going to be any spitting on girls, slapping them around, calling them names, none of that cream pie crap . . ." Sometimes I don't know what's going on with this industry, because some people are shooting the most disgusting, grossest things. I don't know who they're turning on. I don't buy into that this notion that society dictates all of this—*we* dictate to society what's hot and sexy on some level, and I think it's sad that we keep stooping to these levels just because someone else did and we feel the need to outdo each other. I always shot from my point of view because I thought if guys see that I'm having fun they'll like it, and if women see I'm having fun they'll like it too. But the belief that women only want to watch story-driven porn is such bullshit. I think women like many different kinds of porn as long as it's not degrading to them. I get so much fan mail from women, and tons of women show up when I do a signing. I think the reason is because I'm not some kind of sultry, sexy, I'm-out-to-get-you girl, I'm just kind of a dork having fun with a camera and her sex life.

One day my kids are going to find out that I've done porn. I'm just going to tell them straight out. I'd rather they hear this from me than from some kid in the playground. I hope that I raise my kids properly so that they're not judgmental but understanding. I don't think there's anything wrong with what I've done, and neither should anyone else. I've been doing nude modeling since I was eighteen and dancing since I was nineteen. I've been in the sex industry all my life. And believe me, when I was taking time off to have my kids I was wracking my brain to think of something else to do. I know I could go to school and learn anything I want. But I've done porn and I do it well. It feels good to do something that you're good at and that you get recognition from. I don't think it's any fun going to a job where they barely know your name and someone just signs your paycheck as you sit at your desk. I'm not a desk person or a forty-hour-per-week person.

I definitely have a love/hate with the industry, thanks to both good and bad experiences. Unfortunately, my most recent experiences have been negative. Sometimes I think I should lock myself in a room and watch all of my movies from back in the day when I was having so much. I always cautioned people about getting involved with the industry. You have to understand that this will stay with you for the rest of your life. If there's one person that you don't want finding out that you did a movie, I guarantee they will find out. So explore how you feel about that now. Think about it before you do anything. I have no regrets, but I know a lot of girls who have.

In the end, I would like to keep doing what I do and not have anything change my views because of money or pressure. When I quit, I want everything to end on a really positive note so that when I look back, the icky stuff is all in the middle and I have all the awesome, happy, fun experiences in the beginning and in the end. After all, everything has to have a little bad to it, otherwise you don't appreciate the good when it comes along. I never want to do anything I would be ashamed of, because I would never want my kids to be ashamed of me.

NINA HARTLEY

. . . ON PIONEERING THE HARDCORE HOW-TO VIDEO.

I BECAME AWARE OF MY unusual sexual nature when I was a preteen. I suspected at twelve, and knew at fourteen that I was bi. By the time I was sixteen I knew I was interested in group sex, public sex, what we now know as swinging—sex with people who were friendly and nice, but not people I was personally involved with—and naked people. If that part of my dial had been turned down I would just be a nudist, but my dial went all the way up.

I first became interested in pornography when I was fourteen and ran into some books that I found at the bedside of the swinging '70s couple that I babysat for, and I liked it right away. When I was a senior in high school I snuck into a theater to see the Mitchell Brothers' *Autobiography of a Flea.* I had read the book, I liked period pieces, and I wanted to see the movie. I was utterly stunned—I knew what it was that I had to do with my life. I was still a virgin at the time so I didn't know how I was going to get there, but the movie combined theater, performance, dance, sex, and naked people—all the things that I loved! Plus it was directed by a woman. I was very interested in sex, but I was completely unable to have an emotional connection with a partner. For me it was like, Dating? Talking? I didn't want that.

I didn't want to go through the relationship, I just wanted to have the sex.

I went to school to be a nurse. You had to be a nurse to be a midwife, which was my goal at the time. By the time I was twenty-three and a sophomore in nursing school, I started dancing. I got to have sex with women on stage, live, in front of an audience and loved that, too. Fast forward to 1992, and I'm doing live sex shows with a guy in Madrid in a nightclub in front of two thousand people. Nothing beats live performance. If I could sing, I'd be a singer. If I could play an instrument, I'd be a musician. So I love live sex performances. I'll never not love it.

As such I'm in porn for several reasons. One is because of my personal journey to myself and having the option and having the access to a lot of naked bodies with which I can have sex with all of the other bullshit stripped away. No romance. I knew I was going to work with Joe, so I'd meet Joe and introduce myself and get frisky right away with no worries about what are you doing after work or hearing about an ex-girlfriend. And when people hear that they say, oh, that's so impersonal, but no it's not, because I don't have the crutch or the lie of a manufactured personal interest. I was able to see each person individually using their body as a guide, because I'm a scientist. We're biological creatures and I know that if I touch and move a person this way I'll get this response, and if I touch and move a person that way I'll get that response, and it's remarkably consistent.

I've had sex with over a thousand people and I have to say, I'm batting .999. So for an awkward bookish person, I love that the negotiation part has been taken care of. And being a sex performer, you know and I know where this is going. The only question is how are we going to get there? Plus, I believe in body-based theories of therapy, meaning that by putting your body in certain situations your true self will be revealed to you. Martial arts, meditation, dancing, massage, sex . . . if you go through it consciously, all things will be revealed to you. So it's important to me that each of my performances is as emotionally grounded and revealing as it can be. Any performer is that way. I mean, why do people listen to Ella Fitzgerald? She puts her soul into it. Aretha Franklin? She puts her soul into it. Any good artist puts her soul into her work.

Sex has been so maligned in our culture and so distorted and repressed that I determined for my own sake, my own sanity, and my own ability, to become a loving person, to treat sex with the respect it deserves because the feelings it can conjure are real. And as a nurse and a social activist, I was also doing it for all those people who are alone and don't have anyone to say, "It's okay."

Also, at the time, the anti-porn feminists had raised their ugly heads and said how horrible it was for all women. At that time I knew Carol Queen and other women my age who hadn't made that analysis of the situation. If they tell us all women are so horribly abused, I'm going to tell them the rules say my body, my rules. I'm going to decide what I want to be with my body. I *am* this way. I'm not a construct of some man's imagination. I'm not so desperate for male approval that I'm going to debase myself by using my body to get attention from men. I'm a nudist. I have something to say to men about sex, about feminism, and about queer culture, and I discovered that if you're naked, people listen more. So I decided that, within my limitations, I was going to be a performer.

So when Adam & Eve approached me at the adult entertainment expo in 1995 with the concept of doing a how-to line, it was like manna from heaven—it was what I had been waiting to do. I'm not one to go out and create a company to do something like this; I'm the idea person. That's one of the reasons why I love being married to my husband Ernest, because he's a producer person and I'm an idea person. From the very beginning Adam & Eve gave me incredible freedom based on the topics and how I approach them. Ernest helped me with the first two by writing the scripts. We set the format for the scripts for the first two, which were *Nina Hartley's Guide To Fellatio and Cunnilingus*. We said the first section had to be an exhibition of anesthesiology or theory, the middle section me demonstrating and talking to the camera, and the third scene just a scene, incorporating what we've learned today. There are two sex scenes per movie so that people can see everything in action.

When the first tape was released, there seemed to be some confusion about the topic. *Nina Hartley's Guide to Oral Sex* sounds like a teaching tape to me—it doesn't sound like *Gobs of Goo* #72. One reviewer said, "Ms. Hartley talks to us as if we don't know anything about fellatio." Well, yeah . . . it's a guide to fellatio, and I'm assuming you know nothing. Wasn't that clear? A lot of other people think any kind of altruistic porn is crazy, stupid, or not authentic, so there was a lot of head-scratching going on in the industry with the press.

I aim the series at the enthusiastic novice, who has probably sought out one or two things on the subject. So I'm consistent in my nonjudgmental talking—it's very matter-of-fact sex education. With my series, I didn't shy away from the hardcore, so I was a pioneer in that respect because nobody else approached it that way. In my series there's no soft focus, no cutaways, and no tricky camera angles—it was important for me to show everything. But what really makes my guides stand out is that the teacher is practicing what she preaches. It wasn't some white-coated person who you couldn't imagine engaging in sex telling you what to do. I'm talking and doing because there are two parts to sex: the physical skill set and the amorphous emotional aspect. The physical skill set can be taught—squeeze here, tug here, try this. And though we shoot two at a time and consider them companion volumes, they're all stand-alone subjects—you don't have to have seen any of the others to see the one on the issue you're interested in. So far it's been tremendously successful. I'm up to twenty-six titles and 510,000 units in sales over ten years.

Even though the clothes are so horribly dated now, I really like the first two because they're just so pure and sincere. Quite frankly, I think the no-notes-needed anatomical tour without charts was pretty hot! If you really want to see me in my element, forget the big hair and the stupid thing I was wearing. I take you through all of it without any notes, and it didn't even need any alternate takes. I was really proud of that. Another one of my favorites was *Nina Hartley's Guide To Sensual Submission: How To Submit to a Man,* because I had a really sensual scene with Sean Michaels. But of my favorite scene in all of the tapes, I'd have to say my favorite was in the *Masturbation* tape between Lezley Zen and Mario Rossi. It was just so hot! You take two porn performers and tell them they can do everything but fuck . . . and the result was great.

When I first started the series there were other how-to videos, such as the Sinclair and Better Sex titles, but I never watched them because I was afraid I'd plagiarize accidently. The hallmark of my series is that it has a scientific and nurselike forthrightness—I accept that this is behavior people like to engage in so let's teach you how to do it. My information is always solid, it's very positive, it stresses responsibility and privilege. You get to have that, but this is what you need to do for your partner in return.

I tell people all the time that I had all this sex so that others didn't have to, because a lot of this stuff is about things people are never going to do. Very few people have had the number of sex partners I've had at the same time as being a trained health professional and sober. So even if you're not going to have a three-way, you can at least talk about it and see how it's done. My tapes have covered three-way, swinging, toys, dancing, older and younger sexual relationships, submission and domination of both the sexes, G-spot, erotic bondage . . . the list is nearly endless. But we're getting to the bottom of the barrel because as we do more and more, it becomes clearer to me that the sexual thing we really need to be talking about is feelings and emotions. Physically, there's not a lot more I can talk about. Next up is strap-on sex, and I'm not sure what the companion volume to that is going to be.

I made my first porn movie in 1984, graduated from college in 1985, and have been a full-time sex performer/entertainer/educator/evolutionary ever since. I've made about six hundred movies, and after twenty-one years in front of the camera I think this will be my last year in commercial porn. After next year's Adult Expo I have other irons in the fire, and on-camera porn is a young person's game. While I'm still youthful, I'm no longer young—it's just a fact of life, and I have other interests now.

I'm now writing a book based on the series, and that's really different for me. In the Introduction I say that all the guidelines apply. When I was younger I wanted to be good at ballet, but I didn't want to practice. And I wanted to play the violin, but I didn't want to practice. And I wanted to be able to speak French, but I didn't want to practice. I just wanted to be good. I used to spend time thinking about how I just wanted to know something, but I didn't have the emotional maturity to really stick to what I wanted.

Sex has been the only thing that has consistently held my attention and made me want to practice and practice and practice, but to do so you have to have a strong set of guidelines. So it's not an accident that I don't have bad sex anymore—I haven't had bad sex in years upon years, but it's not like some fairy came down and tapped me on the head with her wand. I have a very stiff set of rules and requirements for my sex life, and when all those guidelines are met, it's balls to the wall! There's a wonderful feeling of freedom in that. People say, "Oh, that's not romantic," but I beg to differ. If we have proper negotiation ahead of time and the trust issues have been negotiated so that you understand each other, when you start the session, all those little questions are answered so there's not that little "What if?" ruining your good time. When you have a fence around your playground, it's like having a safety cord on your bungee jump—you really have a lot of space inside your boundary to just roll out the gears. And once I learned how to do that consistently, that's when sex started getting better and better.

In the beginning of my career as an on-camera performer I had my no list, and out of about a thousand scenes I've only done something I didn't like only a few times, because I had that limitation. I say no to things I know I hate. It's a hard job and I have to love what I'm doing in order for it to work. So my consistency has always been because I had a plan and an agenda. I knew it would take twenty years for my message to reach critical mass, but if you take a look at all my movies—take away the stupid hair and all the shoulder pads and cheesy, cheesy jewelry—and look at my performances, they're consistent because I'm a happy person and I enjoy what I'm doing all the time.

I'm here because I want to be here. This is emotionally nurturing and satisfying to me. I've maintained my mental health because I made the decision long ago that rather than waste all this energy on hating it and worrying about it, I'd use that energy to make peace with who I am. Once you make peace with your own sexual nature, you no longer need to judge other people. Judgment comes from self-doubt and shame—it's shame turned outward. So the more you worry about what they're doing out there, the more you worry about what you're doing in here. I determined early on that I don't want to be that unhappy. I've lived that unhappy before, and it just stinks. That was something I was determined to release as soon as possible, and now I've done so. It took me a long time, but my whole career was about learning how to rise above that unhappiness.

Some of the anti-porn feminists say, "Women are used to being sex objects." Well, there's a time when that's appropriate, and that's when I'm horny and I want to have sex. Porn is supposed to objectify both men and women. That's its function. There's a time to say, "I don't want to talk about it, just put your hand on my tit. Yes, objectify me. I'm going to objectify you too, because you have a nice, hard dick. So let's get busy." I don't hate men for their sexual nature. Straight men like to look at naked women, and that's as it should be. The best sex we have is when we turn off all the voices of society and culture and get back to our animal nature, whatever that may be. The more in tune with that we are, the more we can clearly and successfully negotiate our personal relationships.

I can't fuck all night, but I love being the cheerleader. I love giving people permission to be their bad selves. In fact I'm still learning to give myself permission to be my bad self. I'm a work in progress. I've always evolved emotionally, I've always gotten deeper, I've always said to use the power of sex and pleasure in my body and the chemicals it produces in my brain to take myself through my issues. When you really give yourself permission to find and act on your heart's desires, you'll find that your old hurts are revealed to you—things that happened to you when you were a child will suddenly have words that you didn't know to put to them at the time, and then you have clarity. Whatever you can do with all your heart and soul will be the enlightening thing. It just happened to me that it was through sexuality.

I've learned that the magic moment, the key to my personal salvation and my long-term success is to try to get to the point where my partner and I look at each other and say, "Yeah!" And for some people that alone is hugely difficult, because people have all kinds of filters for intimacy—they don't feel they're worthy of that attention. I find a lot of times that when I do access people at that level they're frozen at a very young age in terms of their belief that they're worth anything, and it affects their ability to feel that they're allowed to experience this fun. But once someone lets into him- or herself another's compassion, even if it's only for a second, it's life changing and it's permanent. It's kinesthetic.

Sexuality is hardwired. We are orientation-based—straight or bi—then there is our sexual nature, zero on the scale being vanilla all the way to "you hang from what?!?" being a 10. Then there's your lifestyle: monogamous, swinger, polyamorous. Next is your privacy/exhibitionism scale. They all work together. On top of that our social and cultural layerings tell us our truths about sexuality—our experiences, good bad, or otherwise—and all these things are fighting for recognition. Due to the circumstances of my life I'm a brainy person. I was always thinking more than feeling, so my whole task as an adult was to become a feeling person, to break through my incredibly thick wall to tap into myself. For me, sexuality was the way to do that.

I know I speak for people who want sex to be all that and a bag of chips but it's not. Sex wasn't always like that for me, but I pretended it was. I slogged through all the bad relationships, feeling awkward in bed, all the bullshit . . . I've done it. But through it all I always knew that the feminists were right, that my body would see me through and my pleasure was a good teacher. If I could keep hold of that grail, that goal to focus on, I knew I could get there. I did it in public because I'm a public person, but I also knew that I had to do that because someone had to talk about it in an experienced way—someone had to be able to say, "It's not like those people who hate it say it is, it's bigger than that, and here's my version." If you're unhappy where you are and want to get to the bottom of it, I can be helpful. If you have issues with what I'm doing and don't want to address them, don't waste your time or mine. There are too many people who want to hear what I have to say. People who are sexual seekers respond to me visually and emotionally because they see that I'm one of them. They see that they can enjoy a richer sex life. That's really important, because I believe that adults can choose any kind of consensual experimentation they wish. Period.

WANTON WEBMISTRESSES

THE WOMEN WHO CHANGED THE FACE OF ONLINE SMUT

JANE DUVALL

I WAS A NEW BRIDE at the age of twenty-two and I didn't have much sexual experience—my new husband was only the third person I'd ever been with. Growing up with a mother who was a Planned Parenthood volunteer, I'd heard my share of teen pregnancy horror stories, so I waited until I was nineteen, fancied myself to be in love, and went in for a prescription for birth control. That was the late '80s before the days of STDs being a risk everyone knew about, so I suppose it was riskier than my nineteen-year-old self thought it was.

One afternoon a few months into the marriage, I was looking for a lost shoe and I found a stack of adult magazines under the bed. My husband at the time was a fundamentalist Christian, so I was shocked. It's ridiculous in retrospect. After years in the adult industry, I know now that he was part of a demographic about whom this should have been no surprise. I was curious and flipped through the magazines fairly often. My favorite was *Gallery,* because of "The Girl Next Door," which featured amateur exhibitionist pictures in a contest in each issue. I found myself sort of admiring the guts of the women who sent in their pictures, and they were a lot more fun to look at than the rest of the content.

I was never bothered by my husband's stack of magazines and he never knew that I had found them. The marriage broke up for many other reasons several years later. They say that every stereotype exists for a reason, but the only stereotypical aspect of my participation in the adult industry is probably how I entered it to begin with: trying to make ends meet as a single mom. In 1995, I was going through the divorce and had three very young children to take care of. I worked a full-time job, went to school part time, and then to supplement my main income, I started taking phone sex calls on a secondary line from home in the wee hours while the kids were asleep. That was my first exposure to sex work, and it was not what I expected.

What was eye-opening for me when I started doing phone sex was the dashing of my own stereotypes of the kinds of men who called the lines. Instead of my expectation of a low socioeconomic background or boorish behavior, what I found was that most of the men who called simply had a sexual desire or need that they felt they couldn't share, out of shame or embarrassment, with their partner. For the most part my phone clients were repeat callers, well-educated, polite, truly nice people. I had some definite empathy there, as I had had my own experiences with wanting the less-than-mainstream. I had always had bondage fantasies, and when I finally "came out" to my then-husband, he expressed disgust at my "perversion." At the same time I never regretted being honest about my feelings with him. Yes, it hurt— but it would have hurt more never to have tried. I'd get in all sorts of long conversations with some of my callers about the risks and rewards of sexual honesty.

The other change that I made when I started taking phone calls was to acquire my first computer. I knew nothing about them, but I wanted to take some college credits online and I'd read that it could be done. I bought an old 486 Pentium from a friend who was a bonafide computer geek, and the first thing I found other than school was the long list of Usenet newsgroups. The bondage newsgroups quickly became regular haunts as I started to toy with the idea of actually doing what I'd only fantasized about for so long.

When I think back to that time, it's about all of the things that aligned to drop me into what I did next. I had started to teach myself basic Web design and programming because I wanted a better job. At the same time, I was encountering a group of people who were sexually open, who—if not cheerleaders for it—were at least not judgmental about my part-time phone sex gig. To promote my phone sex persona, I decided to start a Web site which quickly snowballed into a full-fledged Web business. I had a Webzine that had some of my own first attempts at erotic fiction and my own "girl next door–esque" photos, and after months of running that, decided to start an adult link site to generate traffic to it. What I didn't expect was for it to take off so well that the original reason, promoting phone sex, fell by the wayside.

To be honest, I was glad to be done with taking calls. I had started to become emotionally burned out. I will admit that it was my own fault because I didn't have much understanding at the time of how to set boundaries with my clients that would have helped me. Because I genuinely liked them as people, I found myself taking calls with subject matter that I just wasn't into: I was afraid to say no out of fear of hurting the feelings of the strangers I was sharing intimate moments with. I didn't want to make someone feel any more shame than they already felt for whatever their kink was. If I were to do it again, knowing what I know now, I think I have the means to keep within those boundaries without hurting anyone, but it was all part of the process. Happily leaving phone sex aside, I worked full time on the link site, Jane's Net Sex Guide.

The adult Web was still young in 1997. The very first press I ever got was within a couple of months of launching the site, when the now-defunct Web Magazine gave me a "site of the day" pick. They had been impressed with the friendly tone and seemed blown away that it was run by a woman. It was very important for me back then that people knew I was real, that my Web site truly had a "Jane," that it wasn't being run by a bunch of men. I guess it was ego, but whatever the reason, it mattered to me. I had a section I called "The Photo Challenge" to prove the reality of me, where readers could send me an e-mail with a particular challenge. For example: *"Jane, I want to see you eating Wheaties."* So I'd do it and post the picture. Or hold up a sign with something they wanted written, and so on and so forth. In retrospect, it was a little bit of girl-next-door creeping in again.

Of course, running an adult Web site of that nature caused me to be exposed to everything that was out there, instead of just the tiny bubble of the bdsm community that I'd been exploring in my personal life. I was so naïve at the time that I was always genuinely surprised at all of the junk out there. I found myself being outspoken about sites that seemed misogynistic, or sites that were just plain bad—no content, all ads. The early years of the adult Web were also a real Wild West of consumer rip-offs and scams, and I started writing about those as well. It made me really angry to see it going on, because I strongly felt that adult material was marginalized enough as it was without earning a reputation for being shady in its business dealings. It seemed like there were so many companies that were operating on the shame factor: overbill because the consumer will never complain, they won't want to admit they looked (or bought) in the first place.

I had quite a bit of backlash from parts of the adult online community when I started editorializing against the bad business practices that were so rampant. There was an attitude of "we're all on the same team, it's us against them," which was something I truly didn't understand. I'd been brought up to value a strong work ethic and honesty. I didn't understand why that shouldn't apply just because we were dealing with adult pictures instead of toaster ovens. I think it was my own naïveté that helped me make the Web site what it was. I ended up working closely with the Federal Trade Commission to help shut down a couple of particularly egregious adult companies that had swindled people out of tens of millions of dollars back in 1998 and 1999. That was a high point for the consumer protection part of what I did. It was also a turning point in the adult Web, as the industry started to realize that the shame factor was lessening and consumers were going to be vocal about being treated unfairly, not to mention that the same government that wanted to censor adult content would also protect the consumers who bought it.

Meanwhile, the press that had begun with Web Magazine was starting to increase. I was frequently contacted by *Wired,* MSN.com, and others to give opinions and input about the industry, and about that time the New York New Media Association called to ask if I'd participate on a panel discussion in front of six hundred or so reporters in New York. I was thrilled to be asked, if intimidated by the company I was keeping. The rest of the panel included one of the founders of Nerve.com, the Internet head of *Penthouse* magazine, and an analyst from Forrester Research. I was just a suburban mother of three with plenty of opinions. It was an interesting panel, but the best part of the experience was in relating that my first exposure to porn had been "The Girl Next Door" feature in *Gallery* magazine. After the panel ended a woman came up from the audience to introduce herself, and it turned out she was the person who had started that section of *Gallery!* I remember thinking how very unsurprised I was that it had been a woman who came up with the idea.

There were plenty of other fun parts of the job as well. One of the things I truly fell in love with about the online adult industry as opposed to print and video was the incredible diversity of content it afforded people. Where the costs of traditional publishing were so high that nobody wanted to take a risk, the low cost of putting things online made all sorts of independent content producers, amateur exhibitionists, and fetishists able to share their passions with the rest of the world. I felt as if we were all so inundated with one type of airbrushed perfection from mainstream media that we'd forgotten how to eroticize anything else. I remember the first time I went to a women's spa where nudity was the norm, and I was looking around in amazement at all the varied and beautiful bodies around me. I had not really seen many other women nude except in mainstream magazines, and I was enthralled by all the differences. I feel that the Internet did so much for exposing people to more than one concept of what is sexy or beautiful.

I suppose one case in point would be my own personal Web site. It doesn't really exist any longer, but for three years or so I had an offshoot of JanesGuide, which was my own nude and seminude pictures and journal. At the time I started it I was very much in the category of "big, beautiful woman"—or BBW—and the reason I did it was that it actually did help me recognize myself as still being an attractive, sexual human being when the regular day-to-day world made me feel invisible. There online were all of these admirers, male and female alike, who thought those curves were hot! It was interesting to me that over time, as my body changed due to an exercise program I'd started, my site and photos became less popular instead of more so. The closer I got to mainstream standards of beauty, the less real and the less accessible I seemed to be to the people visiting the site.

While the personal site no longer exists as it did once, it was a valuable experience. I felt strongly that I needed to experience being "the talent" if I was going to make money out of promoting the industry. It's funny, I remember that at the time I was doing that site a woman writing to ask me if I felt like I had to pose nude to garner respect in that industry. She couldn't have been more wrong, both about my motivation and about the general attitude that seemed to exist toward "the talent." I'd seen and heard enough at adult conventions to know that the sex-positive attitudes I found in the bdsm community that was my support network were not shared by mainstream porn producers. The Internet clearly has benefited the actors and actresses. More people have been able to control their own material and portrayal than ever before. Independent sites are all over the place, under the general umbrella of "amateur," and they are directly controlling not only what kinds of scenes they shoot, but also how to present them to the world. It may sound like a small thing, the portrayal aspect, but it was brought home to me when I did a photo shoot that I shared with the photographer. I used it on my Web site with my own text and found it beautiful; he used it on his Web site with rather exploitive text and I found it rather hurtful.

Through all of the eight years I've been doing this, I've never wavered in my desire to say whatever is my own truth at the time. I've seen good aspects of the industry as well as bad. I've gotten very involved in the industry and its community, then backed off considerably to regroup. A couple of years ago I split up with my long-term partner, and in large part it was because he wanted sexuality to be a far more encompassing aspect of his life at the same time that I was reprioritizing it in mine. That was the biggest shock and rattling of my belief system that occurred in all the time I've been doing this. In part I blamed the very community I'd been involved in for so long for being overly permissive. There were no rules, there were no boundaries, to say no to anything at all was to be accused of being closed-minded. It's taken me the past couple of years to realize that as in all things, moderation is key. There is a place for adult entertainment, because we are all sexual beings. Whether it's getting turned on by a romance novel,

Angelina Jolie's gorgeous lips in a movie, or the most explicit hardcore sex scene, we all experience some form of it, and I've been happy to be a part of attempting to normalize the experience, to take it out of the brown paper wrapper so everyone has the same chance for growth and experience that I did. What I try to do with my site every day is to remove the shame factor so that all people, regardless of gender and orientation, will start to open up, if not to the world, then at least to their intimate partners.

As for where I am now personally, after two years of regrouping I have found new inspiration in working on the site. I've added two more writers to the staff, both women, from very different backgrounds but both very sex-positive. I continue to find Web sites that inspire me to think, or that just give me grist for my own erotic imagination. I have a new husband, who provides a good sounding board for the mainstream that I didn't have before, being as immersed in sex-positive culture as I was. I find that very helpful, since about 90 percent of my readership is mainstream. What I'm hoping is that the online industry will continue to produce the amazing independent talent that has come out of it in almost a decade, and honestly, the future there looks bright.

EMILY DUBBERLEY

. . . ON STARTING A SEXUAL REVOLUTION IN THE U.K.
THROUGH INTERNET PUBLISHING.

I NEVER THOUGHT I'D END up as a pornographer. When I was a child, I wanted to be a writer; I worked on school magazines from the age of eight, entered every writing competition I could find, and went for work experience with a local newspaper when I was fourteen. When time for university came around, everyone told me that doing an English degree was a waste of time: employers preferred writers who had an additional "specialism." So I decided to study social psychology, and though I didn't realize it at the time, that's when my career in the sex industry began.

In the early 1990s, when I started my degree, porn for women was burgeoning in the U.K. Five new titles had launched, and with them a mass of publicity. But female-oriented porn had a major flaw: you couldn't show a man in a state of sexual arousal. The "Mull of Kintyre" guideline specified that a penis had to stick out from a male model's body by no more than the angle at which the Mull of Kintyre sticks out from Scotland on a map of the U.K., which, figuratively and literally, was a bit of a downer.

Alongside the practical issue of being unable to get off on images of men with flaccid members (if you can tell they wouldn't be in a fit state to perform, it's hardly a turn-on), as a feminist, I was annoyed by the double standard. After all, men could see women in a clear state of arousal—nipples erect and lips glistening—in any top-shelf magazine they wanted. People (mostly men) claimed that this didn't matter, as women weren't aroused by the visual. Their comments were based on archaic research that was invalid in a modern world. And so, I decided that up-to-date sex research would be the focus of my degree.

In my second year, I studied the difference between male and female attitudes toward pornography. Unsurprisingly, for me at least, my research showed that women were just as interested in porn as men: they just had different standards. The material offered wasn't hitting the spot. Erection-free magazines crammed with pictures of buff Chippendale types in fireman's uniforms were too much of a cliché. "Where are the real men?" was a familiar refrain.

However, there was hope in the form of Black Lace books, a new series of erotic novels for women. What they lacked in images, they more than made up for with exceptionally graphic language, busting the myth that women were delicate flowers in need of romanticized sex content. My research found that women were much happier with the erotic writing available: at least with written content, the men could be erect. And, while all but one of the sex magazines withered, Black Lace grew.

By my final year I'd become increasingly fascinated by all things sex. Nancy Friday, the Hite Report, Rachel Silver, and Kinsey all inspired me, so when it came time to choose a dissertation topic I decided to study whether women wanted their sexual fantasies to come true (findings: it depended on the fantasy). I was beginning to see sex as one of life's universals: whether we admit it or not, it has an impact on all of our lives. And when I moved to London at the end of the year to search for my dream job, writing for a women's magazine about sex, I took a stack of sex manuals with me.

Once I arrived in London I discovered that getting a break in journalism wasn't easy. I put sex on the back burner (professionally, at least) while I built up contacts and worked in Internet marketing and the music industry to pay my rent. But I never lost my interest in the area, and, after five years of working with Web sites, I got bored with hearing that the Internet was full of porn when there was nothing out there that seemed remotely designed for women. I interviewed and talked to hundreds of women about it, and none of them had found an adult site that was suitably stimulating and female-friendly, so I decided to create one.

Cliterati.co.uk was designed as a text-based sex Web site for women. We rejected the phrase "porn site" as a description, because at the time it alienated women used to male-oriented pornography. Now porn-chic has made some inroads into fixing the bad reputation of the word "porn" but we wanted the site to appeal to all women, and as such, we wanted to make it feel as safe as possible.

Cliterati lacked pictures for various reasons; the politics of visual porn are harder to negotiate. I believe in informed consent. I wanted to guarantee that if we did run any pictures on the site, the models were fully aware that we were using their image and were emotionally and physically able to consent to the photographs been taken. This was not feasible without setting up a picture agency of my own, something that was outside my budget.

We also wanted to ensure that women could look at the site discreetly, as many women are still embarrassed about masturbation and would be put off by a splash-screen full of big cocks. We wanted the site to appeal to women of all sexualities, meaning we'd need pictures of men and women—but some straight women could be offended by seeing pictures of naked women. Added to this, there were (and still are) very few picture agencies selling naked pictures of straight (or straight-looking) men. And most practically, I'm a writer, not a photographer, and by keeping things text-based I could source a wealth of content myself, simply by producing it.

And so the task of creating the site began. I approached some journalist friends, and we each wrote twenty stories, in five loose categories: straight, lesbian and bi, group sex, sub/dom, and taboo—for the milder end of fetishism—to make it easier for women to navigate the site. I also wanted any woman to be able to add her fantasies to the Web site, as it seemed incredibly arrogant to assume that I, along with five other women, could represent every female fantasy. As time went on we added a further section, fantasies written by men, after site visitors said that they'd like to read male fantasies too. In addition to the erotic material, we included features, vibrator reviews, sex news, and a no-holds-barred problem page that answered the questions women really have about sex, without editing them into a "media-friendly" format.

We deliberately set ourselves a tight deadline of a month to create the site, as all of us had full-time jobs and it's often easier to work to a tight deadline if you want to make something happen. Luckily, my then-partner ran a web design company, userfrenzy.com, and so could do the coding, meaning that we could create a complex database-driven Web site for a negligible sum.

It was never our intention for the site to be a money-making venture: we created it on a damned-near zero budget, paying only for the URL, begging people to provide the original erotica for free and borrowing space on a friend's server. The site was there purely because I felt that women deserved masturbation material. We decided not to charge for access to the site, funding it instead through sex-toy Web site affiliate deals. After all, sometimes a woman can tire of her hand, and we hoped that the site's users would have a degree of loyalty to us for providing them with so much free erotic content, and would buy their sex toys through the site.

The initial response blew us away. It was good that we had a revenue-generating mechanism in place because we soon needed to buy a server of our own. We'd been aiming to attract 100,000 page impressions per month by the end of the first year. We managed it by the end of our first week. An unrelated research report had come out the week before we launched, claiming that 16 percent of people who searched the internet for porn were female. Journalists were looking for female-friendly sites to tie in to this new trend, and Cliterati was the only relevant site in the U.K.

The resulting press interest was immense. By the point at which we launched, we'd gained enough word-of-mouth interest to attract over 100 national press journalists to our launch party (again, arranged on a shoe-string budget and by calling in favors). Stories followed in all the main women's magazines, including *Cosmopolitan* and *Elle,* and a number of national newspapers. Barely a week went by without one of the team being asked to comment on women and sex for some radio station or other. Before long, we'd done interviews with media in Australia, the U.S., and France, to name a few.

But the launch wasn't entirely pain free. We also received hate mail: some relatively naïve e-mails from women claiming that the founders of Cliterati must be male because no self-respecting woman would allow the word "cunt" to be used in an erotic story. Other e-mails were more sinister: men threatening to come around and treat us "like the sluts we were," in many cases going into graphic detail. And then there were the men who tried to intimidate us by attempting to post rape fantasies, incest stories, and worse to Cliterati. Obviously, none of these stories made it onto the site, but at about that time, we decided to remove all contact details from the Web site and only allow reader feedback through the "contribute a story" link. Trust me, few things are less pleasant than coming home after a hard day at work to an inbox full of rape threats and twenty erotic stories containing humiliating violent sex acts, with yourself as the central character.

Perverts weren't the only problem. There were other strange reactions. My family were totally supportive—my mother's only concern was that I might attract stalkers. I never let her know how valid that fear was. But some friends were lost along the way: several said, "I never knew you were a lesbian!" when they saw that the site had a section for lesbian and bi stories and actively avoided homophobia. My response was, "Well, I try not to be racist but that doesn't make me black." Some women seemed nervous about letting me stand next to their boyfriends in case I couldn't resist my base urges now that I was a "pornographer." Other women assumed that I was the "girl most likely" if they wanted to dabble with bi-curiousity. And still others just assumed I was a slut.

And then there was the male reaction when they found out about my job, broadly divided into three categories. They were either intimidated as hell; responded with "Oh, really?" (delivered in lounge-lizard tone with a hand miraculously appearing significantly north of my upper thigh); or (the rare and wonderful few) responded with a simple "How did you get into that?" or similar—as they would if I'd said I was an insurance clerk.

But any negative response was more than made up for by the Cliterati readers who sent in positive letters: one woman said that, age thirty, she'd had her first orgasm thanks to the site. Another said that our advice on dealing with a conflict with her partner had saved her relationship, and hundreds of others wrote in thanking us for showing that masturbation was nothing to be ashamed of.

Over the next few years I met many other people in the adult industry. I was nervous at first, believing the myth that anyone in porn would be a greasy, moustachioed man with wandering hands. It couldn't have been farther from my experience. More women were flocking to the industry, and there was less sexual harassment, drug abuse, and general bad behavior than I'd encountered in the Internet or music industries. The rapidly growing female contingent in the sex industry was having an impact on the way business was done, and there was a fantastic spirit of cooperation between us that continues to this day.

Some of the experiences I had over this time made me think, "I can't believe I'm getting paid for this!" There was the six-week striptease course I attended in order to review it, and the day I spent at "porn school," making a low-budget porn film, with me strictly behind the camera. Some things are too far in the line of work, even for me.

Then there have been embarrassing times: the moment when I inadvertently answered the phone while reviewing a vibrator and just at the point of no return springs to mind. (I was still in work mode and picked the phone up as a matter of habit. I *think* the client at the end of the phone believed me when I said I was having a choking fit.)

And other moments have made me laugh: answering the door to a male porn star friend of mine with, "I don't suppose you know anything about fixing boilers, do you?" when he arrived within minutes of my boiler exploding. He didn't—and I didn't get laid either, which was a bit of a disappointment. (The moral of the story: never believe what you see in porn).

But more than anything, working in the industry has taught me a lot about people. I've had sixty-year-old women come up to me at non–sex industry corporate events and ask me to recommend a vibrator. I've been asked for tips on how to urinate in every color of the rainbow. And I know now that there are more fetishes and quirks in people's bedrooms—and anywhere else you could imagine—than I would have believed before. It's almost certainly true that the quiet ones are the worst.

One of the most pivotal people I met over the years was the

founder of *Lovers' Guide,* Robert Page. He attended Cliterati's third-birthday party and said he loved the Cliterati attitude. I jokingly asked if he was looking for any scriptwriters. After two years of running Cliterati, I'd gone freelance, and I loved the idea of working for the world's biggest sex education video brand. To my surprise, he said, "I do have something that needs writing at the moment, actually." Two weeks later I put my first completed script on his desk: *The Lovers' Guide: Sex Positions.* He loved it, and it started a business relationship that lasts to this day: I have written three videos, edited the *Lovers' Guide* magazine and Web site, and written sex tips that are delivered as text messages to people's mobile phones.

One memorable experience, courtesy of Rob, was spending several days yelling, "Cock out of shot!" when trying to art-direct soft-core pictures for the *Lovers' Guide* magazine. It's amazing how mundane it becomes seeing a man wandering round stroking himself to maintain wood between sets. Of course, the first question male friends asked was, "Did it turn you on?" to which I can honestly answer, "Not most of the time." There was one short period that was arousing, on the first day I was on the set—but not because of any particularly hardcore action. I caught the look between the male and female porn star who were having sex: they'd just met, but clearly had major chemistry going on and were oblivious to the cameras for a passing moment. Now, that was hot.

The advantage of the sex industry is that jobs tend to fit quite well together (no pun intended). While I worked for the Lovers' Guide, I continued to run Cliterati, obviously using my experience gained from the Lovers' Guide to feed into the content, and vice versa. Now Cliterati attracts over 900,000 page impressions per month, and it's still growing. I've written several books off the back of its success: *The Lovers' Guide Lovemaking Deck, Brief Encounters: The Women's Guide to Casual Sex, Things a Woman*

Should Know About Seduction, and *Sex Play*. In May 2005, I launched a spin-off site, www.bibibaby.com—a free dating site for bi-curious women—after we had hundreds of bi-curious fantasies submitted to the site. Early in 2004, I was approached by a publisher asking whether I'd be interested in creating an offline magazine. How could I resist? We met up, and after establishing his credentials (ex-publisher of *The Erotic Review*) and vision (similar to mine, but giving me free reign to create the magazine as I wished), I agreed to take the job of editor. After over a year of research, planning, and building an editorial team, *Scarlet Magazine* launched in November 2005. Terrifyingly, the Mull of Kintyre guideline still stops us from showing an erection, an indication of how little the industry has moved on in some respects. However, *Scarlet* does tackle modern taboos: rimming, strap-on sex for straights, even mundane things like sex during menstruation—along with running some very filthy stories.

When *Scarlet* launched with high-profile press coverage, I was prepared for hate mail, jibes, and lechery. But with the exception of some right-wing press, the reaction has been positive. Women today—a mere five years later—are more accepting of their own sexuality, and men are more accepting of women's sexuality too. We've even had thank-you letters from men grateful for our sex tips improving their partner's performance in bed. As time's goes on, negative reactions toward women in the sex industry seem to be fading, at least in my experience. Sure, there are still people out there who make negative assumptions and judgments, but that's to be expected if you're trying to change things.

Even if the stigma attached to being a woman in the sex industry never leaves, I wouldn't want to give up my job. The world needs people who are prepared to say that sex is a good and healthy thing, and that masturbation is fun rather than something that will make you blind. Being open and upfront about sex helps people realize that they are normal—if such a thing as

normal even exists. Giving people (ethically produced) masturbation material puts smiles on their faces (not to mention all
those glorious orgasm chemicals floating around the body).

While there are times when I'll think, "God, do I have to read
another description of a cock soaked with pre-cum sliding
between soft lips?!' " they tend to pass in a matter of minutes—
usually when the doorbell rings and there's a mailman with a
package full of new toys for me to try. If I'd known as a kid what
I'd end up doing, I'm not sure I'd have believed it. But now, I'm
proud to be part of this world.

KATIE SMITH

LIFE IS THE PURSUIT OF happiness. I am on a journey.

I was an all-star soccer player, with gold and silver medals from the Junior Olympics. I played all the way into high school. Outside of soccer, however, school bored the daylights out of me. I was not challenged. I was more into discussing politics, watching consumer trends, and understanding deeper human and emotional issues. I was also learning that I preferred women, which all in all made me not want to talk with anyone. I thought of myself as a dork. I just didn't connect with anyone. I had to move to Hollywood to find my people.

For the first time in my life I read the want ads. I found an ad that said "Marketing Account Manager Needed." Within one month a company called iGallery hired me. They were a subsidiary of New Frontier Media (The Erotic Networks, TEN). And so my career in adult began. I was hesitant at first. I looked them up before the interview to research the job. It was a bit shocking to see that they were an online management firm for top adult sites. My girlfriend at the time had to convince me to take the interview. If it hadn't been for her, I'm not sure I would be here right now. I did have a slight judgment about the industry and porn in general, and I was worried about who I was going to work with. Well, I was in for another shock.

I was interviewed in a very large, posh conference room with Scott Schalin, President, and Holly Moss, VP of Marketing and Sales. They both wore hip, nice clothes. Both were polite and well spoken. They were 100 percent professional and visionary in how they described the business. I flipped the interview around and asked them where they saw themselves in five years. They said, "We'll be on the cutting edge of the convergence of broadcast and online." That was it for me. "When do I start?"

At first the explicit content was overwhelming. To this day I have seen only a handful of films. I was a little naïve, to say the least, and I guess it was slightly uncomfortable because I was viewing it with coworkers around me. It took me about a month to get over that. The only material that affects me today is the super hardcore kind where the girls don't look like they are having fun. One of the reasons Jenna Jameson, in my mind, is so popular is that she looks like she loves it. Like most people, I prefer that. Everyone should be having fun. Otherwise, I'm uncomfortable.

This was also the first time I became close-mouthed to my family about my career progress. It took time for me to let them in on my secret. To this day, I keep it on the down low in personal situations. My girlfriend is an executive at one of the largest environmental not-for-profits in the country. We just tell her colleagues that I own my agency, which is not a lie, and leave it at that. I don't care what other people think, but if it might hurt someone somehow, then I don't go into details. It's not worth it, and it doesn't bother me.

I was a bit cocky when I started at iGallery in thinking I knew Web sites. I had no idea that every single click could be turned into money, but once I figured it out, I shut my mouth and ran with it. I quickly managed some of the largest clients. I drove subscription sales and e-mail opt-ins, and helped design site tours, members' areas, free sites, CPC campaigns, SEO strategies, dialers, and more. I helped develop new affiliate programs and their B2B website. What I am most proud of is TEN.com. I always thought the standard adult site wasn't good enough for surfers. I wanted to help build something better. My goal was to get as many men off as possible and make the absolute most money doing so.

I became close friends with Scott Strother, VP for Web Development for TEN.com. Over the course of about a year we developed an awareness of the brand and a new way of thinking. Instead of the standard tour, the idea was to open the site up and allow the surfers to get a feel for the real experience. It was the best broadband experience online, and still is to this day. My timing, as usual, was not good. As soon as we started making good things come to life, the powers that controlled us began to fight. New Frontier Media decided that iGallery was too much of a liability for a publicly traded company. They began to slowly shut down the office in Los Angeles and moved their assets to Boulder. They let go a large part of the staff. Michael Werner, the present-day CEO, and Alan Issacman, the infamous lawyer who defended Larry Flynt before the Supreme Court, interviewed me. They wanted me to stay—and even gave me a raise. Many others were not so lucky. It got so bad that I was literally the only person in the Los Angeles office, all alone on the eighth floor of the Comerica building in Sherman Oaks. I didn't want to leave. But I also didn't want to move to Boulder.

AVN offered me a job. I felt that it was the best choice for me at the time, even if it meant a complete change. Darren Roberts and Farley Cahen hired me as their Online Marketing Manager for *AVN*'s network of Web sites. I came in and took about a month to research and analyze the status of the product offerings. I created an action plan that included a complete redesign of the main site, AVN.com, turning it into a portal. I mapped out how the traffic should flow and how we would direct it. I developed an online media kit with ad packages broken down into key section

sponsorships. I had a plan to increase the growth of our partnership revenue. I had a plan for cross-promotions for all the main
business units. I had a clear goal: increase sales. Within one year,
with the help of Jeff Random, and with the same amount of
traffic, we achieved our goal overwhelmingly.

One part of my master plan was to leverage the power of the
brand to help advertising across the board, to help drive eyeballs. We officially launched the AVN Media Network, and I
became Director of Corporate Communications. My job was to
work with each department head and help drive marketing of
each division. I developed and implemented campaigns for
AVN's two magazines; its tradeshows, Internext and Erotica LA;
and the company's online division. I developed the corporate
brand and media kit, and worked with an outside public relations firm. I also managed barter relationships with partner companies to help maintain awareness of the brand and products
going strong in the industry. As this campaign was building,
something else was going on—the market was changing. The
digital media side of the industry was consolidating, maturing.
What this meant for AVN was fewer companies spending money
as the climate became conservative. AVN wanted me to focus on
their tradeshows, which is a key business unit and profit gener-
ator. As much as I will always be loyal and devoted to AVN, the
tradeshow business is not my passion. I love digital media. I love
site and traffic management and marketing. I made a decision to
start my own company, where I could again work with consumer
sites. However, I didn't leave AVN behind. And AVN stood by my
side and became my first client.

(THROB) 3ob.com was born in April 2004. AVN hired
(THROB) and I worked with Renée Johnson, Chad Beecher, and
Tom Hymes to produce their new seminar series for Internext for
both the summer and winter shows. It was my job to coordinate
the industry knowledge into an educational forum. It was a lesson

well learned. That same year I became the first person to produce a seminar in the mainstream conference, Digital Hollywood.

While the show development was going on, I was landing new clients. My main goal was to build my first case study. It's classic how they found me through a (THROB) ad on AVN.com. I received a call from Anh Tran, cofounder of WantedList.com, the largest adult DVD rental Web site. They hired (THROB) to handle their marketing and public relations. The first call to action was the press. They are smart to understand that it is the best, cheapest form of traffic. My job was to get press hits, help them redefine their brand, and develop and coordinate marketing programs. Once they saw that I could offer much more, they got me involved in other key projects. We redesigned their site just in time for *AVN* to review and nominate it for a 2005 Award for best retail Web site. My philosophy stayed the same: open up the site and show surfers what they get. Create an experience. WantedList had great sticky content, so what we did was showcase it better, and cross-sell better. I helped develop a new, fresh brand concept just in time for the 2005 AEE show. I set up Playboy Radio to broadcast live from the WantedList booth with XM Radio. The Opie and Anthony show did a broadcast as well, and we had Tera Patrick driving a crowd, plus we had *Star* magazine following us throughout the show. WantedList.com was written up in *Variety,* and the best was yet to come. The founders of WantedList had worked hard on their product long before I came into the picture, and what happened next was entirely because of the hard work of their team, and their unrelenting vision. They won the award for best retail Web site at the 2005 *AVN* Awards. They shared their glory with me, but it was truly all theirs.

My approach from the beginning was to mix smart consumer product marketing tactics with online direct marketing (data-based) tactics. At first people thought I was crazy. Most people did not think the both could happen at once, unless you were a big brand like *Playboy*. My goal has always been to prove them wrong. I began this approach with TEN and continued with WantedList.com and other companies. I care about customers and want to deliver a great experience. It's hard to convince decision makers that, in the end and long-term, it will make them more money. I pushed my philosophy hard during my Internet seminars. Consumer-centric marketing can happen in online adult. I'm going to make sure of it. That said, others have caught on since and are pushing themselves, which is great to see because it is good for the perception of the industry as well. Smart business people, including the founders of WantedList.com, have come from outside the industry and have begun to infiltrate the industry with a more "mainstream" approach. The bar is rising . . .

Listen, the industry is fun, but for all intents and purposes I could be marketing anything—a star, service, product, movie. A piece of content turns into a unique ID in my world. That unique ID is then turned into a piece of data that I use with other variables to determine outcomes such as CTR (click-through ratio), CPA (cost per acquisition), overall ROI (return on investment), and lifetime customer values. That number tells me which piece of content sells. And with all the other data I look at each day, I keep the growth going.

What has appealed to me from the beginning is that sex sells, and with that comes a wonderful test environment. In this industry there is so much traffic that you can try one thing, see if it works, and keep tweaking it until you find that "happy spot." Adult moves quicker and has the balls to test new technologies and business models. That is the first and foremost thing that attracted me to it from the very first day.

The year 2005 has been great for (THROB). We are working on many exciting projects. I have a great stable of clients and partners, and we are becoming one of the most prestigious marketing firms in the industry. We were chosen to be exclusive partners to such respected companies as Traffic Dude. We partnered with the best companies to offer our clients mobile technology, traffic management tools, DRM, VoD and processing solutions, Web analytics, e-mail solutions, and more. I could not be more proud and grateful for this experience. I remember when (THROB)'s site first went live. I was so happy I just stared at it. I still do. It is my brainchild, and more is on the way.

I have many friends in the industry, although I have to admit I separate personal and business pretty well. I spend off-hours with my girlfriend, family, and friends. I traded soccer for snowboarding, yoga, and hiking. My interests are relatively the same from many years past, albeit better directed. I consume more media than ever. I am a thinker and activist at heart. Instead of a dork, now I just think of myself as a geek. That is way cooler.

This industry has taught me so much. I feel very lucky because I know that mainstream online marketers have a lot of catching up to do. We in adult truly understand the metrics better. No other industry, aside from gambling and pharmaceuticals, can do it as well as adult. I learned from the best. I now know the correct information to seek out, the best tools to use, and the best companies to partner with.

My experience has altered me was by making me better, more knowledgeable, and more well rounded. On top of the numbers side, I was given a chance to work with print and broadcast. This means I am trained to do integrated marketing—and that is second to none. It would have been so much harder to pull this off in mainstream, and it was hard enough as it was. Again, I am very grateful.

What would have happened if I had never gotten into the adult industry? I don't care to think about it, because it was one of the best things that ever happened to me. I get paid to do what I love. For someone who loves technology and online marketing,

I am exactly where I should be. Adult has a strong history of pushing technology to mainstream—we define what works. I was recently quoted in *Laptop* magazine saying, "Porn is like water. No matter how many boundaries you put up, it will always sink in." Society has always sought out adult entertainment. My job is to make that search easier, safer, and more enjoyable. As the market changes, so do I, and that is the most exciting part. I can never get bored.

HESTER NASH

. . . ON HOW A LONGTIME INTEREST IN VINTAGE PORN LAUNCHED A UNIQUE SITE ON THE INTERNET.

THE FIRST TIME I EVER saw pornography I was about seven years old. My best friend's father had a stash of porn, which wasn't hard for a couple of nosy little kids to find. One particular item has stuck with me: a contact sheet of photos of a middle-aged white man with what seemed to be a salami between his legs, wearing a dashing ensemble of black socks, calf garters, and the black mask that always lends an air of mystery. He was applying the salami in various ways to a fleshy black woman in white granny panties and garters (whose face was plainly on view in all the photos). The year was 1965, and my fascination was complete.

It's 2005 and I'm hoping that I'll find those pictures someday so I can add them to my site. Maybe I'll feature them in their own gallery set apart from the rest, and explain why they have special meaning for me. Or perhaps I'll put them up without fanfare, and the little secret behind them will remain mine.

I am a curator. My charge is a vast collection (40,000 and counting) of images charting the history of pornography, primarily over the last 150 years. RetroRaunch.com is a bridge between past and present porn, past and present attitudes. Like most historical archives, it shows us where we've been and helps us understand where we are. In so doing, it plays a crucial role in the politics and culture of porn, and of sex itself. RetroRaunch elbows its way into the discussion about porn and says, "Pardon me, we ain't so different than we were in the '50s, '20s, or even the Civil War, apart from the silicone and digital delivery. So get off your high horse and let's have some fun . . . grandma is *so* busted!"

How funny it is that it began as an afterthought, a quick way to turn a buck while we worked on starting a "real" porn site.

I don't have a terrible tale of childhood abuse that explains my early sexual awareness or my lifetime of dabbling in sex-related work. Nor do I have any stories of childhood repression and religious stifling that would reveal it to be a kind of rebellion. I had nothing to rebel against.

Neither of my parents were in any way uncomfortable discussing sex with me, for which I'm eternally grateful. They were equally frank while being very different in their personal sexual habits, ethics, and taste. How they ever came together to produce me remains a mystery. But isn't that so often the way it is with sex? When nothing else will, sex compels us to cross every kind of gap we may encounter.

Their separate-but-equally open and relaxed approaches to sex created a great balance. Mother was pretty old-school, preferring her sex with love, but the best advice about the whole thing she ever gave me was, "Never marry a man you haven't slept with first." I have never learned whether this was just natural good sense on her part, or the product of her own bitter experience.

And then there's Dad. (He's the man who gave RetroRaunch its name, by the way. We were stumped for the longest time, trying out all sorts of permutations of age-related and sex-related words. I was leaning toward "Yesterporn" when my father called me and offered it up so simply: how about "RetroRaunch"? Of course!) My father is, to put it mildly, sex-positive. He is currently very happily married to one of the most well-known prostitutes and sex work advocates in the country, and it's possible that without certain discussions we had when I was younger (complete with diagrams . . . don't ask), I might not have the satisfying sex life I do today, thank you very much.

I consider it fortunate that I came of age during a time and place that may not come again for many generations, if ever: Hollywood, California, in the '70s. Anything went. No, really—*anything*. While every generation thinks it invented sex, it was undeniably true that ours was uniquely able to take sex to the outer limits, and that's exactly what we did. Freed from fears of pregnancy and disease, living in a town that had the broadest acceptance of alternative lifestyles outside Rio, we stretched the boundaries to the breaking point, and I probably stretched them most of all.

My association with sex work started early. Nearly everyone I knew had worked at one of the theaters on Hollywood Boulevard selling tickets and concessions. I was the only one who worked at the Cave, where the hardcore porn movies alternated with twenty-minute live strip shows, just a few Walk of Fame steps from Hollywood and Vine. The other theaters smelled of popcorn, and so did the Cave, but it also had that special *eau de something extra*.

In addition to selling tickets, I played den mother to the strippers, who were mostly very young women who found themselves in Hollywood without a movie contract but with demanding landlords. I had a natural maturity about me that belied my age, and I was good at holding their hands when they fought with their boyfriends. Or when stripping just wore them down and they had to cry it out.

At eighteen I was already blasé about twenty-foot-high depictions of close-up sex, which was funny, considering my first exposure to filmed sex. When I was fifteen my friends and I did the obligatory sneak into the Pussycat to experience the classic double bill: *Deep Throat* and *The Devil in Miss Jones.* (I vastly prefer *Devil* to this day. *Deep Throat* is just so damn silly.) We entered the theater at the very end of *Devil in Miss Jones,* and if you've seen it you may recall that it ends with poor Miss Jones frantically masturbating in a barren cell with a disinterested man, eternally doomed to remain unsatisfied. This scene included gynecological close-ups of her fingering her pussy, and it was one of those shots we walked in on. Welcome to porn, kids! I was still a virgin, and the experience was . . . indelible.

A mere two years later I got to meet the great and gracious Georgina Spelvin, who starred in *Devil.* She was booked at the Cave for a week as a featured dancer. She was bright, charming, and very down to earth. I liked her a lot, and I still have the personally autographed nude 8x10 she gave me.

I went on to more mainstream pursuits over the next few years, but in the early '80s I got a gig as an "actress" for one of the then-groundbreaking phone sex companies. Back in the those days the work was done piecemeal at home (see Jennifer Jason Leigh in Altman's wonderful movie *Short Cuts*), and during an exceptional shift I might take three or four calls at most. I have nothing but admiration for the girls who these days sit in cubicles for six or eight hours at a time, pounding out the dirty talk on a clock. No, thanks.

Phone sex at its simplest and easiest is three minutes of describing your giant tits and long blonde hair, then hearing a sudden gasp and a click. But for every two or three of those, there's one where the guy wants to make sure he's gotten his money's worth, one way or another. Sometimes it was through brutal repetition of the same few words or sentences for twenty minutes straight—which sounds easy until you try it. Or I'd find myself having to create elaborate scenarios, and characters, and entire storylines, sometimes on topics that were difficult to deal with, depending on one's sensitivities. I have a very high toler-ance for blood and guts, while being intensely squeamish about bodily functions, so no more shit fetish calls for me, please! Although, I must confess that I have never forgotten the coprophile (person sexually excited by feces) who broke down in tears at the end of our call and apologized for being such a freak, expressing his very real and profound gratitude for my sensitivity regarding his needs. That made a huge impact on me and bolstered my already liberal attitude about sexual prefer-ences and fetishes.

Which is why all the so-called "perversion" so readily avail-able on the Internet is actually a life-affirming and healthy thing. Twenty-five years ago, that man felt isolated and alone, a self-loathing freak filled with shame. Gripped by a desire he had no control over, that he was painfully aware was repellent to most people, he was desperate for an outlet, and perhaps to feel for a moment that he was okay. Since his desires are harmless, shouldn't we be happy for him and others like him that they can find each other now? How freeing to learn you aren't alone! So much of what we do is about connecting with others, fighting against the isolation inherent in being alive and self-aware. Sex is at the center of our most secret selves, the source of our greatest vulnerability. What agony it must be to believe that your sexu-ality is intolerably offensive to just about everyone. Why wouldn't we, as a society, want to help people suffering this way?

The Internet is mocked, and not without reason, as one big porn show. But buried underneath the crass commercial excess that makes up so much of that is this wonderful by-product. The Internet is the best possible continuation of Kinsey's work, which was to show us ourselves and tell us we're really okay.

But I digress. Phone sex, for me, was just too draining to pursue for long. I returned to the "straight" work world for a long time, apart from a couple of months spent editing a girlie mag in the late '80s that specialized in women over forty. I enjoyed that, but since the publisher was certifiably insane, I had to move on.

Office work introduced me to one of my greatest loves: computers. It turns out that I was a born nerd. It wasn't long before I found myself in the online world of the '80s and early '90s BBSes, which were sort of a miniature, local, text-based Internet (AOL started out as a really big BBS) where people would dial in to do pretty much all the same things they go online to do now, only more crudely. Play games, exchange messages, debate things, get information.

Oh, and have cybersex. Lots and lots of sex. A girl can't even walk into a *digital* room without the guys hitting on her, it seems. The very first time I entered a chat room I was instantly besieged: "Wanna hotchat?" Woohoo! Dirty typing!

For the lonely, horny, socially inept nerds of the late '80s, hotchat rocked, let me tell you. Totally safe. Not even the pressure of having to speak aloud. Just type your nasty thoughts at them and they type their nasty responses back at you. And as soon as scanners became more common, the dirty pictures started flowing fast and furious, to absolutely nobody's surprise.

It has always been true that as soon as some new medium or technology is introduced that facilitates communication and storytelling, people use it for porn. Drawing? The Chinese dynasties that preceded Christ by a couple of thousand years would make Jenna Jameson blush. Cameras? Naked girls were among the very first subjects photographed, and naked girls bumping bits with naked guys not long after. (Not to mention girl-to-girl and man-to-man bit bumping.) Film? Porn. Home movie cameras? Homemade porn. Video? Porn. Home video? Amateur porn. Cable? Porn. Computers? Digital porn. The Internet? Pornucopia. And that's where RetroRaunch steps in, bridging past, present, and future by being an entirely up-to-the-moment repository for all the porn that came before. Everything old is new again. The first thing we want to do when we can depict anything in a new way is depict people having sex. And it ain't no bad thing.

I have a soft spot for BBSing because it led to the best thing in my life. At thirty-five I'd had plenty of lovers, but I was settling in to the idea that the true love thing just wasn't in the cards. Funny how it happens when you least expect it—in this case playing D&D games on a local BBS and having one of these sweet young men ask me to go to a party. A hot, sweaty, sexy summer later, I was all stupid and stuck on him, and lucky for me he was stuck back.

Fast forward two years when the Internet was really starting to take off. My partner, Chris, was working for a man who had been a pornographer in other media for years but had jumped on the Net and was pulling down pretty serious coin pimping stolen pictures with almost no investment of any kind, apart from the computers and the crumbs he doled out to Chris and a few other brilliant young men who were doing all the work for him. Chris woke up one morning having gagged on all the cigar smoke and exploitation he could stand, so we decided to start our own porn site and keep all those profits for ourselves.

We partnered with an acquaintance of ours because he had a creepy knack for getting strange women to take their clothes off for a camera. A handy talent if you plan to be the biggest porn site in the world, and that's what we were shooting for. I was sure that we still had time and ability to be the number one porn site on the net. Our intention from day one was to be special. We were going to be cooler, more interesting, more compelling. No cheese here.

The planning seemed to be taking a long time for reasons I no longer recall, but in the meantime our partner suggested that we throw together a quickie site of vintage porn material just to generate a few dollars while we were working on the real site. He explained that there was actually a market for this stuff—there were people who preferred it. He also just happened to have a pal who was a collector and would be happy to offer his collection in exchange for a full share of the partnership. (I think now this was sort of his way of balancing power and profit. He considered Chris and me one entity, which wasn't an entirely wrongheaded notion.)

On our first trip to check out the collection, I pretty much fell in love. It was similar to my experience with the Macintosh computer—instant affinity. The vintage material is so exciting and fun on so many levels for me. I've always been a mad fan of black-and-white photography anyway, and how cool was this? It's all just so much more *interesting*. The older nudes are absolutely beautiful as art. The lighting is so very particular to the period, so creamy. You are drawn in to the mystery of each woman in a way that simply can't exist in modern nude photography. Who is she? Why is she posing nude? Is it her lover who has convinced her to do this, or is she a fallen woman?

The hardcore material is even more compelling. Many of us have some familiarity with the "French postcards" of the early twentieth century, but the hardcore comes as a complete surprise to most people. It certainly did to me.

Our knowledge of the past via photography and film is filtered through the prism of the social mores of the time. You know what I mean: that weird, pasted-over fakeness that pop culture had until the '60s. Even the newsreels and documentaries are weirdly disconnected from real human emotion. But hardcore porn of the period pretty much cuts through the bullshit and right to the humanity of the people in a way that little else from that time does. You get the distinct impression that you are being allowed to peer into the private sexual experiences of real people who just happened to have a camera, not professionally produced porn. (Of course, a lot of it actually was professionally produced, since a great deal of it was side work done by Hollywood professionals.) But the women in these pictures look like me. And you. And your best friend. Not necessarily in their appearance, but more about the experience they are having, the way they project a kind of relaxed pleasure, even joy. The world she lived in was so much more constrained than ours in so many ways, and in these photos, naked, raw, fucking, she is her realest self at last. I truly relate to her, I see in her eyes that I have been where she is, and the universality of the sexual high, and the primal nature of it, comes home to me. I never, ever experience that with modern porn.

By this time, 1997, Net porn was already well established and had a certain look to it. Noisy, colorful, in-your-face. There was lots of advertising, popups were becoming the rage, and it was shaking out to be the digital version of Vegas at its worst. We didn't want to do that. We wanted to be something unmistakably different, and to let the material speak for itself. We created a spare aesthetic sensibility that we adhere to to this day, and which has served us very well.

Keeping it simple has also been a boon for our older members, of which we have a large number. (We all tend to prefer what we were exposed to first, and our older members love us for helping them revisit the sorts of things that turned them on when they were young.) They aren't always as comfortable on computers to begin with, so they appreciate the simplicity.

Our partner didn't seem to have the same passion for what we were doing that Chris and I had. He hated the name, he didn't really care one way or another for the material, and we had other conflicts. We dissolved the partnership with him almost as soon as we opened the site, in July 1997. This meant we would no longer have access to the collector's archive, and we would have to set about learning what was involved in collecting vintage erotica. I was faced with a new challenge. Three months earlier I hadn't known anyone cared about this stuff, and now I've got to be an expert?

Panic can be a good teacher. I was lucky to have friends in the photo industry, which is where my search began. That led to a company that specialized in procuring books, photos, and magazines for the movies, and things just branched out from there. There really is a community of people who collect vintage erotica, which of course makes perfect sense. If people are collecting vintage photos of train stations—and they are—you know there have to be plenty of people collecting vintage pictures of naked people.

These days, of course, we are contacted all the time by people who are going through Uncle Arthur's things—and who knew Uncle Arthur was such a kinky bastard? My favorite so far is the couple who were remodeling their newly purchased seventy-year-old house, and got a fun surprise when they found some former owner's forgotten stash inside a wall.

There have been a few instances of men sending us photos of their wives, taken long ago. The men always write sweet messages filled with love, longing and wistful memories. They offer us the pictures as loving tributes to the woman they loved and lusted after. It's very touching to be offered these pictures, to know that they are willing to entrust us with their memories.

Our success has been a combination of things, some lucky accidents and timing, and some I'll claim as our doing. One of the most important instances of lucky timing came right out the gate. A friend of mine had given my name to a writer doing a front page story in *USA Today* about porn on the Net. So a month after we went online, there we were, on the front page of a national newspaper, right alongside Danni's Hard Drive and Persian Kitty. This exposure led to more exposure, as it usually does. Over the years we have been featured on *Marketplace*, Washingtonpost.com, and *Wired*, as well as lots of local newspapers and a few books along the way. Canadian television did an entire segment on Retro-Raunch for a regular series on sex, and I was a guest on the Discovery Channel's Health show *Berman and Berman*. We've also functioned as a sort of educational resource for companies that need access to our archive. We've worked with Showtime and The History Channel, both of which did documentary series on sex and used some of our material.

Along the way we even picked up what I like to call our Porno Oscar, which is actually an award for Best Concept from *AVN,* the industry bible. That was an especially fun and memorable moment in our evolution, although by the time they announced the award (given out at a very nice ceremony in Vegas), we were both pretty sloshed. I don't *think* we embarrassed ourselves, but I know for sure that we were the most giddy and proud of all the winners there that night. (Chris was extra happy because his favorite porn star at the time, Kobe Tai, was the one to actually give us our award. Bonus!)

While I'd never be ashamed of it in any case, RetroRaunch allows me to actually be *proud* of being a pornographer. It's beautiful, it's educational, it's fun, it's different, and, well, it's just cool. On top of all that, I know that it's even something important, in more than one way.

First, RetroRaunch provides the irrefutable evidence that (with the possible exception of the Furry fetish—wow, even I can still be surprised), there's really nothing new under the sun. It's very important that we never lose sight of that. We can't let the would-be censors hypnotize us into believing that we've entered into some new Sodom and we must return to the good old days of purity and chastity and missionary positions (for married couples only). There were no such old days, ever. I was lucky that my mother, who came of age during World War II, told me the truth. So now I'm telling it and showing it to the world: people like to fuck and always have. They do it all different ways with all different people. And they take pictures.

Second, we provide a reality check. The women who adorn our pages, who were lovingly and lustfully photographed for erotic purposes, are gloriously normal. Real breasts in every size and shape, real hair growing where hair normally grows, real flesh. Each one is unique, beautiful, sexy, and honest. Each one looks like women actually look outside of Hollywood, the pages of *Vogue,* and the San Fernando Valley. These normal, flawed women were considered worthy of desire, and rightfully so. That is a message we all need to get, men and women alike.

I used to worry, and an article in *New York* magazine confirmed my fears, that today's young men are developing distorted expectations of what women are supposed to look like and how they are supposed to behave. Rather than attempt to censor what can't really be censored at this point (and I would never wish to do that anyway), I'm glad to be offering an alternative and a different perspective. The best way to battle things you don't want or approve of is not to try to stop them from existing, but to offer something else in their place. So we offer earthy, natural, real porn starring earthy, natural, real people. Who appear to really be enjoying themselves, not just posing for the camera. Now, *that's* truly hot.

I've been going through boxes of material lately, looking to sell some of it. There's an odor to old paper that is so distinctive and evocative. The minute it hits my nose I find my curiosity aroused. I can get lost in the pictures, and I'll make up stories about who is in them and how the picture came to be taken. Like the handful of pictures taken around the time of the Civil War or not long after, which feature a black man and a white woman. Even though I know the pictures were probably produced in Europe, what a thrilling idea to believe he is a former slave, and perhaps this was his former mistress. Longing for each other across the gulf of slavery, each for different reasons, they are together at last, acting out their forbidden passion.

I usually make up happy stories, even though I know better. Not that there aren't good stories, it's just that porn from the past had a dark side. One of the most disturbing things is that some of the pictures were produced under exploitive circumstances. There were cases of institutionalized women being photographed undergoing sexual abuse. I believe that the women were kidnapped for the purposes of the sexual abuse, and the pornography was incidental. Not that it makes any difference. Fortunately, it's not like that anymore. The people who participate in pornography today make the choice freely. Maybe it isn't always a great choice for everyone who makes it, but that just means it's no different from anything else in life.

I really hope that our society can evolve some day to the point where we respect sex work of all kinds, whether it's phone sex or prostitution or pornography. It is pervasive because the demand is pervasive. Looking down our noses at the people who give us what we want is just sickening hypocrisy. It is delusional to imagine that it is merely a handful of pathetic souls supporting a multibillion-dollar industry. It's millions and millions of perfectly normal people with the same degrees of happy, positive adjustment and depressed dysfunction as the part of society that never partakes of any of it. (I could even make the argument for less dysfunction and unhappiness, but not here . . .)

I do enjoy tweaking people with it sometimes when they ask what I do. Most of the time I just say I run a Web site and I buy and sell vintage photography. But occasionally, depending on my audience, I'll just blurt out, nice as you please, "I'm a pornographer." It's interesting to watch people struggle with how to respond to that.

But I really love what I do. I'm making people happy, I'm educating them, I'm broadening their horizons, and I'm contributing to the discussion in important ways. I'm also my own boss, which millions would give their right arm for, I'm having fun, I work with my best friend every day, and on top of all that I get to buy pornography and write it off my taxes. What's not to like?

DANNI ASHE

. . . ON LEARNING HOW TO LAUNCH THE MOST POPULAR ADULT WEB SITE FROM WORKING AT A STRIP CLUB.

WHEN PEOPLE I MEET FIRST learn I'm an adult entertainer, they invariably want to know *why*? How did I get started? What made me do it? Do I hate men? I suspect my answers often fail to satisfy those who are eager for sordid details or for a neat reinforcement of the stripper/porn star stereotype. As it is for most people who make decisions that will affect the course of their lives, the answer to why I started stripping is rooted in a combination of nature, nurture, and circumstance. And, as it is with most of the important choices and events in our lives, the value comes not from knowing how you got there but from what you learned once you did.

I was born in Beaufort, South Carolina, while my father served in the Marine Corps at Paris Island, the product of a brief and unhappy marriage between two young Seattle natives. My mother, married at sixteen, a mother at eighteen, and a divorcée in her early twenties, raised me on her own in Seattle. Like many twenty-something women in the '70s, my mom lived a life of rock festivals, drugs, and free love. I learned about the birds and the bees at an early age and was never taught to feel any shame about nudity or sex. Despite the hippie, liberal environment in which I was raised, I showed an early entrepreneurial streak and was always strongly encouraged to achieve financial independence. At the age of five, I began drawing pictures, rolling them up, affixing prices, and riding around on my tricycle to sell them to the neighbors. Then I started picking flowers in the neighbors' yards and tooled around the block peddling bouquets. Somehow, the fact that I was often selling the neighbors their own flowers didn't seem to matter. I was a born entrepreneur who was told by my mother almost from day one that "MONEY = FREEDOM." And I knew, even in my single-digits, that freedom was what I wanted.

Throughout my childhood years, I was happily independent and ambitious. I did well in school and was popular with my classmates. But all of that began to change when, at age eleven, my breasts began to grow at an alarming pace. By age thirteen, I was wearing a D cup, and the confidence of my early years had evaporated.

The eruption/disruption of my breasts brought with it incessant teasing and attention from children and adults alike. When I reached puberty, I was immediately sexualized, whether I was prepared for what that meant or not. Overnight I'd become a child trapped in a woman's body without a clue about how to handle it. Being a young teen, I wanted to dress and look just like all the other girls, but the little bikinis and tank tops that looked so cute on them made me look like a floozy. So, while my little friends flirted with the boys our age, I was getting hit on by thirty-year-old men. My best friend and her father would tease me about my "boulder holders" and had nicknames for me— "JC" (Jell-O Chest) and "DP2" (Dolly Parton 2). It was funny and I'd laugh along with them, but I was always acutely aware of the fact that my chest was the first and sometimes only thing people noticed about me.

As I tried to learn to deal with the reactions of strangers, schoolmates, friends, and their parents, I prayed that my new-found breasts would just go away, that my body would somehow be transformed into something less noticeable, less awkward, less inviting of ridicule and teasing. I tried weight loss and weight gain, but there was no hiding them. In my later teens, I asked my mother for a breast reduction, but that wasn't an option. I had no choice but to try and learn to live with them.

By the time I turned fifteen, my mother's attitudes had changed with the times from those of the liberal '70s to the more conservative, corporate values of the '80s. She'd become a businesswoman, a busy real estate agent, and I was mostly left to sort out the complications of my new-found figure on my own. Most of the outside world was now giving me the sexual attention appropriate for a grown woman, and I was often left to supervise myself. Since all the perks of childhood were clearly gone, I began to rebel and demand my place in the adult world. After two years of partying, sex, drugs, acting out, and running away, my mother finally gave in and let me move out when I was seventeen.

On my own, living as an adult and making ends meet on only $250 a month, I soon got frustrated with the juvenile restrictions of high school. In my junior year I dropped out, took my GED, and enrolled in community college. I had sincere intentions to get a good education, but I also had some wild friends who were about to take me on a detour. After they won first and second place in an amateur-night contest, two of my best girlfriends started stripping at a local club called Sugars. While I was initially shocked and upset about their decision, the promise of big cash and wild times ultimately lured me in. My first foray into nude dancing was nerve-wracking and alcohol-induced—and the best thing I ever did for my self-esteem. All of a sudden, for the first time in my life, my breasts became an asset instead of a liability.

The first afternoon I worked at Sugars, I was allowed to just do table dances so I could get comfortable with the environment before having to go onstage in front of everyone, but I was still nervous as hell. I felt stupid and awkward my stripper getup—

lace bra and panties, satin gloves, beads, and white pumps—so I just stood around staring at the girls on stage. My two friends had been working there for a couple of weeks and were already pros, working the room with ease and taking the stage with enthusiasm. Finally, one of them decided I needed a push. She asked a nearby customer for a dance and, when he accepted, grabbed me, pushed me in front of him, and left.

There I was, faced with my very first table dance, feeling like the biggest dork on the planet. I was absolutely certain the customer, a quiet, kind-looking older gentleman, would have preferred my slimmer, smaller-breasted girlfriend, and I just knew he had to be disappointed by the bait-and-switch. But I decided to grit my teeth and earn the five bucks for a table dance. That was, after all, why I'd come to Sugars: to make money.

I wriggled around between his legs, trying to imitate the moves I saw other girls performing around the room. As the music blared and I did my surreal little half-naked dance, all I could do was think about what I should do when the song ended. Should I go chew out my friend for deceiving this nice, patient man who didn't have the heart to tell me he didn't want me to dance for him, or should I look for a place to hide? Finally, the song ended and as I stood there dumbly waiting for my five dollars, the customer leaned forward and said, "You have the most lovely figure I've ever seen. Would you dance for me again?"

It was the first time in my life I'd ever been complimented about my body, and I was quite literally dumbstruck. After four dances, I walked away with $20 and a whole new confidence in my stride. Prior to that day, I'd felt my body was nothing more than a freak-show curiosity, and now I knew, at least within the dark walls of Sugars, that my body could be viewed with admiration. That first encounter changed everything, and it was then that I became a stripper.

I continued to dance in strip clubs off and on for eight years.

Numerous times I'd be talked into quitting by a concerned relative or a jealous boyfriend, but each time I left the clubs and tried
to follow a different path out in the real world, I'd end up being
rudely reminded of what a handicap enormous breasts can be. I
was still young and still hadn't learned how to buy a proper bra
or how to dress my figure down for the corporate world. At every
turn my boobs seemed to get in the way and ultimately get me in
trouble. Inevitably, I'd always find myself back in the clubs,
where I could feel confident and secure in a safe cocoon of
acceptance and admiration. I spent many years working on being
the best stripper I could be, and it was in the clubs that I learned
everything I really needed to know about building one of the
world's most successful Web sites.

On the surface, the role of a stripper is pretty simple. You make
money by performing table dances for patrons of the club, and
you pay the club for allowing you to do table dances by paying a
house rent and performing onstage in rotation with the other
dancers. The economics are actually very similar to that of a hairdresser. You pay your hairdresser for cutting your hair and your
hairdresser, in turn, pays the salon a fee for letting her work
there. On the surface, a hairdresser's role is also pretty simple.
They get paid for cutting your hair. But everyone knows that the
best hairdressers are good listeners—people you can talk to,
people who'll offer a sympathetic ear; people who can be objective and supportive—and the same is true of strippers.

In my experience, the strip club environment was divided into
two wildly different worlds: the late-night crowd and the afternoon crowd. Late at night, the clubs would be loud and chaotic,
full of young, drunk groups of guys celebrating testosterone-
soaked rituals and rites of passage. These guys were there to bond
with each other and had very little interest in interacting with the
dancers. To work the late-night shift, you had to be flashy enough

to get noticed among the crowds and you had to be tough enough to handle big groups of young men trying to impress each other. The late-night shift was all about show. A really good-looking dancer with a thick skin could make a whole lot of money working the night shift, but the work was exhausting and burnout was common.

In the afternoon, things were very different. The music wasn't as loud; the men came in alone instead of in groups, and the role of the dancer became much more complex. In the afternoon, men came in looking for someone to talk to, someone who would listen to their fantasies and help them experience those fantasies without passing judgment. They needed a safe place to talk about their feelings and their desires, desires that many of them feared would frighten or upset their wives. I did my time on the night shift, but it was the afternoon shift that I found most rewarding and most lucrative. I enjoyed playing the role of confidante and fantasy facilitator, and I was very, very good at it.

There are, of course, numerous stories of men with strange fetishes—the guys who'd pay for a chance to rub your feet or would pay extra if you'd agree to kick them in the groin while you danced—but the vast majority of my customers shared the same fantasy. They all fantasized about being intimate with more than one woman—a phenomenon that I began to think of as the "harem fantasy."

The men with the unique fetishes often talked quite candidly about them and the events in their childhood or adolescence that they felt had triggered the fetish. But only about half of the harem seekers seemed to actually know what was driving them or what they were really looking for. Often, someone would come in to the club and become deeply infatuated with one dancer, spending all his time and money with that one girl. Then, the next time he came to the club, he'd become deeply infatuated with a different dancer, hardly noticing the first girl was even around. These can be a fairly ego-crushing events for a dancer until she begins to understand and appreciate what's really going on.

It didn't take long for me to realize that when I was dealing with men who didn't understand their own motivations or perhaps chose not to share them, my role was to act as a mirror, to allow my customers to project their fantasies onto me, and that when a customer became infatuated with me it had very little to do with me personally but everything to do with the image he was projecting and the role I was playing for him. Once I took my own ego out of the equation, the patterns of the customers' behavior began to emerge pretty clearly, and I began to understand how to truly give them what they were looking for.

I learned pretty quickly that there was no such thing as being someone's one and only forever favorite stripper. Monogamy doesn't happen in strip clubs. A strip club is all about experiencing the fantasy of polygamy, and my job was to help facilitate that fantasy as much as possible. So, rather than vie with the other girls over who would be the "girl du jour" for a particular customer, I worked on being the trusted friend that customers could count on to introduce them to all the new dancers whenever they came in.

Through years of playing this role, I came to deeply understand and appreciate the disconnect that exists between our modern social needs for monogamy and our more primal desires to be polygamous—to spread and protect our genes by having as many partners as possible. It became my job to help men express and experience their polygamous desires in a safe and accepting environment that wouldn't threaten their wives or the monogamous construct of their everyday lives.

Throughout those years, I continued to try out other careers. Obviously, stripping in bars doesn't allow for much of a long-term future, but I kept finding myself back in the clubs. It was what I knew, where I felt comfortable, and what I was good at. So,

I eventually decided I would stick to adult entertainment, but I had to work my way up the ladder. I made an early entrepreneurial move to try and become an amateur video producer, but in the process I found myself following the typical adult entertainer career trajectory. I went from starting out as a local stripper (a "house dancer") to modeling for men's magazines to shooting soft-core videos to running a mail-order fan club and ultimately becoming a feature dancer.

Modeling was lots of fun, but the fan club came closest to my early stripping experiences. Once again, I had men communicating with me about their desires and projecting their fantasies in my direction, only this time it was happening through the mail instead of in person.

Once again, I encountered countless communications from men seeking to fulfill a harem fantasy—either a request for details about all the other girls I'd worked with or a deep infatuation with images of me they'd seen in a magazine. Once again, I'd often learn from other models that particular fans who'd written to me confessing their undying devotion had also written to them and to dozens of other models with the same devotion. I never had any doubt that those professions of love were genuine at the time they were offered. By writing to a picture in a magazine, these men were just pursuing their primal fantasies about being able to seduce as many women as possible in a safe way, a way that had very little chance of ever leading them into real infidelity.

While the modeling and the fan club were fun and rewarding, the next step for me in the adult entertainer career trajectory ended up being a nightmare. For most entertainers, being a feature dancer is where the money is. You model and shoot movies just to earn credits and name recognition that can be traded for large feature booking fees and headline status in the clubs. Despite my commitment to being a professional dancer, I found the feature circuit fraught with peril at every turn. Week after week I found myself being cheated, lied to, and placed in precarious situations, and I ultimately landed in a Jacksonville jail after a club owner set me up by lying to me about the local dancing regulations. Seriously rattled and genuinely hating life on the road, I once again had to contemplate a career shift.

It was 1994 and the Internet as we know it today didn't really exist. Though the web had been invented five years earlier and the Internet itself was more than twenty years old, it was still a world inhabited mostly by university scholars and techies. While many people used computer services like Prodigy and Compuserve, those companies weren't Internet providers then, they were simply computer bulletin board services. In 1994, the average person had heard of the Internet but didn't really understand what it was for or have a clue about how to use it.

During that time, my husband was working with a large theater circuit. The company's systems administrator, an avid Internet enthusiast named Josh, had decided to build a Web site for the company. He would excitedly tell everyone at the company how great it was that they would be the very first theater circuit in the world to be on the Web. At the time, I'm not sure anyone there truly understood just how prescient Josh's ideas were, but they let him go ahead with the project.

In addition to building the company's Web site, Josh spent much of his free time on the Internet, and one day he mentioned to my husband that there were a lot of pictures of Danni Ashe in the Usenet newsgroups. It didn't take long for the news to reach me, and I found myself burning with curiosity about what these groups were. Who were these people posting my pictures and what were people saying about them? After a quick consultation with Josh on how to get myself on the Internet, I picked up Netcom's Netcruiser software and a couple of books and went home to venture online.

I immediately found several pictures of myself in the alt.sex and alt.binary Usenet groups, so I decided to post a message for more information. My post asked about where the photos were coming from and (always the entrepreneur) included a plug for my fan club. The first response I received came from the moderator of alt.sex, chastising me for my "commercial" post. The rest of the messages came from guys telling me "imposters weren't welcome" and to get lost. Not one to be easily deterred, I fought for my right to post and worked at proving my identity. It took a couple of weeks, but I won acceptance in the group and it was there in the newsgroups that I started to have some familiar, yet this time eye-opening, conversations.

For weeks I'd been spending every waking moment on Usenet. I was debating issues like, "Are Zena Fulsom's breasts real?" but I was also finding myself deep in conversation with men who were fascinated by what I did for a living and basically curious about how to relate to women in general. I found the familiar themes I'd encountered in my stripping and fan club experiences, but this time the guys were not only talking to me about their fantasies and their curiosities but also talking among themselves. As a group, they had a far more sophisticated understanding of what motivated them to hang out in a "sex" forum and why they enjoyed looking at pornography. It was in that Usenet group that I finally gained a deeper insight into what I had first learned so many years earlier in the strip clubs, and where I began to understand what I could do with it.

It was out of these Usenet newsgroup conversations that the idea for Danni's Hard Drive was born, and the day my husband installed a faster modem and showed me his company's new Web site, it all became crystal clear. At that moment, as I watched him click through the hypertext pages, the proverbial light bulb went on over my head and I knew exactly what I had to do. I could see the file structure in my head, how I could create a model directory with pages for dozens of models, complete with photos, bios, and background information—a digital harem—then link all that information to a merchandise catalog. I could fulfill my fans' desires to experience lots of women at once, offer them instant information about girls who grabbed their attention, and use that as a way to market videotapes and other fan club items to them. At the same time, I would make the site light-hearted and welcoming, offer a feminine touch, and create a nonthreatening place where my visitors could experience their fantasies without guilt or shameful feelings.

I quickly began negotiating deals to buy videos and photos I could resell on the site, and worked on convincing models to participate by offering to publish their fan club addresses and promote their upcoming tour dates. I hired a programmer to build the site and foolishly offered him half the business. He fortunately declined the revenue share offer, preferring a payment of $900 to design my pages. Three weeks later, disappointed with the results, I hired another programmer. Four weeks after that, I fired the second programmer too. I was frustrated and ready to just do it myself.

With the encouragement of all my new online friends, I headed for the bookstore and picked up the *HTML Manual of Style* for technical guidance, and Negroponte's *Being Digital* for inspiration. I threw the books into my bag for a trip to the Bahamas and, while everyone else read John Grisham novels and dime store romances on the beach, I sat in the sand and learned how to program HTML.

I took over the design of my Web site, now formally christened "Danni's Hard Drive," and as the site developed, I began looking for an ISP (Internet Service Provider) to host me. I finally zeroed in on a host in Orange County and got the owner on the phone for a discussion about pricing. I explained to him that I expected my site to get a large amount of traffic and that I wanted to discuss prices for a dedicated server. He replied with a paternal, condescending tone and assured me I was getting ahead of myself: "You'll be just fine on our public server." He was the expert, so I agreed and got back to work on the site.

Once Danni's Hard Drive was nearly finished, I e-mailed four friends I'd made on Usenet and told them, "The site's done but please don't tell anybody. I have to go to New York and I don't want to launch until I get back. I'd love it if you could take a look and let me know what you think when I return." I left for New York and the next day I received a frantic call from my new ISP telling me I'd crashed the public server. I was immediately moved to my own dedicated server and within the first month, Danni's Hard Drive was getting nearly a million hits a day. I was selling 15 times more fan club merchandise than I had before. My little Web site had become a big hit.

At the time of Danni.com's launch, it was early July 1995 and the Internet was on the eve of a huge transformation. The Net was about to change from being an orderly, self-policing community of techies and intellectuals who rejected all commercial use of their space to becoming a Wild West gold rush—a commercial free-for-all. I had happened to find myself there at the right time, with the right idea—something I'd understood for so long but, until then, didn't know what to do with—and I embraced both sides of the transformation. I cherished my time in the newsgroups, the clarity and purity of communication that was enjoyed there, a community that would ultimately be drowned out by spam. But I also saw the commercial potential and the opportunity of a lifetime to take my unique skills and turn them into a real business, and I seized the moment.

By 1996, just a year after its launch, Danni's Hard Drive was among the top ten most trafficked Web sites in the world, and year after year it has continued to enjoy a success that was beyond my wildest dreams. There was, of course, a lot of blood, sweat, and tears, and a lot of heartache.

JOANNA ANGEL

. . . ON BEING A FEMINIST WITH A PORN SITE.

THERE ARE TWO KINDS OF sluts in this world: the kind I used to be, and the kind I am now. The former sleeps with guys for attention. She craves guys with status because they make her feel better about herself, and she won't admit to anyone that what she really wants is for one of the guys to want a mean- ingful relationship with her. The latter sleeps with guys because she really genuinely likes having sex. She openly admits she wants a relationship, but she knows it's not going to happen because all guys are scumbags and her porn site is far more important to her than any of these assholes. Okay, that last part might have been just about me.

I was sitting in our grimy college-apartment kitchen sur- rounded by homemade bongs and mounds of dirty dishes in New Brunswick, New Jersey, snacking on organic rice cakes, and reading *The Paradox of Feminist Criticism,* when my roommate Mitch asked me if I'd help him start a porn site. I'd been waiting tables for the past two years and had just lost my job in a screaming fit with my manager over a wrinkled apron. I was nine credits short of a piece of paper from Rutgers University that said I was good at reading books, I had no money, and some strange breed of self-respect that was really turning into an unsatisfying diet. I decided I had nothing to lose; at least I'd be doing something that didn't involve Excel spreadsheets and a dress code, and that was the ultimate goal. "Sure," I replied, "why the hell not?" I had no idea what I was getting myself into.

BurningAngel.com was the indie-punk-porn site thrown together with Mitch's friend's 2.0 mega pixel digital camera, my topless photos, a few other cute girls with tattoos, my self deprecating stories about my sex life, and a friend who was kind of okay with HTML. It grew faster than a Vivid Girl's cup size. After just a few months, I was bombarded with questions I didn't know how to answer. People really expected me to stand for something, and truthfully, I knew I did, but for what I wasn't so sure.

I tried to deal with my career anxiety like most people do in their early twenties—by getting stoned—but this made my identity crises more daunting, as questions about my life's meaning replaced the more familiar questions about which movie channel to watch. Why am I suddenly surrounded by porn? Am I a feminist? What exactly is BurningAngel all about? Why am I doing this? Is this *punk*? Do I even care? Unfortunately, one bowl and two slices of cheeseless pizza later, the urgency to search for answers hadn't left me.

I had struggled with feminism for so long, I even wasn't sure I knew what it meant anymore. I racked my brain for all those important issues I'd talked about in my gender studies classes. I thought about Take Back the Night, sobbing on my ex-boyfriend's doorstep, and my brief, not-so-empowering experiences with lesbianism. I tried to put it all together, but it didn't add up. I couldn't explain how, but I knew deep down that I was, and always had been, a seriously real, honest-to-god, hardcore feminist. If anything could ever tie up these loose ends of politics, rage, and sensitivity it was going to be this Web site; I just didn't know how.

No one in the porn industry had a clue as to who we were, but

BurningAngel was the sexiest new topic of discussion in all the punk-rock-indie media, not excluding their message boards. Some people were ripping up the BA postcards handed to them, and others were hanging them up on their walls. Boyfriends were getting angry, and girlfriends were getting recognized. I was either a hero or a disgrace to feminism and punk, and I didn't know how to react. I had never made porn, watched porn, or had friends in porn, so who was I to say what this was and how it was affecting gender roles, the state of underground music, or anything else that mattered?

Perhaps I should start at the beginning, with the person in every girl's life who shapes her idea of femininity: her mother. Sometimes I doubt my legitimacy as a porn star, because my mother didn't abandon me at a young age. The problem was more that she was *always* around. I can assure you that as you are reading this, there are at least four messages from her demanding a phone call back. I always wished there was *something* more important than me in my mother's life, but all she ever really wanted out of life was to have kids, and now that she has three grown ones, she's wants grandkids (and I'm sure she'll remind me of this when I return her phone call later).

My mother isn't a native English speaker, and as a result has a hard time communicating with anyone she isn't related to. I won't pretend to know how this feels, but she blamed my father for her inability to find a job and fit in somewhere, which was especially crucial because he is always at work. Maybe my father is partly to blame, but she would have been a lot happier, and even more respected by my father and her children, if she could have done these things on her own. As a young girl, I wasn't sure what I wanted to be when I grew up, but whatever it was, it wasn't my mother.

Out of compassion for other girls, I didn't want anyone else to be my mother, either. I was in the sixth grade when I learned that other people who felt this way called themselves "feminists," so I fancied myself one as well. In high school, a feminist was Susan B. Anthony. In college, it was Emma Goldman, and now it's Nina Hartley.

BurningAngel is a porn site with tattooed, pierced girls, alongside band interviews. I wasn't turning away my bleach blonde, silicone-breasted friends because I'd discovered a secret, untapped resource in porn; this was just what I knew. By the same token, I had no desire to mimic the editorial content of some sophisticated men's magazine by writing about changing carburetors, or Sarah Michelle Gellar's favorite position. So I worked with what I had and gave people what I could, by interviewing hardcore bands and writing about having sex with the members.

Mitch became nervous about what was happening. The Web site had been up for just a few months and the number of people I'd slept with had jumped from under five to over twenty. Mitch had overheard a guy at a show say to his friend, "Yo, get an interview on this Web site and Joanna will totally fuck you."

"So *what*?" I responded. "Any publicity is good publicity."

That first summer of BurningAngel's existence, I went to lots of shows in many different cities, to interview bands, hand out BurningAngel flyers, and have sex. The PR, the bragging rights to say, "I interviewed AFI," and those tattooed boys who hadn't gotten laid since they left their girlfriends behind to go on tour, were enough motivation to make me drive to Kentucky in a car with over 200,000 miles on it, in the summer's heat, without a working air conditioner.

I walked around with a tape recorder and a shaved pussy, and I wasn't afraid to use either. I had sex in parking lots, tour vans (or buses if I was lucky), and underneath merch tables. I had a threesome in a bar bathroom, and one time gave head to a drummer while he was on the phone with his wife, wishing her a happy anniversary.

My band interviews were like foreplay. I'd get guys to talk about sex, strip clubs, and porn; I even asked bands if they'd jerked off to my photos. That was more than enough to get them worked up, especially the ones who were on the road for a few months. Not to mention the fact that "press" in the hardcore/ punk scene is usually conducted by some guy wearing khakis and a Black Flag T-shirt. Believe it or not, I was the only girl with topless photos on the Internet working for the press.

I transcribed these confessional band interviews and posted them on BurningAngel. People liked them, and I got to have sex with guys who never used to give me the time of day. I considered myself some kind of *Sex and the City* feminist: I was proud to be a slut with a really cool career.

BurningAngel had been up for a year, and we were barely making enough money to get by. I found a part-time job answering phones at a piercing place about four blocks away from my house. The management was lax enough to let me skip work when I had an interview or photo shoot, and nice enough to pay me with free piercings along with the $5.25 an hour. BurningAngel wasn't putting money in my pocket, but I was able to brag to the other cute girl receptionist at the shop about all the famous dick I'd sucked. She envied me, and that was payment enough.

I was nothing like my mother. I was really making it in the world all on my own: men were nothing but sex objects to me, I was a self-published "erotic writer," I'd interviewed (and slept with) people on the cover of *Rolling Stone,* I knew a whole lot about "artsy photography," I had big natural breasts, a skinny waist, a part-time job, and a career—and I was barely twenty-two. What else could I possibly ask for?

So the one guy who didn't try to make out with me right away was the one guy I liked enough not to try to make out with right away. There were bands I'd interviewed because everyone else liked them, others because I had crushes on particular members, but Dyllan's band fell into the select category of bands I interviewed because I really respected their music. The sound was brilliant, and the fact that he wrote all the songs was a far greater turn-on than a story about getting a lap dance from a girl who shot ping-pong balls out of her pussy at a strip club in Georgia, or the usual diatribe on preferring natural, girl-next-door types to Jenna Jamesons. The inane stories and false statements were enough to get me in bed, but believe it or not, they didn't impress me. Dyllan actually was really smart, possibly even smarter than I was. He made me laugh in ways that challenged my sense of humor, and asked me questions that made me reevaluate what I was doing. He not only wrote the music and played in his own band, he also managed it. It was kind of like being naked on your own porn site.

I didn't want to fuck Dyllan; I wanted to kiss him. It had been a while since I had felt that way about anyone. We took a "strictly business" vacation to Miami, to an annual indie music conference open only to people in the music business. He got me in to the convention, and on our down time we ate junk food, went for walks, and watched the three channels our hotel room had to offer. One night, we made out. He didn't kiss me and I didn't kiss him, it was one of those things where we really just kissed each other. When it was over he whispered, "Please don't tell anyone this happened."

The next night, I went out to dinner with him and the rest of his bandmates. I got a phone call from a guy I was kind of seeing at the time, and we got into a petty fight about why I hadn't called him, which I totally dramatized in the hopes of making Dyllan jealous. When I hung up, Dylan looked at me and said, "I don't know how guys do it."

"Do what?" I asked.

"Date you," he clarified.

"What do you mean?" I asked.

"Your entire life revolves around making other dudes horny. I mean, good for you, you've got nice tits, but if I was your boyfriend I'd freak."

The entire table laughed. Not sure of what I should do, I laughed with them. After the laughter died down, I excused myself, ran to the bathroom, and cried. I didn't even have it in me to write an antagonistic story about him and publish it on the Web site, changing one letter in his name. I didn't want to tell his girlfriend or attempt to sabotage his relationship, I just wanted to cry and get angry at myself for being what I was. I wasn't proud of being a slut anymore. I'd have been better off in an arranged marriage with one of my mother's friend's sons. People were reading my writing, looking at my Web site, and letting me interview their bands . . . and yeah, that was an accomplishment. But did this make me a feminist? I wondered how much time Nina Hartley spent in her lifetime crying on the floors of seafood restaurants in Miami, and this made me feel pretty stupid.

BurningAngel wasn't feminist, and neither was I. The Web site was one big cry for attention. I wasn't fighting the patriarchy, I was giving it blow jobs and letting it break my heart. I was running a Web site that barely made any money, I was naked on the Internet, and no one in their right mind wanted to date me.

My lease was running out in less than a month and I was sick of living on a college campus. I wanted to do what every unsettled college graduate in central Jersey wants to do: move to New York City. I didn't want to give up on making it as a Web entrepreneur, but realistically, I knew I wasn't going to make enough money in the next three weeks to cover my first month's rent. I had a few options: I could 1) settle for another year in this beer-guzzling, Santana-listening, fast food–infested town; 2) move back in with my mom, make a résumé full of things I'd never done, and pray to get called back by places I didn't want to work in the first place, or 3) become a stripper.

Interviewing bands was always fun, because I was the one calling the shots, and sex was fun for the same reason. But thirty-plus hours a week in a room full of men who wanted so badly to fuck me but settled for a $20 cock tease because they couldn't worked wonders for my confidence, not to mention my bank account. My vagina was worth a lot of money, I realized. I was so angry at myself for giving it up so easily all this time. I had never even had someone pay for my dinner, and now they were paying for my car. I made a lot of money quickly and moved out of Jersey before my lease was up. I didn't even stick around for the big fiasco over our security deposit. I could have wiped my ass with $700.

I made the club a lot of money, too—$100 off every VIP room I sold—and in exchange, I was treated like a celebrity: anyone who looked at me, touched me, or spoke to me the wrong way was thrown out of the club by a 250-pound bouncer. It was awesome. I wished one of them would had been there when Dyllan told me he wouldn't date me. Maybe I wouldn't have felt so pathetic. In an interview the other day, I was asked if I ever get approached by "creepy guys who recognize me," and I answered honestly when I said, "I feel pretty comfortable around creepy guys. It's the nice ones I have a hard time dealing with." I've been totally submissive to most of the men in my life, but I could get the men at the strip club to do anything.

I want to make clear that there is no answer to the question I get asked on a daily basis, *Is porn feminist?* I wish people would simply ask me about *my* porn rather than leave it up to me to make an assessment of a $20-billion industry. I can confidently say that BurningAngel in its current form, and everything it produces, is feminist. As for the rest of porn, some girls (like the ones writing chapters in this book) are feminists, and some girls aren't. Some porn isn't labeled feminist, but has feminist elements in it, and some porn (cough: Max Hardcore) has nothing feminist about it even in its loosest interpretation.

In every strip club there are a handful of serious, hard-working girls who *always* make a ton of money, and their "bad nights" amount to what the average clothed worker makes in a week. So, while I can't make a broad generalization about feminism and porn, what I can say about feminism and the sex business is that *every* one of these top-notch strippers is a fucking feminist, whether she calls herself one or not. I speak from experience when I tell you that that making this amount of money regularly at a strip club requires not only an intense hatred for all men, but the ambition to buy a house, a car, have a family, invest in real estate, and have a solid retirement plan by the age of thirty-five without the emotional or financial support of any man. I haven't met many dancers with the intelligence that Nina Hartley or Tristan Taormino have, but I have yet to see this brutal demand for independence anywhere in porno.

Take Chica, for instance: the deathly hot, Hispanic, real dirty stripper—and by dirty I don't mean that she rubbed extra hard on her dances. In fact, they usually sucked. But she knew how to get that money, whether it meant telling customers that she liked to get pissed on, that her day job was being a secretary for a law firm, or that her mother needed a heart transplant. In the three-day period when the two of us shared a customer, Chica laid down the rules: it was me or her. He chose her. And she chose $5,000 rims for her Escalade, a $1,500 Fendi bag, and a house in northern New Jersey for her two kids. "Bitch," she said when I asked her if anyone was helping her pay child support. "I got my own house, my own car, my own yard, and my own kids. Ain't no one putting their name on any of my shit, because this way if I lose a man, all I lose is a piece of dick, which usually ain't that great anyway."

I too wanted to buy superfluous name-brand bags one day, along with some property and a car that takes up three parking spaces, but I didn't want to do that at a strip club. Stripping is a drug: I was powerful and successful, but it was all fake. The minute my shift was over, I was nothing but a girl who could order Grey Goose instead of well vodka with my tonic, and that doesn't give you anything, aside from a really nice drunk. Anyone who's decided to cut back on drugs knows it's really boring and difficult at first, but better for you in the long run. I changed my schedule from four nights a week to one and put my efforts back into the site, but this time I had a strategy. If I could be just as successful on BurningAngel as I was at the strip club, I could take over the world.

My manager invited some of us girls to a porno party in Atlantic City. I brought BurningAngel flyers to the party, assuming the crowd (like the crowd at the strip club) would be really easy to please. All this time I'd been promoting BurningAngel to hip rock 'n' roll kids who had never bought porn (in fact, a lot of them were morally opposed). Imagine how many memberships I could get if I were exposed to people who actually *liked* porn? I was excited.

The party wasn't all it was cracked up to be. Everyone I spoke with, whether a director, a distributor, a cameraman, or even just a guy hanging out, had the same response to "Hey, check out my Web site!" and that was, "Take your shirt off." I should have known there was something shady about this party when I was asked to sign a release form at the door. I was the only girl in the entire place who wasn't drunk and topless, and having spent half of my week at a strip club, and the other half running a porn site, I'd decided that if I wasn't getting paid or getting PR, there wasn't any point in contributing to this scene. Jersey's finest men were groping the girls, and the DJ was spinning hip-hop songs from 1995. If there is anything that doesn't get me in the mood, it's *House of Pain*.

The great thing that came out of this party was getting to see Nina Hartley. The emcee announced her presence, and all the men who had laughed in my face and thrown my flyers on the floor cheered for her. The dance floor cleared, she made her way into the center, and Sunset Thomas followed her in.

Nina pinned her down, and got to work: she ate her pussy and licked her asshole. Sunset Thomas's orgasm was drowned out by the crowd's roar, but it was clear she was enjoying herself. Watching them, I knew that I wouldn't have been able to put on such a performance; the whole episode would have appeared visibly amateur, and sloppy, if I had tried it. Nina had this really amazing way of concentrating on Sunset and the crowd at the same time, and she didn't need any bodyguards to tell the crowd that groping her was out of the question. The difference between Nina Hartley and me was that she was a porn star, and I was just a stripper with some topless photos on the Internet.

Until I saw this, I was stuck in a sort of porno purgatory. I wasn't sure if it was feminist to make hardcore or softcore porn, or if BurningAngel was punk because there were punk bands on it, or because we didn't give a shit. Did I put my photos on BurningAngel to make recruiting girls easier? Or did I really like doing porn? I was growing up, and I needed BurningAngel to grow up with me.

After the party, I told Mitch we should buy a video camera and start making hardcore movies. Even he was hesitant to move in a hardcore direction, because he hated confrontation and was scared it would induce even more antagonism. We brainstormed ideas and decided that the DVD should be just like the site: band interviews and tattooed indie girls, only this time they'd be having sex.

"Oh, and Mitch . . . I want to be on this DVD," I said.

"What? Are you sure? You know, you don't have to be . . ."

"Well, yeah, I know. But it just wouldn't make any sense if I wasn't."

"So . . . do you wanna do girl-girl or something?" he asked.

"No, I think I'll do anal," I said. I mean, if I was gonna do this, I figured I should really do it. Mitch laughed. He was kind of like a brother, and he still felt weird about seeing me with my top off.

"Why anal?" he asked.

"Because there's nothing wrong with doing porn," I said.

I've read most of the porn star memoirs in the bookstore: most begin with poverty and desertion, and end with love and money. So, reader, I hope it doesn't disappoint you that there weren't any rags or riches in this story. Interviews with me have appeared on TV, Web sites, and in print magazines, all with the angle of demystifying a "porn revolution" that I've apparently started. I'm not driving an Escalade, and I don't have a swimming pool, a black credit card, or a boyfriend, but BurningAngel has earned itself a nice office, a full-time webmaster, some very dedicated interns, a lovely photographer, lighting equipment, a really good camera, and finally, *BurningAngel.com: The Movie*. I'm not so sure I started a revolution, but I know I started something pretty awesome, and most important, I feel like a real, true, honest-to-god feminist.

SESKA LEE

. . . ON TAKING THE AMATEUR PORN APPROACH TO THE WEB.

MY PRIMARY MOTIVATION IN CHOOSING to work in porn was and is personal, not commercial. However, the route I took to become a porn performer may be a little different than one might expect. I was never a sex-crazed teen or a glue-sniffing streetwalker. That may be what adult Internet sites would like you to think amateur porn performers are all about. It doesn't represent the truth—certainly not my truth. I am a regular gal who came from happy family. I went to college, received my degrees, and worked as an educator. Then I realized I wanted to explore different things. And so I did.

I became interested in porn later in life than most, both as a viewer and as a performer. I was in my mid-twenties when I saw my first adult video. It belonged to my boyfriend James. He was open with me about having a collection. It piqued my interest, so one night I sat down and watched various people having various kinds of sex. I was worried I would be uncomfortable seeing the images of thrusting penises or the "money shots" because I had never seen these acts close up. I thought they would overwhelm my senses. They didn't. Instead, what distressed me was much more self-centerd. My insecurities. Were these videos a represen-tation of what my boyfriend wanted in his life? Did he want me to look like these women, to act like these women? I felt I had very little in common with them. I had small natural breasts. I wore little makeup. I was a preppie dresser. Beyond their appearance, I could not imagine myself being as comfortable with my body, or as comfortable with my sexuality as the women in the video seemed to be.

After I had watched the videos, James and I had some serious discussions and I did a lot of soul searching on my own. There were two key things I came to realize. Porn was about fantasy and fantasies are not necessarily what you want in your everyday life.

I began to see porn for what it was—a commercial representation of sexuality, not the reality of sex. In most productions bloopers were edited out, sexual acts were orchestrated in advance, and the actors were giving a performance. They were well aware of the camera. What the pornographers chose to show was based on what they thought would sell the best.

Everyday sex is not a commercial enterprise. We do not have makeup artists and hair stylists to make us over into porn starlets, exaggerating our feminine traits. Male partners are not chosen specifically because of their penis size and their ability to stay hard and ejaculate on command. There are no cameramen in our bedrooms. The primary motivation is not money. The primary motivation is pleasure. Or at least one hopes it is.

I also came to appreciate the role fantasy plays in our adult lives. Our imagination is always at work. It offers us a safe way to explore other possibilities. We can be in complete control of a situation; what we imagine serves us. It does not make a relationship with a partner any less meaningful. It is not something to feel guilty about. I think fantasy helps keep us sane.

And so, with all that porn stuff figured out, James and I began to explore our sexual horizons. We made our first attempt to have sex in front of the camera. It was to be for a personal video that was just for our viewing pleasure. I personally did not enjoy watching this particular video, but James enjoyed it immensely. I found it difficult to watch myself be sexual in combination with the imperfections I saw. I was quite critical of the low production quality of our tape (poor sound, poor lighting, and poor camera angles), as well as the faults I saw in my physical characteristics. I was very hard on myself. James was much more generous. He watched the video with the expectation of flaws and naturalness. He knew that what he would see would be raw and real, but arousing as well. While I did not enjoy watching the video, I realized I very much enjoyed having sex on camera. It excited me. I discovered I was an exhibitionist.

At around this time we also became interested in the alternative lifestyle scene. I found that the Internet was a perfect place for me to explore my desires. It was in the privacy of my own home. I could go at my own pace. It was safe. I was eager to read up on some of the areas of sexuality that appealed to my erotic mind: fetish clothing, bdsm, and swinging. I started local. I surfed for stores and clubs in my area. I read everything I could get my hands on that pertained to the rules and etiquette of the different scenes. It was very educational and gave me insight into a world that is most often shrouded in myth and mystery. After my education phase, James and I began attending fetish nights, and we experimented with swinging. Overall, it was a learning experience that helped us figure out what our turn-ons were and what suited us best as a couple.

Around this same time I discovered a link to Carol Cox's personal XXX Web site. It was a rich resource for me. Not only did it have pictures of real people having sex, which I found to be arousing and accessible, but it was also a door to another world for me. One I was terribly intrigued by. Amateur porn.

So what exactly is amateur porn? You cannot be an amateur if you are making money, right? Well, it depends on who you ask. Look at sport. With all the sponsorship deals people are getting these days, there are few true amateurs left. The same can be said about porn. But the label remains because it differentiates the performers who work in the mainstream porn industry, fall under the conventional porn standards of beauty, and have made a recognizable name for themselves from those performers who do not fit the mold or who have gone the independent route. Amateurs are the unknowns. They are people you would never expect to be in the adult entertainment industry: older women, fat women, housewives. They are regular folks who get their kicks being sexual exhibitionists in homemade porn movies and pictures, which they share with a consensual audience. It began with the video revolution; with the Internet they moved onto the World Wide Web.

At first, these amateur sites were free, but then came the bandwidth bills, and people had to get a little more savvy if they wanted to continue having their Web sites. Now it has become big business. Most porn corporations hire unknown models and create Web sites featuring their pictures. Other Internet entrepreneurs buy pictures of a given model and create a Web site around this content. The Webmaster makes up their biographical information more often than not. They all fall under the umbrella of amateur porn. Yet, there are still many personal Web sites that are run by the people they feature. Folks who keep trying to find a balance between being an exhibitionist and paying the bills. I like to think that these genuine amateur websites are the mom-and-pop sites of online porn.

James and I were quite excited that one of the most well-known and successful Amateurs on the Internet happened to live in our city, and we had the opportunity to meet her. We decided to attend one of her advertised gatherings. It was held at a local swingers' club. We approached her at the beginning of the night and said hello. She introduced us to her husband, and the four of us hit it off. In short order, we became good friends. It was with their encouragement and support that James and I decided to create an amateur adult site of our own. We were now to become pornographers instead of just viewers of photography.

When deciding to expose my self on the Web I knew that, based upon my experience producing that personal porn video, I would have to get past my body issues and worries about being imperfect. In the beginning I was concerned that I would feel insecure about my breasts. Porn is notorious for massive boobage, something I just don't have. I thought I would feel pressured to get breast implants. I was delightfully surprised by my opposite reaction. I became very happy with my body and felt celebrated for my own natural attributes. In fact, I rarely ever wear my old Wonderbra anymore. Porn has been good for this girl's self-image.

Part of that has to do with the talks I had with James, as well as the feedback I have received from members of my Web site. James helped me realize that there is no such thing as the perfect woman or man for everyone. We all have our distinct tastes and preferences when it comes to erotic material and who we find attractive. Some people find me attractive and enjoy my pictures and others do not. It isn't anything personal against me, but more about the diversity of human beings.

One expectation I had that turned out to be correct was that running my own adult site is work. Yes, I get to have some crazy sexual experiences that most people can only dream about, but it is still work. If I have a cold, I still have to do those updates, perform for my Webcam shows, and write those journal entries. We also can't be away from home for very long because James and I update the site very regularly. If we vacation, we must be able to get online. That leaves out more exotic places to travel to. However, that is the boring stuff.

More fascinating is the sex part of the work. Now, I am letting you in on a big secret here. Having sex for a living is not always very glamorous and it takes some effort to make fantasy come to life. Even with an amateur site that reflects my actual sexual lifestyle there is some artifice to it. For example, I never used to schedule my sexual activities. Having a site has caused me to do so. My photo shoots and especially my webcam shows are scheduled. Every Tuesday night at 9 P.M. I know I am going to be participating in some sexual activity. It is not as spontaneous as the rest of my sex life. Lucky for me, I work well with planning. It helps me to get into a sexual frame of mind and then give a good show for the viewers. I know that some performers get bogged down by the aspect of running their own personal porn Web sites.

The other reality of pornography that I learned early on is that what looks best in still pornography is the most uncomfortable position possible for the model. Yes, if you see someone in a sexy posed shot, chances are their backs are killing them. With the live shows I don't have the same problem because I am in motion. This is a good thing, as it lets me enjoy the sex itself. However, as a performer who is also the cameraperson (as James and I are), in the back of your mind you are always thinking about the camera. For me this is mainly a turn-on because I enjoy performing for interested parties. However, you do have to focus on the camera angles and choosing positions that will give the viewer the best possible show. Nonexhibitionist sex tends to be just a blur of humping bums, and this does not make for the best porn.

This being the case, my experience as a pornographer has greatly influenced my view and appreciation of porn. I know the inside scoop. While the sex isn't faked, it is contrived and it isn't perfect. Accidents happen. One time I fell over while having anal sex on camera. It was hilarious and real. With amateur porn you can't always edit out such bloopers. Yet leaving them in can make the porn very accessible to the viewers. My life may be a fantasy for them, but it is one they can share and understand. It is not out of reach.

Some people are disappointed by what they perceive as flaws and mistakes in porn. It bursts their sexual bubbles. For them, mainstream porn is a better option. It can have a beauty and an idealness that allows them to escape for a short time. Nevertheless, I think it is healthy to have some reality mixed in with your fantasy. It helps you see the performers as the complex people they are and see yourself and your partners in comparison as just as sexy and arousing.

When I am old and gray (or more likely still a brunette, covering it up), I think I will look back at my life in porn as being a good experience. As a viewer of porn, I have been given the gift of seeing sexual possibilities and enhancing imagery. As a pornographer, I have been able to share my experiences and insights with others and offer them a gift in return for their support. On a selfish note, all of it has allowed me to feel better about my body, my abilities, and my value as a sexual being. Most important, it has allowed me to see the same qualities in others.

SEX SELLERS

THE WOMEN BEHIND THE COMPANIES
WE BUY FROM

THERESA FLYNT

I WAS IN COLLEGE WHEN Columbia Pictures started making the movie *The People vs. Larry Flynt*. It was right in the middle of midterms, so I never saw much of the filming. But it was during a private screening of the movie in New York that I truly came to realize what it meant to be a Flynt.

Just a few people from the film were there, Woody Harrelson, my dad, the director Milos Forman . . . there were maybe a dozen of us in the room. I remember knowing that my dad was famous and I knew all about the Falwell case and everything else that had happened. But when I was sitting there watching the story unfold before me, it felt like I was seeing everything for the first time. What the film did was take my father—who is now 62—and his whole life and all of his accomplishments and condense them into two hours of entertainment, and I was able to see why someone would take an interest in making a movie about him. It was then that I understood what the world sees in him, how the world perceives him, and how the world *should* perceive him. When it was over I started crying so hard that I couldn't breathe. I stood up. Milos came over and hugged me. He said, "I hope the rest of the world reacts as you just did."

"Well, they can't—that's my family's life," I told him. "That's my father's life, and nobody is going to react the way that I did."

I think it was that moment that made me realize my dad's impact on the world and journalism, and how big a hero he really is. Regardless, it wasn't my intention to be a part of his company. I actually wanted to be a news broadcaster.

My parents divorced when I was about two, so I spent most of my life going back and forth between my dad and Althea (my step-mother) and my mom, so I had dual parenting. I had friends where both my parents lived. I remember once when I was six years old I was playing with a neighbor's kid. Her mother came out of the house and was really nice to me, asking who I was and making small talk before asking me what house I lived in. I pointed to it and she grabbed her kid and took her inside as she told me, "You can't come over here anymore—you might as well just go back inside." Back then I didn't get it. I remember my mother telling me, "She doesn't like our family." I didn't understand why.

I lived with my dad steadily from thirteen on. I always knew what he did for a living. I knew that he was self-employed and I saw what was going on, but for me it was normal because it was my world. So by the time I hit junior high and high school I was the cool kid because I knew more about things that other kids didn't. I helped so many girls who didn't know how to use a pad or tampon because their parents hadn't even told them about their period. I helped a friend through an abortion because she didn't know any better about safe sex. I helped my friends shop for their first bras. So many of my friends' parents couldn't talk to them about sex, so I talked to them about it. It baffled me that those parents weren't buying their daughters bras when they started developing, or sitting down with them and a box of pads to explain how to use them when their periods started, or even just explaining what a period was. So I became a resource for a lot of girlfriends. And although guiding my friends through these things was something of an adult situation to be in, it felt good because I had the answers they were looking for.

But even during that time I had some girlfriends whose parents weren't completely comfortable with where I came from. They'd say it was okay for me to spend the night at their house, but would forbid their daughters to come over to my dad's house because they thought we had topless maids running around. People thought crazy things about my home life, and really we were . . . well, I wouldn't say a "normal family" because I don't think a normal family exists. But we would go to the movies together, eat dinner together. We weren't like the colorful stories that people imagined. I was always aware of what *Hustler* was, but it wasn't on our coffee tables. In fact, the raciest thing that would happen—if you want to call it that—is my stepmother used to walk around naked sometimes, but it never bothered me. I could talk to my parents about anything, whereas my friends couldn't. So I felt lucky to grow up with the family I had.

When I was nineteen I took my GEs at Santa Monica College, and then I quit college because I didn't know what I wanted to major in. I was really indecisive. I had taken a few journalism classes, but it wasn't for me. Journalism writing was very structured, so I hated it. I never wanted to work in publishing; it never made sense to me. I didn't want to write because it wasn't something that interested me, so I didn't want to work for my dad's company, Larry Flynt Publications. I worked there off and on during semesters in college in the subscriptions department, at reception, or assisting editorial a little bit, but it wasn't stimulating to me. I took a psychology class or two because I was really trying to figure out what I wanted to be.

At one point I quit school and signed up with a temp agency, working as a secretary and doing random office jobs until I finally decided one day that I wanted to go back to school to get a degree in business. I thought that if I got my degree in business administration and marketing I could apply it to whatever I wanted to do, which was still something I wasn't entirely sure about. But at that point it didn't matter what career I chose in life, because I knew that if I had a business background it would help me. So I transferred my units and went to Mount St. Mary's in Los Angeles.

So I graduated from college, earning a degree in business and marketing, but I still wasn't interested in working for my dad until he decided that it was time to diversify the *Hustler* brand. He felt that he wanted to get into the retail sector. One afternoon I was sitting in one of the offices in my dad's building talking to him on the phone, and he said, "You know, I'm driving by this Blockbuster on Sunset and I'm thinking about putting a store there."

The light bulb went on. "Really?" I asked.

He said yes and hung up. I thought about it for a few moments before calling him back to tell him, "You know, if you don't have anyone to run the store it might be something that I'd want to do." And then I hung up.

He called me back. "You know what," he said. "You'd be great for it."

I was married for sixteen years, and my husband and I would go to adult stores occasionally to look for things to spice up our sex life. I hated those stores. Hated them! I can remember going into the stores and thinking how I didn't even want to buy anything—I didn't even want to touch the box because there was dust on it, and then there was this creepy old man behind the register who'd look at me like I was a freak for being in there. I always felt so uncomfortable. So when my dad decided that he wanted to open a retail store in West Hollywood on Sunset Boulevard, I said it was something that I could do because I could see the need for it.

I was always looking for something nobody was doing, and I thought nobody really had any clean, pretty sex stores that made people feel comfortable in their environment, so that's how I got involved. It was a natural progression, and the timing was perfect. I saw something new for the company other than just relying on publishing. I saw it as *Hustler* going mainstream and breaking new ground, reaching a new market, doing something that was rewarding, and helping couples spice up their sex life in a clean, educated, light, bright, friendly environment.

The path to opening the store wasn't smooth. We're a family business, so there's always family involved. My dad set a budget and said, "I want a store where even a schoolteacher would feel comfortable coming in to buy a sex toy." I totally identified with that. Even though I'm not a schoolteacher, I knew that I wanted people to walk in and not feel like they were in a traditional adult store, with the windows blacked out, featuring neon signs and peep-show booths. We hired a team of designers—a man and woman in Los Angeles—that helped us go for that "department store" feel. We worked together. They would pitch colors and then my dad and I would sit down and talk about it, eventually ending up choosing purples and reds.

And then it evolved. I was responsible for the products we carry, because I went to all the conventions and picked out what we were going to sell. The buying is done with the philosophy that as long as it's sexy, quality, at the right price, trendy, and in demand, we'll have it in our store. So whether it's candles, massage oils, crystal earrings, or flavored lip gloss, you'll find it in our store because we sell sex, and sex isn't just what's in the bedroom! We also decided to have a coffee shop in our store, but it didn't happen quite the way we thought it would. The coffee shop happened because nobody—not Starbucks, not Peet's, not The Coffee Bean and Tea Leaf—would lease next to us because they thought we were going to be this seedy adult store. So I decided we could run a coffee shop ourselves. We wanted to have one because it would relax the atmosphere, and then we could have a newsstand where people could read magazines and drink coffee and eat sensuous desserts.

We also wanted to make the stores someplace fun to have events. So in addition to hosting book readings, classes, and other fun happenings, the stores also provide a venue for our customers to meet their favorite adult stars and get their autographs. Our *Hustler* Hollywood store hosts our Porn Walk of Fame, where we have handprints from Ron Jeremy to Jenna Jameson. All of this was important to us to ensure that we would be considered on a different plane from other adult stores, but that doesn't mean that there aren't still problems with running this type of business.

I run into issues with the *Hustler* name every time I open a new store. When people know we're coming they get up in arms. The media and community pull together and picket because of the negative connotation associated with the traditional adult store. But once we open, the picketers are gone. Not only because we're not what they think we are—with our big, bright windows they can see that we showcase clothing, candles, and so many other things aside from sex merchandise—but because I make sure that our stores are very active in the community. We make sure to get involved with community chambers of commerce. Being active in the community, being an asset to the community, and being an attractive store helps create word of mouth.

Though I was happy with how the first store looked and felt, it wasn't until a realtor I was working with sang its praises that I knew I'd created exactly the tone I was looking to strike with Hustler Hollywood. We were scouting for locations in Portland when he told me, "When I came to L.A. I couldn't believe that I had three generations in your store. My two daughters were looking for T-shirts in the apparel section, my mother and father were having coffee and reading the paper in the café, and my wife and I were looking at the sex goodies. I should've gotten a picture of the three generations in there because there's no other store like that!"

So that's how I found my niche in the *Hustler* empire. There's now six Hustler Hollywood stores, from L.A. to Lexington, Kentucky with two currently under construction. Though my title within the company is Executive Vice President of Retail Operations, my job encompasses so much more than that. I oversee our retail development, our mail-order division, our online store, our sex toy license, and then I help my dad when he needs it with projects, promotions, and marketing. We recently started making our apparel ourselves, so I oversee that as well. I love every minute of what I do; I just wish there were more hours in the day to get it all done.

There's something about retailing in the sex sector that is infinitely more fulfilling than traditional retailing. I don't think that I could go work at the Gap now, even if I wanted to. I'm selling things that help people with their sex lives and their desires. So if they're buying condoms at my store and they know the right lube to go with those condoms, or if they're buying a toy to switch things up or a movie to have some fun with, I feel like I'm helping people. I wish people knew more about sex, because there's so many people who know nothing about STDs, that you can't use certain lubes with certain condoms . . . people just don't know this. I've had people tell me that *Hustler* is just a smut peddler, pushing porn to the masses. I look at it as educating the masses. I'm not selling what I'm selling just to make money, I'm selling what I'm selling because it's rewarding.

Sex is not trendy. Whether you're eighteen or eighty, you're either thinking about doing it or you're actually doing it. So as long as I sell quality products in a clean but sexy environment, I know I'm doing the right thing.

LINDA JOHNSON

I DON'T WALK AROUND ANNOUNCING that I work for Jenna Jameson. Of course, there are times when I'll be on flights and get into conversations with people who, inevitably, ask me what I do. You don't know how someone is going to react when you tell them you work in the adult industry, and I don't want someone shoving their religion at me. However I'm not ashamed of it or I wouldn't be here. So when people ask me what I do for a living, depending on the situation and who's asking the question, I'll say I'm either a booking agent or talent manager, or that I work in Internet. And they always push it—they always want to know more.

I've come to the point where I can gauge who's going to be comfortable with the true answer. Very few people have said, "Oh, I can't imagine how you could ever do that." One person said that to me once when I was waiting to get on the plane, and I said to him, "Well, it's a good thing that's not a job you choose to do." I thought that was so closed-minded, but this was probably the same person who went home and jerked off to one of her films. But most people say, "Oh my God, I love her!" Or, "I read her book! I saw her on VH1!" Then they want to know if she's really that nice, that genuine, that fun. But there was one time out of all those times that I've gotten into that conversation that shocked me.

There was an older couple sitting next to me in first class on a flight I was on heading to New York. Jenna was with her husband, Jay, a few rows up, so I wound up chatting with the older couple. They were going home to see their son and they asked me, what are you going to New York for?

"I'm actually going to see Howard Stern," I told them.

"Really?" said the woman. "Are you famous?"

"No, no," I said. "That wouldn't be me."

So we got to talking, because here's the thing—you either *know* who Jenna is or you don't. So I told them that I worked for Jenna Jameson, and I'll never forget the look on their faces. Both of them stared at me blankly, then they looked at each other, and they burst into laughter. The woman leaned in and said, "Okay— in our house, in our closet, we have this secret box and in it is all of her movies." And by looking at them, you'd never guess that they were fans of Jenna, let alone porn. About ten minutes later Jenna walked back to see me and I introduced her to them, and they were just absolutely in awe. They couldn't wait to tell their friends. It was probably the coolest thing I'd ever experienced, and I walked off that plane thinking, *I love people who have minds that are open.* It was the most pleasant trip I'd ever had.

I started working with Club Jenna in the very beginning. Jenna's husband, Jay, and I have known each other for sixteen years. I met him back when I was managing bands—I worked with people in jazz, r&b and hip-hop. His brother owned a travel agency, and I used to book all the travel for the bands through him. When I moved on from that, I worked for his brother for a number of years. When they started Club Jenna they called me and asked if I would come along and help start the company. At that point, I had never met Jenna—I didn't even know who she was. So when I finally did meet her, it was the craziest thing—it was like I'd met my long-lost sister. We just clicked. We have a lot of similar things in our history: our families, being on our own, our professional dedication. It's really pretty cool, because I understood a lot of things that nobody else understood about her.

I left home when I was very young and did the one thing that I knew I did well: work. I threw myself into every job I had. Jenna did the same thing. She left home and started working right away, and said from the very beginning that she was going to be the best she was going to be. I was the same way—I was determined. I was adopted at birth and grew up in an abusive home, so I left home when I was fifteen years old. I knew my home life was a scene I had to get out of because it just felt wrong. So Jenna and I were both out there by ourselves. We both relied on our survival skills; we had no choice. Unless you've been through those things it's hard to understand why someone would act or react to certain situations the way that they do, and I understood it because I had been through similar things. Obviously, we chose different paths, but ultimately we came together on the same one.

Now, before I started working in the adult industry, I didn't really have an opinion on it. I mean, I was on the road with R. Kelly for two years, so it's not like I'd never seen an adult film or been to a strip club. It wasn't something that I personally sought out, but it was something that was always around because the guys in the bands had an interest in it. Being on the road nine months at a time, they're going to hit a strip club or two. Until I went to work for Club Jenna I never really gave it much thought, because it just wasn't a really relevant thing in my life, but that changed when it became a part of my everyday life. When I got into the industry I was initially shocked at the hardcore until I'd been around it every day, and then I fell into this mode where I critiqued it—that lighting is bad, the angle is bad . . . you get to a point where it's just a way of life. It's who we are. Now I think it's funny for people to be so offended and up in arms about something that, if we didn't engage in it, we wouldn't be here. It's quite the double standard that people should be ashamed of.

Club Jenna became a corporation in December 1999 and I started working with them the following March. We started by creating a Web site. None of us had ever created a Web site before—none of us had any idea what we were doing. The first day I went in, there were boxes and boxes of slides and content from all the stages of Jenna's career. We wanted to shoot new photos of her for the site, but before we could get to that we had to scan and categorize everything so it could be put online. Initially, Jay's sister, Chris, and I spent all of our time organizing everything, physically scanning every slide and picture Jenna had into the computer ourselves. We scanned for a year. I'd be scanning until 10 or 11 P.M. every night, one by one, getting everything organized so we'd have everything where it needed to be. It took us a year of scanning and working with designers to get it all done. Then, finally, we started shooting exclusive content of Jenna. The whole process took about a year and a half, scanning the old content, creating the new content, and launching the site. It was such a process, but really, it was a fantastic learning experience. We look back now and think of how far we've come . . . it's amazing that we even got off the ground.

After the site launched we started focusing on promotion and building the company name—with Jenna at the helm, naturally, because she's the CEO of the company. She knows what she wants to do and what direction she wants to go in, just like when she first started. Her attitude was simple: now that she had the company the sky was the limit, so we made the decision to focus on mainstream. Jenna capitalized on her hosting duties with the E! Channel, and soon everyone wanted to do shows, books, and radio with her. Everyone told her, "You made this all work and everything you touch is gold. Let's do more!" It gave her the opportunity to choose, just like she's always done in her career. Jenna has always been the smart one to say, "This is what I want to do and how I want to do it—this is what I'm going to be."

My job was basically to run her life, and it was during this time that I discovered what a good team we make, because we push each other. We're both really driven, which is one of the reasons why we work well together. Back in those days, we'd be on the road for twenty-six to twenty-eight days out of a month, and we'd be exhausted by the end. She'd be dancing and shooting, and there were days when I didn't know how she did it, but she did it because she had people counting on her. She did it because she likes it. And in the entire time I've worked with people in both the mainstream and adult industry, I've never seen anyone who likes meeting her fans and the people who support her as much as she does. There are very few times when we'd be in public and people wouldn't approach her. And no matter what the situation, she'd always smile and sign an autograph. Always. I think that's the reason people care about her so much, and it's also the reason she's a star—she truly appreciates the people who put her there. It's amazing to me. There were times when I'd be, like, "Get the hell away! Se's trying to put a morsel of food in her mouth!" It just never ceased to amaze me. And the types of people who would come up to her were equally amazing. Sure, there'd be young guys, but after the book came out, everything changed. Everyone approached her: older women, couples, people you'd never think of as porn consumers would come up to her and say, "I read your book and you have no idea how it touched my life."

That book was, of course, *How to Make Love Like a Porn Star: A Cautionary Tale*. It took three years for her to complete the book, and it was a grueling project because she threw herself into it—she bared all. She struggled with it while she was writing it because she revealed intense things and she didn't want to hurt anyone's feelings. Jay and I were her cheerleaders during that time. We told her, "If you don't tell your whole story, it's going to be missing your feelings and passion. It's not going to be believable." But for her to sit down and open up her life like that to someone . . . I don't think I could've done that. I don't think I could've sat down with someone and said, "Okay, this is me." The fact that she did it was good for her. It took a lot of nerve for her to say, "Look, this is who I am and these are the decisions I made, and I have no regrets. The end. I made these decisions because this is what I wanted to do." And you know what? It was amazing. But none of us were prepared for what happened next.

I don't think any of us expected the reception that the book got, and when it hit, the book tour was unreal. I have chills just writing about it! I was with her through the whole tour. We did ten cities in twelve days, and the lines of people were just insane. People brought their babies. The crowds ran the gamut from kids to the elderly. I was floored. People would tell her, "I read your book and it gave me hope; now I know I can decide things for myself," and we'd hear that in every city. Sometimes I'd be brought to tears, because who would've thought that a book by an adult star would touch people like that? And look at the press that it got. We appeared in every show imaginable—every show loved her. And out of all that press, there was only one interview that was negative. Out of all of that press—one. It was crazy. But I was never as proud of her as I was on that tour, because she sat there and signed every one of those books at those signings.

The thing about Jenna and signings is she wants to know about everyone. Every person is her friend, and I'm the one sitting there saying, "C'mon, girl, there's four thousand people in line!" She'll sit there and say, "Hi, how are you? Where are you from?" She really wants to know about them, and they'd stand there for hours and hours, waiting to have that one-on-one time with her. She'd tell each and every one of them, "Thanks for coming. You have no idea how much this means to me." Every single person she talks to she genuinely cares about, because she means it. But there was one particular time where we were at a signing and this guy said to me, "It must really be hard traveling with someone so beautiful." It stuck with me and I thought about that over time. It makes me laugh now, because not only did I find it strange that someone would say that, but I don't think that I ever felt like that with her. I know her. I know the person she is, and she's my friend. Sometimes you forget that she's a beautiful woman everyone refers to as a beautiful woman and an adult star. She's just a dork. All I see it as is we're on another trip doing another gig, and that's my girl.

When I started at Club Jenna we were putting the company together and I was working on Jenna's scheduling. It's basically all I've done for the past five years, but things have evolved since then. Two years ago at Christmas I was made a partner in the company, so now it's Jenna, Jay, me, our attorney in Colorado, and Mo, our vice president. In addition to the five of us running the company, we have twenty-five employees, because we run the Web sites for all the top girls in the business, like Briana Banks and Tera Patrick. A year and a half ago we signed a contract girl, Krystal Steal. Until a short while ago I was doing all of the accounts payable, payroll, and human resources, not to mention all of Jay's and Jenna's scheduling. It's been crazy, but we've come a long way in the last five years.

For as popular as Jenna has been, and how far she's gone above and beyond the role that everyone else has played in the industry in a totally different way, she evolved with the company. Club Jenna was her vehicle to see and do everything that she wanted to do. Jay's the president of the company, and he's the one who sat down with her and said, "We want to go in this direction." It's something we built as a team and each of us had our roles. We all determined how to take things to the next level, but it took Jay and Jenna's business sense to bring the team all together. Jay is ten times the workaholic we are. He's very driven and it was very important to him that Jenna succeed; it was important to him that he give her every tool that she needed to achieve everything she wanted to achieve. He's driven. Make no mistake, Jenna's a hard worker. I'd look at her schedule and there'd be literally two days in a month when she'd be in town. Everyone wanted a piece of her, but all of that hard work paid off. Look at how well her book did! It allowed her to do everything she wanted.

Now everyone who enters the industry wants to be Jenna Jameson. All the girls say, "I want to be like Jenna," but they never want to work that hard to get there. They don't understand that she didn't just laze about to get where she is. A lot of hard work went into this, and I have five years of scheduling to prove it. I look back at some of those days and think, how did we get through it? But we did it by cheerleading. Jay would tell her, "I know you can do it, baby," and I would tell her, "Look, I know that you're tired, but . . ." She'd get on camera and sit in that interview, and I've never seen someone who can just turn it on like that. She's just Jenna—she can get in there and sit in that interview, and she's just on. There were days where she'd be sick as a dog throwing up, and I'd tell her we'd have to do this, that and the other thing, and she'd get out there and be just dazzling. I don't know how she did it. People don't realize that Jenna created herself. But along the way, a lot of people have helped. It's amazing. It's amazing when people support you and believe in you and want you to succeed. Jenna is blessed because there were a lot of people who wanted her to be all that she wanted to be, and that's really important.

So, over the years I've had more than a couple of things to do, and now that we have all the new contract girls, I'm managing and scheduling them as well. Jay and I are working on getting all the scheduling done for all the filming, and I'm working on all the promotions for them with our publicist, T.J. So now I've become more of a manager for the girls rather than Jenna being my whole life. Back then, wherever Jenna went, I went. And now it's different with our girls. We'll send security with them, we're working with T.J. and he'll be setting up the promotions. It was hard, but I reached a point in my life when I decided I can't be everywhere at once.

When the girls did their first promotional tour in Chicago, it was really hard not to go. It was the first time that I haven't had to do a promotional trip, and I was suffering some anxiety over it because my job has always been to make sure that they never have to worry about anything other than being beautiful and who they are. That was always my job with Jenna: I never wanted her to worry about doing anything other than showing up and doing what she had to do. The company always had to handle everything else. So I'm very particular in my travels and organizing. I have a tendency to want to mother the girls because I want this to be easy for them—I want them to want to do this and I want it to be fun. The easier it is for them, the more they'll want to succeed. I don't want them to worry about their travel, whether the promoter is happy, where they're going and what they're doing . . . it's my job to worry.

However, I wouldn't change anything for the world. I look back on these past five years, and the biggest lesson for me has been that you have to believe. If you believe in yourself and you surround yourself with people who support you, there's nothing you can't accomplish.

I've seen marked changes in myself over the last five years. I've always been behind the scenes. When they're filming I don't like to be on camera, I don't like to be interviewed . . . let Jenna be the front person. But I think the more we're involved in other things—and I can't even begin to tell you the things we've done, the places we've gone, and the shoots we've experienced—and the more I do this, the more confident I've become, because that I've been a part of something tremendous. It makes me feel great. I'm one of those people who believes I can do anything I want, and I'll work as hard as I have to in order to get it done. I like working. It's what I do. But I think it's also helped me realize that there's more than just work. You have to have a balance, family, and friends who really care about you so that you can have fun. I'm really to that point now because yes, we worked, but now it's time to enjoy it. Not that I didn't enjoy the work, because work has always been fun for me, but that's not how I get my kicks. I'm trying to be a little less work-oriented. Jenna got to that point too. You go and go, and at some point you have to say, "Okay, can I have a vacation?" You have to take a second to breathe.

But one of the best parts of this whole journey has been helping change society's perception of the women involved in this business. I think it's about time there was a shift in the way people viewed the women performing in front of the camera. It's taken a long time, but I think it's great that women are stepping up and opening their mouths, claiming their power, demonstrating their power . . . I love it. My biggest thing is that I hate fear, and I think that the fact that they're not afraid of doing what they want to do or creating a product that they want to create speaks volumes. It takes balls to say, "This is what I want to do and I'm going to do it, not because I'm a woman, but because I want to do it." I think people who try to make a statement just to make a statement miss the point. Talk is cheap—you have to have a heart to back it up. And I think women being involved and doing the stuff we want to do . . . it's time people started acknowledging that we're equal to men and to give credit where credit is due.

So, when people say that women aren't porn consumers, it makes me laugh. I mean, come on! No man could ever be that creative in bed—where do you think we get all of our ideas? It's just time we got the credit for it. When I go to signings and promotions with Jenna, the women are far more aggressive than the men ever are. I remember during the book tour we did a signing in Rochester, New York, at Guitar World, and there were girls showing their boobs to get people to let them advance in line. It was the most hilarious thing! The line went all the way down the block and around the corner, and these girls were flashing people in line just to get a few more people ahead so they could get closer to Jenna. If I had a dollar for every time a woman propositioned her, you and I would both be in St. Thomas right now. There are people who would say, "My boyfriend really wants to have a threesome, but the only person I'll have a threesome with is you." It would happen all the time! And nine times out of ten, the men are shy and quiet. The girls will yell, "Oh my God, I love you! Sign my boobs! Sign my underwear! Sign my ass!" The guys will be, like, "Hi. To Tom. Thanks." I think it's because Jenna is fun and real. Women connect with her because she doesn't come off as fake and plastic. And she's not always Jenna Jameson, she's also Jenna Massoli, but she lets enough of the Jenna Massoli blend with the Jenna Jameson image that it makes her real.

I'm excited about my future. We now have five contract girls. I'm excited to promote them, I'm excited to get some movies shot for them, I'm excited for them to experience the Club Jenna life. I think we're lucky. We have a great company and a great team, and I'm excited for the girls we've brought on to our team because I want to help them realize their dreams. They want to be the star that Jenna is, and I'm the first one to tell them they'd better be wiling to work, sacrifice, and throw themselves out there. And I'm happy to give them that opportunity, because they believe that dreams will come true. I hope to be here until the end, if there is one.

It strikes me that the result of all this hard work is that people seem to think if Jenna's name is attached to something, it makes adult entertainment okay, because she's done so much. She's been on Howard Stern, she's been on mainstream television, she has a book . . . it's not just adult entertainment. So I think that when people look at Jenna and the Club Jenna name, they don't think of it as being "just porn" because we do so much more: we do a lot of merchandising, have wireless content, we have all of these other things. Plus, Jenna and the person that she has become enables people to want to be better and want to have more. She doesn't have this magical, mystical success gene. She went out there and did it her way. So I say, grab hold of your heart, get out there, and make things happen.

JENNIFER MARTSOLF

. . . ON HELPING CREATE THE SEX TOYS THAT MAKE IT
INTO YOUR BEDROOM.

I HAVE ALWAYS ADMIRED HIGHLY sexual people. They seem to have a secret zest for life that I somehow lack. I feel tremendous pressure to reveal myself as the ultimate sex kitten, given my extensive résumé. Thirteen years ago, at the tender age of nineteen, I began my foray into human sexuality as a clerk in a condom store. I then progressed to video/DVD buyer for a chain of adult bookstores, finally running head first into a position as director of product development for one of the largest importer/exporters of adult novelties in the world. It may seem that I have a bountiful sex life. Regretfully, I am fully clothed for most of it. I am, however, able to take great pleasure in alluding to the possibility that I might be ahead of the pack in the quest for carnal knowledge.

I am, actually, quite shy by nature. To look at me you would never guess that I spend my days up to my elbows in cockrings, clit ticklers, and fifty-five-gallon drums of lubricant—not literally, but if you are interested, I can arrange that for a bulk price. I am also psychic. Well, not really, but I can probably guess what you are thinking. "So what kind of novelties?" "Do you have to test every item?" "What does your job entail exactly?" "How did you get into that?" "What's your best seller?" "Do your parents know what you do?" Over the last thirteen years my jobs have changed, but the questions are always the same. The conversation always begins with, "So, what do you do?"

Sometimes the way in which I answer that question is immediately clear to me. For instance, it is unlikely that I would be completely candid with one of my grandmother's bridge club girlfriends. However, at other times, I have to decide quickly how I wish to reveal myself to the person asking the question. I can go one of two ways: If I paint myself as a regular gal who does product development for a "toy company," I set myself up for a lengthy conversations involving children and children's toys, neither one being a subject that I know anything about or have any interest in. I also have to explain that I don't work for Mattel and they have probably never heard of any product I've ever worked on. At this point, the conversation usually takes an awkward turn because I don't lie very well and it's obvious that I'm skirting some issue.

The alternative response is always more entertaining for me. I, being proud of what I do, and a closet attention whore, generally opt for the truth. "I do product development for an adult toy company." "Say that again?" they say. I say, "I do product development for an adult toy company." "That's what I thought you said." Then the standard questionnaire unfolds, in exactly the same order, every time:

What kind of toys, exactly?

Finding a delicate balance between brainiac and total bimbo, I say in a girly voice with a coy smile, "My toys are for grown-ups." We carry every type of adult product you can imagine and some you couldn't. In our warehouse, you will find everything from Liquid Love Massage Oil™ to Mr. Thick Dick Erection Cream™, from Seymore Butts' Tushy Rocker to Red Light District Toys' No Cum Dodging Allowed Masturbator, along with Meme the

Midget Love Dolls and Legend Toyz Bondage Balls. We are pioneers in the gag gift industry with Glow In The Dark Erotic Dice,
Bachelorette Partyware, and Furry Love Cuffs.

"Put a pecker on it, it will sell" is our mantra. We have over two
thousand items at any given time, including lubricants, lotions,
potions, edible undies, candy, games, wind-up toys, condoms,
french ticklers, cockrings, vibrators of every shape, size, color, and
material available, strap-ons, masturbators, pumps, blow-up
dolls, kits . . . you get the idea. Our catalog has one of the most
extensive selections of adult-related novelties in the world.

I'd like to paint a little picture of my office life. I have fun on
occasion. A woman I work with was grumbling about her job one
day. I was quick to offer her a different perspective: "Are you kidding me? You're looking at it all wrong. See this item right here?
This Lil' Butt Buddy, pearly pink, ribbed butt plug with the easy-
to-grip 'Contour Control' battery pack, is going to end up in
someone's ass and they are going to be overjoyed about it. Do you
fail to see the beauty in that? We're making the world a better
place for some lucky guy or gal who just wants a little pleasure
in the end. How can you be dissatisfied in this wonderland?"

This discourse on my life's work brought her little concilia-
tion, but it left me thinking that I had finally found my place in
the world. I was also thinking she could use a Lil' Butt Buddy all
her own, but I kept that to myself. She could have one or six
already. One never knows. I then pondered if she would like the
light-up model or if the basic one would suffice. Hey, you may
have caught yourself wondering similar things about your
coworkers, but it's a valid question for one in my line of work.

Do you have to test every item?

This is where I like to have fun with people. I can see it in their
eyes. Most people seem to want to hear me say that I lounge

around and masturbate at work all day or that I host corporate product testing orgies every weekend. Perhaps I should, but it hasn't been a necessity (or even a possibility) up to this point.

I do take home samples that I find particularly appealing. I've had many a one-night stand with items over the years. Not that I wasn't satisfied enough to add them to my bedside kit; I just have an endless supply. So why get attached? I'll admit I have fallen in love with our 7th Heaven Platinum Rabbit Pearl™ more than a few times. To keep our romance fresh, I request samples in other colors and shapes, hence the Rainbow Rabbit and the 7th Heaven Platinum G-Spot.

All of the massage oil, lubricants, lotions, potions, and erection creams are tested by me, our office staff, and assorted friends and lovers. We also send them out to our big home party customers to get feedback from "the field." Think Tupperware Parties Gone Wild. Those girls tend to be the toughest critics, so if a product makes it by them, we are fairly confident about the quality.

Let me just say that we release anywhere from 150 to 300 items every six months. In reality, if I tested every one of them, I would 1) have way too much time on my hands (and knees), 2) have calluses in strange places, 3) have to have a penis part-time, 4) be completely exhausted, and 5) probably be a lot thinner, which, I admit, could be incentive enough for me to warrant points one through four.

So what does your job entail?

At this point in the conversation I usually find it necessary to reveal that I do indeed have a brain and a legitimate job. Despite the fact that I have denied personally testing every item, I can see by the smirk and slight glazing of the eyes that they don't necessarily believe me and they are having a hard time picturing me in a job analogous to any other corporate executive.

I have the best job ever. It's analytical and aesthetic. It's science and fantasy. It's all of the senses and nonsense. It's BIG business.

A piece of rubber from China can be the highlight of the perfect date. A defective circuit board from China can be the downfall of the perfect honeymoon. It has to look enticing, smell inviting, sound provocative, and be pleasing to the touch. That's a huge responsibility for a piece of plastic. This inanimate object has to turn you on without turning off mid-moan. It has to produce powerful, titillating vibrations without sounding like a lawnmower that ate a sprinkler head.

The lotions have to taste good, feel good, warm well, be nonsticky, nonstaining, fantasy-fulfilling love potions in attractive packaging that will sell over someone else's taste-good, feel-good, warm-well, nonsticky, nonstaining, fantasy-fulfilling love potions in attractive packaging.

People will do and pay anything to feel better. The challenge is how to tap into that in a unique way. The best-selling Rabbit Pearl™ is my boss's invention. How many different ways can you sell a Rabbit Pearl™? How do I make my heavily copied Rabbit Pearl™ look different from everybody else's pearl rabbit? How do I relay to the consumer that our Rabbit Pearl™ will give them the ultimate sexual experience? How do I make it big enough to appeal to a lube-logged vibe virtuoso without frightening a first-time buyer? How can I package it smaller and cheaper so the retailers will be happy? These are questions asked by anyone developing any type of product for the mass market.

My boss and I make a trip to China and Taiwan twice a year. During that trip we work on new items with our factories over there. The rough samples are then sent to me. We decide if the material is of good quality, if the color is right, if the vibration is sufficient. Is it quiet? What does the rubber smell like? We then decide how to package it. Our art department designs the packaging and we have it printed overseas. I then coordinate all of the parts coming together around the same time so we can assemble the packaging here in our factory. We also have tube and bottle filling capabilities at our factory in Chatsworth. We manufacture a lot of private label massage oils, lubricants, lotions, toy cleaners, and sexual energy drinks, not only for ourselves, but for many others in our industry as well.

We sell globally. We're trying to get as much exposure as possible. Licensing names seems to be the route. We currently license Seymore Butts Toyz, Red Light District Toys, Legend Toyz, Pussyman Toyz, Jodie Moore Toyz, Monica Sweetheart Collection, and Playgirl. We also purchased Las Vegas Novelties, which will enable us to pour our own rubber goods. We will be opening a trading company in China that will offer thousands of items worldwide.

I think at this point, people start to realize that I may have some credibility and I might even be an upstanding taxpayer.

How did you get into that?

Deep breath. Long story short . . .

At nineteen I was in floundering about in community college, trying to figure out what a degree in sociology could do for me, a question I still have no answer for. What was I thinking? I desperately needed health insurance more than anything else, so it was off to work I went. I had a friend who worked at a "gift shop" called Condoms Plus.

I thought I was so open-minded—besides, the shop didn't have any adult merchandise so it wasn't like I had to see any seventy-six different condoms, whip them out of a box, blow air ever so gently into the tip, and lay them on the counter on a jeweler's mat, all the while maintaining a banker's reserve.

I took my job seriously. I took copious notes. I wrote a training manual for all of the employees because I thought it was important that we all be condom connoisseurs. I do believe I was crimson for three weeks, but I was a professional.

This was a new store, and it soon became apparent that profits lay in the adult merchandise. The owner decided to open a small adult section in the back of the store, with toys, videos, and magazines. I was mortified. I couldn't possibly sell that kind of stuff. What is a Ben-Wa ball? You put them where? To strengthen what? Who is Ron Jeremy? What is *Behind the Green Door?* I don't dare watch and find out. Is *Edward Penishands* as good as the original? Oh my God, that vibrator is huge! Who is going to buy that? Well, this gentleman, apparently.

I could have gone out and applied for a regular job at this point, but I was starting to enjoy the shock value of my work. I was strangely fascinated by the things that people revealed to me. I had a customer who came in every Friday night for several months. He would pick out a new cockring and then go into a story about how he broke his last one because he was so well endowed. Some people might find this rather creepy, but I found it fodder for all kinds of speculation. Did he realize that he was telling the same story to the same person every week? Did he fantasize about coming in to tell the story? Did he fantasize about making his new purchase when he got home? Did he just want me to know that he was hung like a horse or did he feel some strange guilt over what he really did with all of the previous cockrings? He really threw me for a loop when I started to see him out at some of the gay clubs. What pleasure would this gay man take in this ritualized behavior? The truth is, it's none of my business. That was his thing and he was not harming me in the process, so I would sell him his cockring and send him out into the night with a smile and a thank you.

It was here that I developed a talent for reading people. Some are very open about their needs and desires and others have to dance gingerly around the subject so as not to be so embarrassed that they can never return. Selling a consumer something that will really satisfy them, without ever making them verbalize what they desire, is an art form. Knowing what not to suggest, so as not to offend a potential customer, is vital. If you had ever tried to sell a condom to a lesbian, you would know. It is not a stare you would want to endure twice. To this day I have stellar gaydar.

Being a clerk at Condoms Plus was a typical "college job" for me. It was not a position that I ever imagined would put me on the path to a career. Condoms Plus is owned by F Street, a twelve-store chain of adult bookstores that is very well known in San Diego County. Fortunately for me the owner of F Street, Alma Vasic, recognized that I was motivated and interested in doing more with my life than the average clerk and that, with a little time and effort, she could mold me into a great employee.

Alma has been an invaluable inspiration to me. She inherited her business through the unfortunate loss of her husband. At the time of his death, she was inundated with offers to sell the business, but she swore she never would and she has been true to her word. I have seen her suffer an incessant number of legal battles defending her right to sell, and your right to purchase, adult merchandise in San Diego. She has an incredible passion for fighting the constant pressure from the City to cleanse itself of all things sexual. There have been cases involving vice squad raids on the arcades, constantly changing city ordinances regarding the types of doors on the arcades, losing two stores over zoning laws, having difficulty obtaining licenses to open new stores. Over all of those hurdles, in addition to all of the regular headaches associated with owning a 24-hour retail chain, she has never given up defending her rights and those of her customers.

While I was still at Condoms Plus, Alma's secretary went on vacation. Alma asked me to fill in as a temp. She had bigger plans for me, but I had no idea. That same day she fired her video buyer. Fate seemed to deal me a lucky hand. I was in the right place at the right time. Neither Alma nor I had any clue who Jenna Jameson was or what a reverse cowgirl might entail. I was never a fan of adult video, and suddenly I found myself responsible for a greater part of the selection of adult content flowing through "America's Finest City." I was about to get a speed course in sexuality that would cover everything from softcore bikini girls to hardcore, cumshot compilations; from straight, to gay, to transsexual, to bisexual, and everything in between. All races, all predilections . . . there are an infinite number of ways you can insert unit A into slot B, and there is money in every one of them. I thought for sure that a triple penetration including a double anal must at least offend the laws of physics, if no one else. Not only was it not offensive, but it was hot and people would pay top dollar to watch it. The more hardcore, the better.

I learned a lot about human nature from working for F Street, as well as learning how one can draw on that understanding of human nature to make adult entertainment a very lucrative business.

Not many people realize that the transsexual videos are always top ranking in the peepshows, though you rent or sell very few. It seems that men have a thirsty curiosity for things they will never tell anyone about. They can watch the peepshows without anyone knowing what they are watching. No rental forms, no credit card charges, no possible way to search their Internet cache. It's completely anonymous.

I love to know what people do when they think no one is watching. We all do exactly as we please, whether we speak of it or not. What is to some considered "deviant" sexuality exists on a far greater scale than anyone will ever admit. I find it far more interesting and healthy to study and celebrate it rather than deny and legislate it.

I learned that the government is tough to argue with and you will find very little support from your best customers. When you are on the front lines of the community you get to see how they are constantly trying to shut you down and fine you and zone you out, even though it is obvious that people in the community support your store by patronizing it. You see how one person complaining beats out the multitude who buy from you everyday, because those customers will not admit that they support you. It's very frustrating. So much so that I felt it was time to move on.

My favorite workdays always involved product meetings where we had a round-table discussion on all of the new toy samples that had come in from various vendors. That was something I could relate to. Something tangible that I could take home, and play with and share and use creatively, by myself or with my boyfriend. Toys had nothing to do with someone else's fantasy, or getting through a scene of some girl squeaking like a dolphin, or wasted time fast forwarding. They didn't require any heavy electronics or late fees. Toys were instant gratification—just add batteries.

I was saturated and completely desensitized to adult video. It was like watching static on the screen. When I started buying in 1996, there were approximately twelve hundred titles released. When I left in 2002 there were well over twelve thousand. I think Vivid releases that many a year now. (Just kidding.) Well, perhaps it could be true if you consider Internet content.

I started to realize that I couldn't take another day of looking at Tom Byron's wrinkled balls over breakfast. "Let's see, I'll take two scrambled eggs on an English muffin, with special sauce, and a double anal with some girl/girl on the side. Oh, and I really need to order Dirty Debutantes 256. The first 255 did so well." Get me out of here.

Fate was about to deal me another winning hand. On a Wednesday I put the word out that I was looking for a change. I was thinking about, perhaps, selling videos, which I clearly see would not have been any better for me, but I really didn't have any idea as to what else I could do. I just knew I was ready to move on. That day I received a call from Legend Video, one of my video vendors, urging me to call Pipedream Products Inc. Legend had just signed a toy deal with Pipedream, making them the first adult toy company to offer a free DVD with an adult toy. They were looking for an assistant to Nick Orlandino, the COO of Pipedream Products, who is the often misunderstood genius responsible for all product development and marketing for one of the most extensive lines in the novelty business. Nick is a brash New Yorker with a mind for business and the sense of humor of a twelve-year-old. This is a guy I can learn from. What an opportunity!

I set up an interview on Thursday in Los Angeles. Would it be worth it to leave San Diego and move to L.A. for this? Why not? I can always go home if I don't like it. Was I up to the challenge? I wasn't sure, but it was a great opportunity to find out. I always make it a policy to say, "Yes, I can" before I figure out, "No, I can't." I called him on Friday morning and accepted. Could I start in two weeks? "Of course!"

Now the hard part: go to work that morning and tell this woman I so adored, who took a huge risk more than a few times by believing in me, that I am deserting her and I'm giving only two weeks notice. I wrote out my resignation letter and took it to her with all the courage I could muster. She cried and I cried and when it was all said and done, I rejoiced in the fact that I would never have to look at *Cum Drenched Fuck Sluts From Hell* over breakfast again. I knew I had made the right decision.

I packed up my little apartment and I moved to the San Fernando Valley. Which is, of course, where one must go to reach the hotbed of all things adult. Where else can you see an eighteen-year old, fresh out of the trailer park, grocery shopping in Juicy Couture with a real Louis Vuitton bag? I figured if I didn't make it at Pipedream, I could always get myself a porn career, complete with a heavily tattooed suitcase pimp to shuttle me around the Valley, while he funneled all of my earnings into his burgeoning Ultimate Fighting Championship career. It is always good to have a backup plan, right? At the ripe old age of thirty I could only get work doing "Mature Kink," but there's a niche market for everyone.

What is your best seller?

Glow-in-the-Dark Erotic Dice. It's a simple dice game. One die gives you a body part and the other die tells you what to do to said body part. They are great for those of you who need a structured set of instructions to give you permission to suck your lover's nipple or for those of you who have never put "lick" and "toes" together. Judging from the number sold, everyone on the planet must have at least one set. Turn out the lights—you may even see a pair in your bedroom.

Our Waterproof Finger Fun is quickly running a close second. Apparently, on a global scale, vibrating fingers seem to be an essential element in unlocking intense sexual pleasure. Who knew? We'll see how the Waterproof Finger Fun Tongue and the Waterproof Finger Fun G-Spot turn out.

Do your parents know what you do?

I'm thirty-two years old. I should hope so! Although, my earlier days were spent under the guise of working in a "lovely gift boutique" for the sake of my grandparents, who have since passed away.

My mother has always been very supportive of everything I do. Well, everything I tell her about, anyway. I count myself so fortunate to have a strong woman like her in my life. She is my rock and my ultimate source of love, inspiration, and self-respect. I hope to be able to pass that strength to other women I meet along my way.

My father, on the other hand, quietly informed me a few years ago that my grandfather would roll over in his grave if he knew what I was doing. I find it amusing that he hasn't uttered those words once since I showed up for Christmas driving his dream car. Suddenly my job has become a respectable career. It puts me on the path of achieving the goals of any other self-respecting American.

Forgive me, Dad, when you catch me on this season's episode of Showtime's *Family Business,* molding Seymore Butts's cock. You just keep your eyes on that car in the driveway. It's all in a day's work. Sometimes I have to take one for the team.

Let's hope my grandfather doesn't get cable in the afterlife.

SHEILA RAE

. . . ON RUNNING AN ADULT SPECIALTY STORE, BOTH ONLINE
AND BRICK-AND-MORTAR.

I GREW UP, LIKE MOST American kids, in an average American family, thinking that my next-door neighbors were perfect and my family just the tiniest bit off. My dad grew up in Queens, my mom in the Bronx. This is was a New York City that doesn't exist anymore: a city built on neighborhoods and old-world mores and values. My family fit right in, and then some. Dad had a master's in the '60s at a time when high school graduates were the norm and backbone of an American economy and society about to hit a big change. He was a high-level executive at General Electric, traveling around the country for most of the year. This scenario didn't seem too promising for my parental matrimonial union, and sure enough, they parted ways while I was still in elementary school. Mom, God bless her nurturing soul, raised us to what my two sisters and brother are today, for better or worse, and earned her Ph.D. while doing it.

I graduated college with a Bachelor of Science in Management Information Systems and a minor in computer science from the University of Lowell (Massachusetts). After graduation, I moved to Boston with three roommates, and here the story really begins.

I had a computer-programming job for Grossman's Inc. I traveled around the country installing software and explaining its usage to employees. During these, my Gulliver days, I met my future fiancé.

A few months passed and I grew bored. Someone had mentioned trying to get a job at the Naked Eye, the largest strip club in Boston, the closest thing the Hub had to a Vegas revue. The Crows was a mixture of Damon Runyonesque characters. Wise guys, Chinese, Vietnamese, policemen, and street hustlers all sat together every night to toast the girls and recount their exploits. The Naked Eye was more of a private gentlemen's club than anything else. You could always count on meeting your particular crowd of friends on any given evening and the party to continue at two or three favored restaurants in Chinatown 'til the wee hours. It was there that I met my future husband, in the midst of this atmosphere of sex, money, alcohol, and laughter. Throughout this sojourn I was still naïve about how the rest of the world operated. I was soon to be brusquely awakened.

I had my first date with my future hubby at the age of twenty-four. It was a memorable experience, punctuated by the fact that the FBI pulled us over to question him concerning the Isabella Gardner Museum heist. Meanwhile, time rolled on at the Naked Eye and months became years. Our circle of friends became smaller. Bobby Price, a renowned storyteller whose father, Elliott, ran Caesar's Palace and was featured in the book *Casino,* died. Frank Salemme, dashing, handsome, and loved by the city, also died. There are enough stories about our close friends, like these two, to fill volumes, stories dealing with humor, close calls, and honor to friends and family. On an optimistic note, some of our cronies gained fame and fortune at the same time that others faltered. David Fioravanti became a recent reality show winner and aspiring actor. Brian Goodman (nephew), who after defending his sister from her boyfriend was accused by both, ended up incarcerated. Upon his release, he answered a casting call while having coffee with my stepson in South Boston and wondering what job he could get to satisfy the conditions of his parole. This led to a bit part in *Good Will Hunting,* and then good fortune progressed in the form of *Blow, The Last Castle,* and the series *In the Line of Fire.* Proof positive that sometimes karma does not bite you on the ass, but walks with you arm in arm and gives you hugs and kisses.

The climate in Boston was changing in the nineties. Real estate developers were beginning to look at was then known as the Combat Zone, our own little red light district. The Chinese community began to protest strip clubs in their midst, since Chinatown was expanding in every direction especially south. The funny thing is that the civic leaders who protested the loudest during the daytime licensing board hearings could be seen any night with their cronies occupying booths and sipping cognac at the club. I had it on good authority that the landlord would not renew the lease on the building because of a deal with the city of Boston that would allow him to build parking lots. The license had no place to go, since the owners were too busy with their own agendas to pursue a new cabaret. I sensed the potential for impending catastrophe and started to formulate my personal evacuation procedures. It was obvious the future of burlesque entertainment in Boston was less than certain. The mayor, the media, and the police department all began to blame all the city's ills on the Combat Zone. The Licensing Board was not about to bestow its blessing on an enterprise that was, on the one hand being maligned, and on the other occupied one of the highest-valued real estate areas.

I had noticed the amount of business that the local "bookstores" (as they were known at the time) were doing. The overflow from the clubs, sailors, college students, discreet gentlemen, and a very few ladies from the fringes of "normalcy" would frequent the bookstores in an almost cloak-and-dagger manner worthy of a secret agent. You could see them peering in the storefronts, walking up and down the sidewalk before making their dash inside. You have to understand that during that period, most stores that catered to our sexual nature were often clandestine, backwater operations, managed by cigar-chomping heavies in dimly lit rooms. I had also noticed the lack of couples and the presence of only the most adventurous women. As I began to investigate further, I was told that the adult industry had no place for women except as performers. This business was rough. The customers were usually in their cups and stores were only to be found a stone's throw from each other in the infamous Combat Zone. All this was about to change.

The year was 1996 and my dancing time had empowered me with self-reliance and resourcefulness. My schooling and corporate résumé had prepared me for the business world. I was thirsty for success, and I knew that I wanted to remain in the adult business. I also knew that the strip club business had seen its hey-day in Boston. The "bookstore" venture had no appeal to me in its present form. My plan was simple: to reinvent the concept of an adult store. Make it couple friendly. Make it upscale. Give it aluminum floors. Give it in-vogue lighting. Stock it with the last word in fetish wear. Line its walls with extravagant, hedonistic toys. Make it sensual, sensuous, and splendid. Best of all, make this rakish, swank palace available to all on that invisible conjoinment—the Internet. And so Eros Boutique was born.

I hit the ground running. The first thing I did was secure a locale in the South End, the trendiest, most up-and-coming Boston neighborhood. A place where women, even if alone, would not be in fear for their personal safety or their property. I advertised. I attended fetish conventions. I had my wares displayed at S/M club nights. I appealed to the everyday woman who in this modern era was assuming responsibility for her own orgasm. I secured the most exclusive vendors in the United States and Europe. I fired and hired. I truly learned the meaning of woman-owned and -operated.

It hasn't all been a bed of roses. My son's first day of kinder-garten at Saint John's in Boston's North End was marked by a pro-motional phone call from KISS-108, a national radio station. As my child howled his reluctance to stay in the church vestibule, I was trying to conduct a radio interview on my cell phone. Let me tell you, it's not easy whispering answers to questions on bondage in the sanctuary of a basilica surrounded by nuns. During my first vacation in years, which I took with my mother and sisters, I was contacted by the *Ricki Lake Show* as a consultant. It is very hard to answer questions and try to book guests for a "swingers" segment while you're in a water park surrounded by children and watching your mom go down the water slide.

The adult business is extremely competitive. I spend long hours both at the store supervising the retail concern and at my office maximizing the performance of the Internet. ErosBou-tique.com was one of the pioneers of the affiliate program con-cept, and that fortunately has also been a success. We have been featured in magazines from *Jane* to *Marie Claire,* from *Skin II* to *Hustler* and *Taboo*. We have been interviewed on radio programs from *Berman & Berman* to Howard Stern. We have appeared on shows from *Ricki Lake* to features on Showtime. All in all, it's been a long sweet ride and worth every bump. I'm proof positive that a woman can create and operate an affluent sexual emporium.

JOY KING

. . . ON WEARING MANY DIFFERENT HATS BEHIND THE SCENES, FROM PR TO SALES AND ALMOST EVERYTHING IN BETWEEN.

ON A WARM AUGUST MORNING in 1985, I walked apprehensively through the front door of a typical San Fernando Valley office building to apply for an accounting position. The job would pay more than the one I had, and the thought of working for a mainstream video company was exciting to me. At twenty-one, I was a hardworking, street-smart kid with plenty of ambition but no real direction. I had no idea how my life would change that day.

As it turned out, this mainstream video company, which sold Gumby and Strawberry Shortcake videos, also had a not-so-mainstream division, Caballero Home Video. During the interview, the 250-pound woman who was grilling me for the position questioned me about my views on sex and porn. At the time, all I cared about is that I would make more money; sure, sex and porn are great. So, when do I start?

I started the following Monday and stayed for ten years. During those ten years I grew not just to like porn, but to love it. During my tenure I had quickly moved from accounting to sales and then finally into public relations. It was PR that I really excelled at, and I quickly realized that I could make a difference. Back then, adult companies ran from the press, afraid of their negative stories and intimidated by their influence. I was too new to have these preconceived ideas, and took the press on eagerly. It didn't hurt that I was a young, attractive woman pitching sex stories to men. And as a woman who embraced sexuality and porn openly to women in the media, I shattered the myth that only cigar-smoking, scumbag men worked in this industry. I suspected that my unique position to gain the trust of both men and women in media could help me. At the time I had no idea how right I was.

So, now that I was handling public relations for Caballero it meant that I would be dealing with people who actually *made* these movies: directors, actors, actresses. It was certainly something that I was far removed from while doing accounting or selling the product on the phone, but I was up for the challenge, and since we had signed Tori Wells and Tami Monroe, it was my job to get press out to meet these gals.

As you can imagine, I was a little nervous about showing up on the set of a porn movie in the late '80s. It was still the taboo business that many were trying to make illegal, so I was somewhat apprehensive when I first arrived on the scene. That day's set was a warehouse that had been converted into a studio in a low-rent part of town—the kind of area my dad always warned me to avoid at all costs. Now here I was parking my car and walking into the building where porn was being filmed. What would Dad think? And let's not even ask Mom. . . .

Fortunately I had decided to go to the set of a director that I had met several times and truly admired, F.J. Lincoln. He and his production assistant, Patty, are really great people and immediately made sure I was okay. It wasn't anything like what I imagined, but I'm not really sure what I was thinking it was going to be like, anyway. There were a couple of crew guys hanging around smoking and talking while two completely naked people sat taking a break from the action. I settled into a spot hidden from view, trying to take it all in. While I tried to get my heartbeat back to normal, Freddy was going over the next couple of shots with his cameraman and cast. It went something like this:

Freddy:	"Okay, so now we're gonna change positions and shoot from the back."
Cameraman:	"Um, okay, so from over here?"
Freddy:	"Yeah, that's good. Okay, honey, now you're gonna be over here and I want you doggy style."
Porn Girl:	"Doggy? I hate doggy. Why can't we just do reverse cowgirl or something?"
Freddy:	"You hate doggy? Why do you hate doggy? No, we need doggy!"
Porn Girl:	"God, I hate this shit. My pussy always farts when I'm in doggy. God, why can't we do something else?"
Freddy:	"Oh God, come on! No one cares if your pussy farts, now let's just do it so we can move on."

Definitely not the kind of conversation that most people would overhear at work. But in the end, Freddy got his doggy and the girl stopped whining. For the record, her pussy did not fart during the scene, much to my disappointment. I was just dying to watch that scenario.

While I enjoyed working at Caballero, specifically for Al Bloom and Howie Klein, they had made some difficult decisions and sold the company in 1994. Although I was loyal to my employers, I was not thrilled with the new owners, who quickly pilfered the product and lowered the standards of quality that had made Caballero one of the true legends in adult. The need for PR had declined and I found myself back in sales.

Unhappy with my current situation, I started to look elsewhere for a new home. A good friend of mine, Steve Orenstein, had started his own production company in 1993, Wicked Pictures. We had discussed the possibility of having me join his company but had been unable to figure out where I fit. Finally, in January 1995, Steve signed a new girl and had the vision that I could promote this girl, do sales to the mail-order giant Adam & Eve, and become part of his growing family at Wicked. In February I became the fifth employee at the company and met the girl I would be working with for the next five years, Jenna Jameson.

Wicked had just finished an eighteen-month contract with Chasey Lain, and Jenna had a lot to live up to. There had been a great deal of buildup before I actually met Jenna. I wouldn't say I was disappointed, but let's just say that she wasn't what I expected. Short and slightly mousy, she was shorter than me by seven inches and I felt like I should squat down to speak to her like a child. But that quickly changed when she started talking. Her sense of humor and quick wit was a perfect match for mine, and we quickly became close friends. More important than her sense of humor, Jenna knew exactly what she wanted. She didn't know exactly how to get there, but there was no question about who she wanted to become. I remember sitting in my office and listening to her say, "I want to become the biggest and most successful porn star ever." That was that. Whatever she needed to do to make that happen was what she would do. It was my job to make that happen. I was ready for the challenge, so we got to work.

In the beginning, Jenna would plop herself on the other side of my desk and wait for me to give her something to do. It was usually a lot of hanging around doing nothing, but eventually pounding the phones paid off, and she did a few phone interviews with some adult publications. I was aggressively pitching her as the next big thing, and when I was successful in scheduling the interviews, she hit it out of the park, backing up my boastful claims. Her charisma and passion were easily conveyed over the phone lines, and soon we had hordes of press desperate to get on the set and meet the new Wicked Girl. Everyone soon became convinced that she just might be the next big thing. If we had only known . . . .

Our sets became a three-ring media circus. It got to the point where directors were more than a little annoyed with my open invitation to the press. Hey, I was just trying to do my job, but looking back, I can see why my pack of photographers and jour-nalists were a pain in the ass to a director trying to film a movie in a short amount of time. I was constantly pulling Jenna away for a few minutes with a magazine or a photographer, holding up filming to get a few more stories or pictures out there. I can't even tell you how many times my press guys outnumbered the crew, but I'm sure there's a director or two who can.

I'll never forget when we shot the movie *The Wicked One*. This was a going to be a big movie for Wicked, and especially for Jenna. One of the things Jenna wanted to do was establish herself as not just another fuck bunny, but a talented actress who could win awards. This movie would be her most challenging, and she was ready for it. At the time, she was dating Brad Armstrong, our big director, and they worked tirelessly on it. Because it was such a big movie for us, I invited an arsenal of press to cover the event and get as much exposure for the project as possible. By now Jenna was a media darling and *everyone* wanted to come. And come they did. I don't want to exaggerate, but let's just say that we were not prepared for the onslaught of press that day.

I spent most of the day in the kitchen trying to help catering deal with an extra twenty mouths to feed, something I hadn't anticipated. In the past, the press would show up, take a few shots, ask a few questions, and move on. This time, everyone showed up and dropped anchor. I was simply not ready for it. Neither was the crew, who had to constantly step over them and remind them to keep quite while filming was going on. Through all of the chaos, though, Brad Armstrong somehow managed to pull it off, and Jenna shone like the star she was becoming. In the end, no one else remembers the stress or chaos I created on the set, because the only thing that matters is that Jenna was nominated for and won Best Actress for her role in *The Wicked One* that year.

At the end of my road with Jenna, I think we did okay. We went to Cannes, did the Howard Stern thing, shot for mainstream magazines, photographers, talk shows, Web sites, newspapers, and news programs. When all was said and done, Jenna was becoming a household name. In my heart I know I had a hand in it, but I also recognize that the stars had aligned just right to allow it all to happen. Steve Orenstein was generous and had immense vision. Jenna was everything we said she was, her projects for us, mostly at the direction of her ex-husband, Brad Armstrong, were a notch above everything else out there, and I had started the ball rolling with marketing and an aggressive public relations campaign. Hard work and determination had paid off. I'm very proud of what Jenna has accomplished in her career. I feel like I watched her grow up, and in some ways I guess I did. But Jenna wasn't my only responsibility for Wicked. Let me tell you about a company called Adam & Eve.

Back in my days at Caballero I had learned a great deal about selling to mail-order companies, and in particular, the largest adult mail-order company around, Adam & Eve. Because Adam & Eve is a complex and extremely successful company, if you strive to learn as much about their business as possible you can greatly improve the amount of business you do together. Over the years (fifteen and counting) I have amassed a great deal of knowledge about their operation, and it was been one of the most enjoyable journeys I have had in this industry. I've never encountered a company with more integrity and more honest employees than Adam & Eve. It most certainly starts at the top and works its way down the ranks. Read their company mission statement and you'll understand.

Let me explain why I wave the Adam & Eve flag so high. A couple of years ago, our sales manager left Wicked. Steve had to find a replacement, and his first thought was me. After all, I had met Steve while I was doing sales for Caballero. It seemed like the perfect solution to him. However, it wasn't an easy decision for me. Not because Steve doesn't have a great product—on the contrary, what Wicked produces is much better than most. The bigger issue was something that I had experienced while doing sales at Caballero, and I feared that it might still be an issue. Unfortunately, I was right.

Being a woman in an industry dominated by men isn't easy. Especially since we're selling sex, so to speak. I have been fortunate to work for some really great men who treat women with respect. But trust me, they are the minority. I mean no disrespect to the "nice guys" out there, but believe me, I was faced with more sexual harassment doing sales than in any other position I have held in this business. I don't know why that is. In any event, I wasn't anxious to jump back into sales considering what I had dealt with in the past. On the other hand, I was much older and wiser now and thought that maybe it wouldn't be an issue.

Doing national sales for any distribution company requires quite a bit of travel. In our business it means trade shows, sales trips, store signings, vendor shows, etc. I was used to traveling, since public relations requires the same type of trips, but here's the difference. Doing PR, I'd deal with some press (sometimes at night clubs) do photo ops, hang, and then head back to the room. I'm not suggesting I didn't do my share of partying and occasionally watched the sun come up, but rarely, if ever, did a journalist or photographer imply that they should get laid for their story. But that's exactly what happened when I did sales.

Let me share one particular incident with you.

I'm in Las Vegas (or maybe it was Atlantic City—these shows tend to blur together) during one of the trade shows. All the usual suspects are hanging at the bar after the show trying to figure out who they're having dinner with and what to do after that. It's a typical scenario. If you're in sales it's pretty much required, since *all* of your customers will be there. Go, buy them a drink, and hang. Not tough work by any stretch of the imagination; in fact, it's kind of fun. So I'm there along with some other sales folks (we tend to hang together since we have to talk to the same buyers), and a group of us decides on dinner, and gambling after that.

Dinner is an overpriced, entirely too-long event that always turns into a yawn fest. I enjoy great service and delicious food, don't get me wrong, but three hours is two hours too many. However, it provides an excellent opportunity to really get to know the people you're doing business with, so you endure. My harasser that night was a fairly new customer that I didn't' know too well, so I was anxious to spend time getting to know him better. I wouldn't have guessed by the dinner conversation how the night would end.

After hearing about his wife and kids, life in the suburbs, and vacations in the Caribbean, the check arrived, and the ten of us headed to the casino. The wine had flowed at dinner and everyone was feeling A-OK. We split into smaller groups and found tables to play blackjack. My new customer seemed interested in staying with me, and since he was a potentially large account, that was fine with me. Until he made his move. At one point while at the tables he put his hand on my knee. I was startled and jerked my leg out from under his hand. How rude. I glared at him and he smiled back. At this point there were other people around so I didn't want to embarrass him, but he was out of line.

I'm not sure who coined the phrase "what happens in Vegas stays in Vegas," but I wasn't entirely on board with it that night. My harasser didn't give up easily, and I finally had to create a scene in order for him to leave me alone. I'm sure the alcohol had a lot to do with it, but it was frustrating to be ten years older and dealing with the same bullshit. "You're an attractive woman working in porn, surely you: a) put out, b) have no morals, or c) have worked in front of the camera, so who cares?"

I hope I'm not coming off like a victim or a whiner. I knew going in that working in the adult entertainment industry would bring me face to face with certain stereotypes and situations that wouldn't be pleasant. I accepted that, with the hope of changing it. But the situation I described happened to me more times than I care to recount. It's unfortunate, but it's what it is. It is scenarios like these that make me proud to work with a company like Adam & Eve. In over fifteen years of meetings, tradeshows, parties, signings, and dinners, I have never felt uncomfortable or awkward. This is truly a testament to their professionalism and ethics. I applaud Phil Harver for his body of work on behalf of this industry.

So, here I am now. It's 2005 and I've been with Wicked for ten years. My position has changed several times over the years, but at this point my business card says "Vice President of Special Projects," which is fancy-speak for "I handle sales to Adam & Eve, put together comps, and screen our movies for final approval."

Last year Wicked decided to start creating and selling four-hour compilations. For anyone who doesn't know what that is, it's basically editing scenes together from existing movies, packaging them, and selling them. Sort of like a greatest hits music CD, but much more fun—it *is* porn, after all. At the time, I had the most extensive knowledge of our library and eventually ended up with the job of putting the projects together. Let me give you a typical day in the life of Joy King.

I generally get to the office between 8:30 and 9 A.M. and spend about an hour deleting spam. If I'm lucky, I actually have some *real* e-mail to answer, which only takes a few minutes. Usually it has something to do with a shipment to Adam & Eve—maybe masters have been approved on something I created for them. Easy stuff. I send some e-mails to let my contacts know what's coming up, schedule meetings for my upcoming trip, and send e-vites for my biannual dinner that we have when I come to their town. But we'll get to that a little later.

Once the e-mails are done it's time to start making porn. My biggest challenge is coming up with titles for compilations. I'm afraid that I'm not really very good at it, although I have had a few winners (*Taco Flavored Kisses* was my personal favorite). Our sales manager, Tony, is the most creative at it (*Trading Races* and *Sweet & Sour Porked*). I lean on him heavily for help, although lately our director of new media has had some big winners too (*Amazing Lace* and *Vertical Blondes*). So after I get a title, I pick scenes, create edit notes, coordinate materials, and voilà! A comp is born.

After I complete that list, I have to watch it to make sure what I asked for is what really ends up on the tape. So, just to give you a perspective here, I'm creating four four-hour comps a week, or roughly one a day, if you factor in re-edits, changes, and pulling the visuals for the box. If you combine that with our standard production schedule of movies, I watch roughly twenty-five hours of porn a week, or thirteen hundred hours a year. That's a lot of movies. Thank God I work for a company that considers quality to be an important factor when producing films. I can't imagine watching this much adult entertainment if it wasn't good quality. I honestly don't think I could stomach it.

That being said, I don't consider myself a pervert or addicted to porn. It's just my job. I happen to think it's a pretty cool job, but it's still just how I make my living. It's a good living, but still my living.

In the end, I would like to think that my life and work has had a positive impact on the adult entertainment Industry. I have tried hard to overcome negative stereotypes and hope that in some way I have helped to accomplish that. The things I have done seem trivial to me, but I am constantly reminded that I have helped legitimize porn on a mainstream level. I am too humble to accept that my role has had the impact that some suggest.

With all of that being said, my twenty years in the adult entertainment industry have been a mixed blessing. I say mixed, because although I've enjoyed tremendous success, it has come at a price. I think any career mother with a career understands what I'm about to say. As the main support of my loving and wonderful son, Greg, I often put my career first and justified it in the name of supporting him, when all he needed was for me to be home. I have missed family gatherings, funerals, weddings, and other events because I was working. I can't go back, so instead I move forward and try to be more aware so I can balance my personal and family life with my career.

I have met some of the most incredible people on my journey in this world. My friend turned boss, Steve Orenstein, is now my brother-in-law. I am grateful that our paths crossed and equally grateful for my sister, who is now happily married to him. Matt, Sydnee, Devinn, Gina, Kimbirly, Jenna, Dana, Juli, Theresa . . . It's a short list, but thanks for being my "true" friends.

The adult industry taught me many things. But the most profound is that if you have ambition, whether you're willing to be naked or not, you can succeed.

JEWEL DE'NYLE

MY STORY ISN'T UNLIKE THE others. I started dancing at the tender age of twenty-one at a little club in California that was connected to an adult shop. I wanted money, pure and simple. I wanted to make enough to save so I could open up my own business someday, whether it be a boutique, a floral shop . . . what it was going to be didn't matter—I just wanted to be self-employed. Every day when I'd arrive to work to dance, I'd walk around the store and look at all the beautiful women on the box covers of porn movies and think, "Wow, I wish I was as beautiful as they are." Of course, I didn't know at the time that airbrushing was a big part of the illusion. Either way, I never thought in my wildest dreams that I was ever good enough or pretty enough to step into their world. I thought of myself as a house girl stripper and was content with that, until the day a porn star was featured at my club and saw me onstage. She was blown away by me.

Her name was Selena Steele. Selena was the door that opened up a whole new world. She approached me and we talked about the business, and then she gave me some contacts. I went for it. It wasn't long before Jewel the stripper was left behind and Jewel De'Nyle was created.

My first scene was with Peter North for Joey Silvera, and they were very taken by me. In fact, Joey hired me several times after that, and Peter dated me for two years, so I guess I had a talent. That was a rare thing that only came along once in a while, but I didn't know that at the time. I just thought I was the new girl and everyone wanted a piece of me, but as it turned out, they never stopped wanting me. When I got into doing scenes, I had a goal from the gate, and that was to run the show. I knew someday I would do whatever it took to get what I wanted. The price was high, but I didn't care. What else was I going to do or put on a résumé? If I was going to use my pussy as a bank, then I damn sure wasn't going to do it for nothing.

From day one I saved every dime I made. I looked at it from a gambling standpoint: my body was a slot machine that companies and people were willing to keep putting money in, and I'd be damned if I was going to go bust. I had a brain and an ass, and wasn't afraid to use either of them. I made sure I gave everything I had when I did scenes to ensure I never looked burned out or sick of what I was doing, because I knew I had to keep my fans wanting more. After winning over twenty-five awards in this industry in six years' time, the first being in Cannes in 1999 after being in the industry for only eight months, I won Starlet of the Year and never looked back.

Years passed quickly, and I needed something different. I wanted more than just spreading my legs—I wanted to be the one filming it. I approached Jill Kelly Productions because I knew they were a company that aspired to hire women talent. So Jill Kelly and I had a meeting at the Four Seasons in Vegas, and boom! The next step of my career was accomplished. I was now behind the camera and not just in front of it, and wow, what a rush it was, being 100 percent in control only two years into my career! My JKP days didn't last long, though. I finished out my contract and then I was let go, as my movies were considered too hardcore. For the life of me I couldn't figure it out—why am I too hard? I was naturally hardcore, so I never looked at it as being outside the norm. In fact, all the fluff stuff that was out on the market bored me to death and I wanted no part of it. In my mind, I never wanted to shoot masterpieces, I wanted to shoot masturbation pieces. So for me, being hardcore wasn't an issue. And as it turns out, it wasn't an issue in the sales department, either.

Within a day of finishing up at JKP I was hired by Puritan. Puritan liked my hardcore sensibility. Of course, JKP eventually did too as they realized that my movies were chart toppers, but it was too late. I'd moved on to a company that let me have the freedom to be my natural nasty self and didn't want me to shoot the fluff I was bored to death with. I stayed with Puritan for almost two years. They were fantastic, and they gave me an opportunity to shoot gonzo porn, which not everyone was doing at the time. I was looked at as being a bit eccentric, but anyone who had worked with me knew it was my style and didn't expect fluff from me from the get-go. You have to realize that back when I started as a director, I was one of the only women shooting hardcore. All the other female directors were shooting features, and I was doing something different and edgy. Not that there were a lot of female directors at that time. At that point I could count on one hand how many of us were behind the camera.

So after shooting my series *Babes in Pornland* for Puritan I was finally recognized by the porn world as one of porn's leading ladies—not just for my performances, but as a director, as I was given an award for one of my movies at the 2002 *AVN* Awards for Best Sex Scene—Video for *Interracial Babes*. I won for a sex scene I did with Lexington Steele in that movie, but not just for the scene. It was also a scene I directed in a movie I created. I couldn't believe it. Out of the thousands of movies reviewed, I won, and to this day that was the moment when I knew I had what it took to be a great pornographer.

The time had come—I was ready to venture out on my own. I

had accomplished everything I set out to do except for one goal: to have my own company. I put my directing and performing for other companies behind me, as they were getting rich off my name and I was getting just a small piece. I couldn't settle for that—I needed more. After years of hard work and not living lavishly or driving a fancy car, I put my money back into my name and Platinum X Pictures was born.

I started out with three business partners, but now it's only me and one of my best friends, David Joseph, running the show. PXP had its share of hard knocks in the beginning, as I was a female running the show in an all-boys-club industry. Pussy ruled in front of the camera, but it was pretty much not excepted behind the camera, let alone behind a desk in an executive position. I'm a powerful person in this business, so I always get someone who likes to run their mouth and say how I don't own PXP or that I didn't start the company. I'm vice president, and I make all the decisions along with David on all company policies. So for those who think I'm just using my name while others run the show, they are very mistaken. Many of the good ole boys talk down to me and have hurt me any way they can, but all it did was to put me on the map. The more shit they talked, the more press they gave me. I had a name, and no one was going to stop me from building my own empire.

But I had other reasons for wanting to launch my own company. I started PXP instead of fully retiring off the money I made so that I could give my parents a job. My father had lost everything, as he was a politician, and porn and politics go together like oil and water. I remember when the FBI showed up and raided their home for child porn just to smear my father's name because he had a famous porn daughter and someone wanted his seat in the legislature. It was a total setup. Nothing was ever found. At one point they showed up at my house and tried to get me to say something, anything bad, about my father, and even threatened me personally to try to get me to talk. All I did was slam the door in their faces after I told them to come back with a warrant or I was calling the police and would have them escorted off my property. It was all a fine mess. Can you believe all this over doing adult films? As I slammed the door in the face of the FBI, all I could do was yell, "Stop spending tax dollars on bullshit!"

At any rate, I couldn't stand seeing my mom and dad getting crushed by the media and the public for having a daughter they supported in a legal industry. Porn cost my family everything. But after all the madness, it gave back everything and then some to me and my family. My parents stood by me when I was ready to fall and they came to California to help me out with my company. Without them, I wouldn't have the success I have today—they kept me strong when it seemed the whole world was trying to break us down. I have the strongest parents one could have. They lost every dime—their house, their credit—and never once did they blame me. Instead, they dusted themselves off, moved on, and started over. Porn is not as glamorous as one is led to believe. Once you're in, you and your family are marked for life—especially if you have family in high places, like I did.

But not only did it cost my family's well-being, it cost me a marriage.

I started PXP with my then-husband, Michael Stefano. Working together and being married took its toll over time, and my marriage failed. Michael and I were a dream couple, the powerhouse couple in the business. I got him out of a bad situation at another company and put all I had behind him to help him build his name and reputation so he could ride to the top with me. But lo and behold, I created an egomaniac. All of a sudden I lost my husband. The man I loved became a man obsessed with himself and his money. I somehow got lost in the shuffle. I gave him the world, and without my money or name he wouldn't have been the star he is today. No doubt he's a good performer, but he wouldn't be as recognized if it weren't for my backing him every step of the way. Michael forgot one big thing—us—and cared only about himself and his stardom.

I couldn't take it anymore and filed for divorce. The man I helped create turned against me and did everything in his power to ruin PXP. I couldn't understand how a man's ego could get so big that he'd want to destroy a company we created together, so I had to let him go, as I knew it was a lost cause. The man I married vanished before my eyes and Michael Stefano the porn star took over. Michael had to be let go from PXP for the good of our company. He had let his resentment of what I had created get the best of him and would never acknowledge the success of the empire I'd created. Anything I'd done that he didn't do on his own he couldn't stand, as he was the star, and no one else was as good as he was. Some nights I'd lie in bed crying and ask myself, "Why? What did I do to deserve this?" Okay, I fucked for a living and filmed people fucking, but was it really fair that my personal decisions had such consequences?

But once the smoke cleared and my thoughts got back on track, there was no stopping me. I was now more determined then ever to prove I would make it. I'd come too far to turn my back now, and I'll be damned if I prove my critics right. The harder people tried to knock me down, the stronger I got. Now I've never been so happy. I have a huge company, one of the top companies in porn. Our numbers doubled in less than a year, we're in almost every magazine, and everyone wants our product all over the world. And my parents have never been happier.

I believe everything in life happens for a reason, and my reason is that I had to go through what I did to give my parents a life they could only have dreamed of and to open the door for all the other girls who have come after me. Only the strong survive, and it was a test of survival. I felt this was my chosen path— to be a leader, so the females in line behind me have it easier than I did to prove they are more than just a pretty face.

LAINIE SPEISER

. . . ON PROMOTING SOME OF ADULT'S MOST
RECOGNIZABLE BRANDS.

IT WAS TRULY A SCENE out of the film *Boogie Nights,* complete with its supporting actress and real-life porn star Nina Hartley. It was my promotional party for the hardcore rag *Fox* magazine, a closing party for the East Coast Video Show. I was proud of myself because all the greats were there—Ron Jeremy, Jill Kelly, Jewel De'Nyle, Gina Lynn—and hosted by my all-time favorite porn couple, Anna Malle and Hank Armstrong. At *Fox,* we had our own special shtick: the actual porn personalities were also the editors and publishers. It was a great tool for a publicist, an easy way to keep the media machine going, because the girls were in the magazine every month. Anna Malle was the stripper editor, a sexy, outrageous, horny, and happy woman who adored being the naughty center of attention. One of the reasons I loved Anna so much was that it was immediately obvious to all who met her that she was truly a fun-loving, crazy nympho who was lucky enough to find a forum that would allow her to behave like this and get paid for it. For a promoter like me, it is these women whom you most want to work with, because they loved what they did as much as I did.

Anna and Hank made the perfect swinging sex couple. She looked so different from the other women in this business. In a sea of blondes, she was dark and exotic, with an American Indian lineage. Her high cheekbones, dark hair, caramel-colored skin, and wiry, rubber band of a body that screamed high energy set her apart from the rest. She loved to fuck. She loved men and women, and even in our off time she always managed to make every occasion a celebration. Hank was the yin to her yang. He looked like a retired football player, big and blond, mellow and likeable. Of course, he also had a humongous cock, and whenever anyone in the office happened to have a big banana we would take a pen and write "Hank's Crank" across it. When they came to town we would all be excited and giddy because they were so much fun to be around. "The Malles are coming!" we would jokingly cry, "The Malles are coming!"

My party with "The Malles" was held at a duplex suite in the Sands Hotel and Casino, outfitted with booze, food, a bartender, and a big pool table. By midnight the place was in full effect, and I could tell that even the publisher, Russell Orenstein, was pleased. Then again, what Italian-Jewish heterosexual wouldn't be? The soiree was dripping with tanned, tight bodies that were topped off with big fake tits, their nipples out and proud in their flimsy dresses and halters, standing at attention like a cherry on top of a frosted cupcake. Anna glowed in a Bebe number, which was really just a very fancy, silky, gold robe with two buttons fastened at the waist, a matching gold G-string, and spiky fuck-me heels. She ran around the place like a squirrel on amphetamines, laughing and talking and charming the shit out of everyone. At one point, she was hopping about with an empty champagne bucket, begging tips for the bartender, who was swarmed by heavy drinkers like flies on a giant turd. "Everyone! Everyone! I just want you all to know that RON JEREMY just put FIVE DOL-LARS in the bucket!" She waved the fiver high over her sleek, dark head. "FIVE DOLLARS! RON JEREMY!" And of course we all laughed and cheered because everyone in the business knows The Hedgehog is one cheap mofo.

My boyfriend, Tom, was there, too, taking photos of it all and looking like Jimmy Olsen turned rock star, with his black leather pants and ribbed black turtleneck offsetting his shiny blond hair and teenybopper angel face. He took a photo of me and Nina Hartley, whom I gushed at in admiration. The well-preserved, middle-aged sex pot purred and ran her hand inside the blouse that exposed my midriff. "Ummm . . ." she said in my ear. "You're soft and smooth like a woman should be." Nina ran her tongue along the outline of my ear and Tom happily clicked away while my face turned hot and red. "Awww, you're so sweet." I said, "Thank you." Anna jumped to join us for a pose, grabbed Tom's leather-clad package for a tight squeeze and shouted, "DAMN, HE'S HOT!!!" Then she turned quickly to me. "I hope that's okay, Miss Lainie. I'm just goofing around." I was touched by her good manners and I elbowed her narrow torso. "Oh, Anna. You know you're the only one I would allow a free grope."

Tom and I had met on the job. He worked as a copy editor, and our big romance, we suspected, was an object of scorn among some of the higher-ups on staff. It was one thing to have a fling, but this was an exclusive relationship, and we were in love. Tom and I were quiet and discreet about it, but he was coincidentally fired soon after we were spotted by the office manager cuddling on the number 6 train at 8:00 A.M. His presence at this party made my boss, Russell Orenstein, quite uneasy, but I just decided to ignore it. Yeshiva schooling had taught me a few things. The biggest was never to act guilty about anything you're doing, whether it's wrong or right. Besides, there were plenty of provocative nubiles around, treating him like an emperor. By 2 A.M. it was time to break it up. Anna and Hank were going to use the suite to shoot "Swinger Party" footage for their Web site and possibly to sell it as a DVD. She had her heels off at that point and stood on the glass coffee table. "I want to thank you all for coming! I want to thank *Fox* magazine! I want to thank Russell Orenstein! I want to thank Miss Lainie for throwing this wonderful party!!" There were claps and hoots among the guests. Then Anna clapped her hands together and said, "Now, for those of you who are here to fuck, please stay! And for those who aren't, please collect your coats in the upstairs bedroom!" Tom looked hopefully at me, but I quickly dashed that. "Okay, Bud, let's go," I said. In the upstairs bedroom Anna and I hugged and I thanked her for being her wonderful, sweet self. Anna, thin and small-boned, somehow managed to catch me off guard and knocked me over, landing me on the bed, where she promptly jumped on top of me, straddled me, pinned me down, and yelled, "YOU WILL LIKE GIRLS!!!!" Of course, she was joking and we laughed and rolled around like kids. Tom took photos and said, "That's what I keep telling her, Anna, but she doesn't listen."

Outside in the cold, damp, Atlantic City October night, Tom and I strolled on the boardwalk looking for beer and burgers to bring up to our room at the Tropicana. "We could've stayed," he said. "We could've just watched and fooled around only with each other." It is a letdown to be dating a career porn person like me. You think I will open you up to a world of freewheeling sexual experimentation, only to find I'm just as uptight and old-fashioned as any other woman, maybe even more so. Because I really don't care about the pornography itself. I just love the women and the business. I'm like a drug dealer who doesn't touch the stuff, making me able to achieve a longevity. I shook my head and fished out a Marlboro from the pack. "No, no way," I said. "That wouldn't be professional." A year later we were no longer a couple, but we would still be together, both of us working at *Penthouse* magazine, and still friends.

Fourteen years ago it started as a mistake. I was twenty-two, fresh out of college and having trouble finding and keeping permanent employment. I had just been let go from Harry Abrams, an art book publishing company, for being weird and refusing to take a drug test. I was broke, and there was a recession going on.

Magazines were on the decline, folding right and left. I had two respectable internships under my belt, *Spin* magazine and the *New York Press,* but at both places I'd found the experience to be dismal, boring, and generally negative. Everyone in publishing seemed nasty and bitter, and it wasn't what I thought it would be at all. It was corporate and uptight, filled with WASP trust-fund kids who had their families supplementing their paltry publishing incomes. Everyone was tense and tenacious, yet happy to eat shit for just a chance to write a measly record review and have their name in print. Everyone took it and themselves very seriously, and it was totally different from the kind of person I had grown to be. All I had to offer was creativity, enthusiasm, ideas, and a loud, bodacious personality to go with my loud, bodacious appearance. I was not at all wanted. But I kept plowing through the want ads and answered everything that had anything to do with magazines, books, or newspapers. I had a B.A. in journalism from the School of Visual Arts in New York City, and I was in love with publishing. Some company just had to appreciate that, and one finally did.

I had sent out so many résumés and cover letters that I just stopped keeping track, so I was thrilled to get a call from Montcalm Publishing's director of promotions, Cecelia Giunta. Montcalm produces smut titles raging from mild to hardcore (*Gallery, Fox, and Lollypops*), and through my ten years there I would gradually rep them all. But when I got that call I didn't know squat about the place. Cecelia Giunta informed me that I had answered an ad looking for a promotion assistant and it would be for *Gallery* magazine. "Do you know what kind of a magazine *Gallery* is?" she asked. I only knew of *Gallery Guide* and said, "Sure, it's the art magazine. I know it well." Wrong. "No." she said. "It's a men's sophisticate," she explained. I had no idea what the phrase "men's sophisticate" meant, but this time I chose to stay silent. "It's like *Playboy,*" she went on to say. "Do you have a problem working with erotic material?" A nudie? Porno? Edgy, provocative, rebellious, under the radar and underground? "That sounds perfect for me," I said with a big smile. "That is completely fine with me." Even on the phone, before we'd even met, I knew I had the job. Not only a job, but a career, an identity, a family, and a home.

You can smirk, sneer, and giggle all you want about my choice of business, but you can't deny that pornography is the purest and most old-fashioned form of entertainment that will ever exist, and it will exist until the end of civilization as we know it. It is shameless but real, hocking not just sex, but beauty, glamour, and fantasy. The best entertainment gives you the promise of escape, and no industry delivers that better than porno. I've always been a dreamer and I loved this industry right away because of that, but it is hard for my fellow journalism alumni to take me seriously. They work for the *New York Times, Vanity Fair,* and PBS, respected institutions that perform important services in regard to the media. I bring models to *The Howard Stern Show* to talk about their lesbian experiences, write press releases that always include cup sizes, and take phone calls from women at 2 A.M. about filling their Valtrex prescriptions in the remote areas of South Dakota. Of course, in knowing me, my friends find an ornament and conversation piece for every cocktail party, introducing me to their friends as "Lainie Speiser, the sephardic porn peddler." Maybe I'm not respectable but I am interesting and chic.

Can I admit this? I'm embarrassed to admit this, but it's true. There are so many times through the years that I've wondered why anyone bothers to come to any of my autograph signings, club events, radio contests, and trade shows. Scores of men always show up and I wonder why. They're all kinds of men, not just weirdo Star Trek types who live in their parents' basement. I've met wealthy men, businessmen, young men, old men, married men, single men, fathers and grandfathers, Americans, Europeans, and Asians. They stand and wait there in a crowd or a line just to meet a *Penthouse* Pet for one minute, only to say, "Hello," tell her their name, and have her sign a magazine or an 8x10 glossy. Sometimes they pay for me to snap a Polaroid of him standing with his arm around her, and she signs that too. I wonder, "What's he going to do with that? Stick it on his fridge with a magnet? Put it in a frame and display it among the family photos? Keep it in a box with his other centerfold keepsakes?" I understand the fascination with celebrity, with sexual fantasy, with silly crushes on people you will never have in your life, but when faced with the object of your daydreams, isn't the reality of being just another fan in line, another face in the crowd, another person in a meet-and-greet, just a huge letdown? Of course, the *Penthouse* Pets are every bit as beautiful in person, many times even more breathtaking, because no photo or Webcam can capture, say, the *Penthouse* Pet of the Year for 2003, Sunny Leone. How Sunny's eyes dance when she laughs. How her skin glows. How sweetly charming she is. But the fact that they will never have Sunny, for this moment of "What's your name?" or "Where are you from?" would crush my fantasy forever. To me, it's best not to break that barrier. Also, the fact that if any of these men linger too long I will always make sure they know it's time to go. I am part of that letdown, and it's a strange position to be in.

I really don't worry about it too long though, because none of the fans seem to care anyway. Their fetish for collecting pictures and autographs easily outweighs their emotional desires and needs. When I took Sunny Leone to Rhode Island for appearances at the erotic retail chain, Amazing Superstores, I met some characters who were so obsessed by her photographic two-dimensional image that they barely acknowledged her when she spoke to them. They came for serious business, completing their Sunny Leone collection. One frequent customer to all Amazing Superstore celebrity appearances came with is own cardboard box of Sunny: her magazines, her slicks, her DVDs, and her trading cards. He also supplied his own special markers and felt-tip pens, the ones he knew would not fade, far superior to my black Sharpies. He did accept the free *Penthouse* publicity photo that comes with the purchase of the magazine. But I swear, he did not look at the real flesh-and-blood Sunny once. With his head bent, he instructed her on where to sign on each precious item and what to say. I hoped she wouldn't make a mistake and drive him into a freakout where he would run around the store screaming and flailing and knocking over displays of strap-ons and vibrators. Fortunately, as always, Sunny was a pro, and after he left she rested her pretty head against my hip and asked me if I could run across the street to get her some chocolate. Which, of course, I did.

I played and slept with dolls past the age most girls get bored and discard them. Even though I had breasts and was menstruating by age eleven, I still hugged my baby doll Nigel and my red-headed replica of myself, Lainie-Doll, to me every night, and my mother encouraged it, visualizing my future as an excellent wife and mother. What she got instead was a full-grown woman who, at the age of thirty-six, is still single and childless but very maternal, using these skills on porn stars and centerfolds. Being on the road with the girls is like a never-ending slumber party, and I credit that to keeping me looking and acting young and fresh. We choose outfits together, swap beauty tips, complain about men, confide in each other, and sometimes we even cry together. When I visit my mom and see the saved drawings from my childhood—all of the girls in outlandish clothes, heavy makeup, and big hair—I can't help but wonder if I just got the calling from an early age the way some people get when they become priests or nuns. A beautiful woman to me is not just an object of sexuality or titillation, but the representation of success and happiness.

I grew up in a dingy working-class town and spent a lot of my time alone the first few years of school because I was a sickly kid. All I had were my drawings and watching the soaps with my mom while she did her sewing. All those women on those soaps in their sexy clothes and perfect makeup and hair. I wanted to grow up and be just like them. In the afternoons, my mom and I watched a lot of old movies, and I got turned on to Marilyn Monroe, Joan Crawford, Lana Turner, and Jayne Mansfield. These women were pure sex and fantasy, far more than the actresses of the twenty-first century.

Those women were more pinup than anything else, and they personified what all females were supposed to be. To this day, I'm much more comfortable in a skirt and nylons than I am in jeans and a T-shirt. My family knows how I've been making a living all these years, and it hasn't phased them one bit, but I also attribute that to being raised in a European family, as I am a first-generation American. Nudity was never a big deal in my home anyway, but sometimes I laugh when my mother says, "It's not that I mind that you work for dirty magazines, but I wonder why you love it so much. It disturbs me." So much for the dolls, soap operas, and old movies.

I once dated a long-haired, crunchy guy who was an organizer for a musician's union. He was totally my physical type: tall and stocky, with a sweet voice and low-key disposition. I thought we'd have a good relationship, but I thought wrong, because he was very repelled by my choice of vocation. "You know," he once told me, "you are exploiting women. No matter how you slice it, that is what you're doing." Sometimes the far left can be just as annoying and narrow-minded to me as the far right. We were drinking beer out of paper bags and sitting on the grass in Tompkins Square Park, and I was tipsy and feeling arrogant and said, "No, no way! I exploit MEN! It's MEN who get exploited, not the women! The women are in complete control. It's the men who get the shaft. I play with their emotions with this crap." I don't think I made a good case for myself either way. When it comes to heterosexual sexuality, women do hold all the cards. Women don't need porno mags and movies to get off. Men do. Women don't buy porno because they can have sex virtually anytime they want, and when they want it they aren't afraid to ask for it. It's not because we're prudes. It's because it's at our fingertips. Anyway, I've never seen women suffer from low self-esteem at the hand of any *Penthouse* magazine or Jenna Jameson DVD. Women in porn come in all shapes, heights, races, ages, and sizes. There are all kinds of ideals. It's the fashion magazines that make women feel fat, ugly, and unattractive. Don't blame *Penthouse,* blame *Vogue.* All the women are five foot eleven and weigh a hundred pounds. Their bodies look like boys. You are being dictated to by men who don't even have sex with women, and by women who don't shop at department stores. I felt like an ugly duckling before I became the Sephardic Porn Peddler. I thought I was too chubby, too short, too busty, too unconventional-looking. But in this business I bloomed and became confident, self-assured, and happy. When I walk down the street, women look at me because they wonder, "Why does she seem so content with herself?" I've been allowed to grow as a person and to be myself without anyone slapping me down and telling me to conform.

I made a good friend and coworker in Pet of the Year 2004, Victoria Zdrok. We had more in common than with the other Pets because we are both in our thirties, educated, and European, and the only time we ever wear sneakers is when we work out. Victoria is the most unreal-looking, real-acting centerfold you will ever meet. That is to say, she's had lots of plastic surgery and has no problem talking about it. In fact, she loves to talk about it. Tall, blonde, and Ukrainian, Victoria has been in this business as long as I have. She started out as a *Playboy* Playmate and became the Pet of the Year ten years later at the age of thirty-one. Some Pets like to brag about their ability to get any man they want, but Victoria likes to brag about her education. "My hobby is col- lecting doctorates and degrees," she loves to tell the press. But it's no bunk. Victoria has a J.D. and a PH.D. and got those degrees with high marks. Because of that, and the fact that she's incredibly fun and free-spirited in a classy, put-together package, I've probably achieved my greatest media successes with the commercially-friendly Victoria. And never has a centerfold actually given me a to-do list—repeatedly. I would get five or six e-mails a day from Victoria, asking me to get her in *Maxim, Jane* magazine, CNBC, Fox News. You name it and I did it for her. She pushes me and inspires me and I adore her for that.

But we've also had arguments, passionate ones the likes of which I've had only with my sister or mother. "I don't want to do that motorcycle rally," she once bitched. "It's not my kind of appearance." I told her all *Penthouse* appearances, as far as I was concerned, were her kind of appearances, besides which she had committed to do this months ago and her face was on all the posters and advertising. "I know, I know I agreed, but I don't want to," she whined. "Send one of the other Pets to do it. I know the other girls like this stuff," she said. "Its too low-class for me. I don't like being around low-class people. It depresses me." Now, I consider myself to be above average in the patience department. I will listen. I will pamper. I will indulge. I will stroke. But one thing I cannot handle is hypocrisy, and I let my friend and talent have it, but good. "You know what's low-class, Victoria?" I said to her. "What's low-class is shimmying out of your panties at the Webster Hall promotion and selling them to a fan for two hundred dollars! Don't give me that shit about class! What was classy about that?" At which Victoria, instead of getting offended, burst into giggles. "Oh, Lainie! What was I supposed to do, give the guy my panties for free?" She knew she had got my goat and was enjoying it big time. "How about keeping your panties on?" I shouted in my cubicle. "How about that?" The whole office hears my booming voice all through the work day, but luckily they find what I talk about quite entertaining.

Victoria is now slowly phasing out of nude modeling and reinventing herself as what she calls a Sexy Sexpert, using her certification as a sex therapist and her Ph.D. in psychology to do some good for her fans, both male and female. She's *Penthouse* magazine's new sex columnist, and she tells everyone that one day she's going to tie me up and use all kinds of sex toys on me. None of the girls can believe I don't own a vibrator, but I tell them, "I got two hands, don't I?" Once when Victoria and I were doing a tour of Chicago, she went on a toy shopping spree at an adult store called Frenchy's, which was generous enough to let her raid the store of their goodies. Like a mother to a spoiled child, I told Victoria, "Mind your manners. Don't be so greedy." Which of course made everyone laugh, and as we exited the store Victoria told them, "I can't wait to get to the hotel room and try them all out." To which I said, "Yes, and by the way, we happen to be sharing a room." Which made the store employees laugh even more. When we got back to our Holiday Inn suite, she hit the bathroom and I lit a smoke, both of us embarrassed about what the other one was doing, but doing it anyway. Victoria also doesn't drink alcohol, do drugs, drink coffee, smoke cigarettes, or anything else, because she doesn't want to cloud her mind. Sex, she says, "is my ultimate high." God bless her.

Just for the record, this industry isn't made up of only madcap hipsters such as myself. It's all kinds of people of all ages, races, and creeds who make your pornography. When I worked at *Gallery,* there was a sixty-year-old Italian Queens grandma named Terry who headed the advertising department, and at *Gallery* that was entirely composed of phone sex and sex products. Terry had gotten married while still in her teens and never had sex with anyone but her husband, and there she was, a good Catholic woman, reading sex ads and checking to see if they were clean enough to be printed in Canada, which has stricter guidelines than we Americans do. The only problem was that Terry didn't understand what half the lingo meant. "Lainie, can you come in here?" she'd call to me. "Can you tell me, hon? What does 'rim job' mean?" She'd sit at her desk with her pink cardigan wrapped around her shoulders and her half glasses sliding down to the tip of her nose. "It means tonguing someone's asshole," I said, flipping through her ads. I loved the video ads that were so dirty there were black bars and circles hiding half the action. It made it seem super-duper dirty and bad. "You're kidding. People really do that to each other?" I'd nod and she'd shrug. "Okay, that can go through."

I've made friends in porn publishing who, although they have long left it, still remain very close to me. There's Paul, the former art director of *Gallery* and *Fox* magazines, who bears a striking resemblance to Pee-Wee Herman. Since he always knew he was gay, he has never seen a naked woman up close in his life. But he was great at his job, although sometimes he would get tired of staring at spread pussy all day and would yell, "God damn! If I see any more roast beef I'm gonna lose it!" Now he's the top art director at *Adweek* magazine. "Porn, advertising, it's the same thing." He dismisses the difference. I guess he has a point. Another good friend I made was Rose, a left-wing earth mother who doesn't shave her legs, wear makeup, or care about fashion trends. She was the copy editor at *Gallery* and would constantly bitch at her boss about giving the readers a lot of biological misinformation. "What's all this with women coming in squirts and gushes and buckets! Women don't orgasm like that and we shouldn't say they do! It's our responsibility to give the correct information. These guys have enough problems." Her boss didn't listen. I think he thought Rose to be a Femi-Nazi, but she was absolutely correct, although her griping did her no good.

In fact, in all the naughty magazines, you can always read about women squirting and gushing and coming in great buckets. I wonder if men wish we could physically react as dramatically as they do? When I started working at *Penthouse,* I was told that the publisher, Bob Guccione, ran photos of women urinating for that reason. Because when a man is sexually excited there's motion, there's action, and when a man has an orgasm, there's proof with the squirting of semen. But when a woman is excited or has an orgasm, well, you can't really capture it well on camera, hence the peeing pictures. Men could get excited by seeing the woman's vagina in motion. I know, I know, it seems pretty farfetched to me too, and it obviously didn't set the world on fire. Mr. Guccione slowly watched his empire crumble until he lost *Penthouse* late last year. It was sad, but inevitable. With *Maxim* and *FHM* beating us porn peddlers at our own game, the world just doesn't want to see hardcore in print anymore. It's too embarrassing, too expensive, too one-dimensional, and now it reigns supreme on the Web and in DVDs. I myself might have to accept that there will be a time when I shall have to say good-bye to all of this, but for now, thank goodness, this isn't the case.

I always tell the girls they have to offer the fans more than their pretty faces and perfect bodies. With thirteen-year-old girls running around in hip huggers so low you can see both their butt cracks and their pubic bones, flesh is everywhere. I try to encourage them to cultivate their personalities and their interests. So I have Pet Crystal Klein playing piano in the nude on Howard Stern or I have Victoria Zdrok offering sex advice to Victoria Gotti on television. Still, there are girls all over the world who want to peddle their wares and show the world how gorgeous they are, naked and proud.

For Spring Break 2004 I was doing a promotion in South Padre Island, Texas. It was absolutely wild, with girls ripping off their bikini tops and mugging for the cameras. Sunny was on that tour and she was running around with her digital video camera, taking content for her own Web sites and making me think about how the exploited are becoming the exploits—what a great twist of events. Sunny was dressed in tight jeans and an equally tight *Penthouse* ribbed wife beater, encouraging the drunk, young things, saying her baby-soft voice, "Can you show me your pussy?" Later, we were on a boat, a booze cruise, with some bikini contest winners. It was dark and chilly, and I'd had a few beers and needed to pee like a racehorse. "Go ahead and piss then," Hot Carl, the host of the bikini contest, said to me, and gestured at a naked girl with her bush in the breeze, urinating off the side of the boat. "No," I said, "I don't think so." I asked, "Do you know when we're heading back to the club?" He informed me, "Not for a while," so I climbed on another boat and begged them to take me back to the club Parrot Eyes pronto. They did and I barely made it in time, but I made it just the same. I flushed, washed up, and touched up my burgundy lipstick. Then I heard a voice behind me yell, "Oh, *Penthouse* lady! *Penthouse* lady!" I turned around and saw a nineteen-year-old blonde, beautiful and naked and standing with the toilet seat between her long, slender legs. She let out a long stream of urine and said, "Do you think I'm good enough to be in your magazine?" I smiled and said, "Well, you certainly are, except for one thing. We don't do pee shots anymore." But I wished I had my camera with me. It would have been a great shot for my monthly promotional column.

Oh, well. There will always be others, that's for sure.

JODI MARIE LINDQUIST

. . . ON LENDING AN ARTISTIC EYE TO THE INDUSTRY.

WHEN I WAS ABOUT FIVE years old, I discovered the bottom shelf of my parents' bookcase. This is the shelf that I called the "sexy" shelf—and as difficult as it was to get to (I had to pull a footstool, rocking chair, and stack of photo albums out of the way), I found myself sitting there in awe about three times a week. To accompany my introduction to the naked line-drawn human figure, and close-up insets 2a–4b, I would take a well-deserved bubble bath, which subsequently led to my introduction to self-discovery. After being discovered unexpectedly in the bathroom during one of my "bubble baths," I swore off the sudsy for a good four years. This was my first true introduction to shame, falsely placed upon myself because of family values, or some kind of religious dogma that stuck during a Sunday service when I was too young to decipher right from wrong for myself. Regardless, I caught wind of my sexuality at a pretty young age. And my curiosity for sex and everything related grew greater with every inch of my adolescence.

My family was really pretty closed lipped about sexuality. My father would like to think that I am still a virgin, and I rarely tell him anything to the contrary. I'd prefer to remain the perfect little baby girl, youngest of five, smart and determined, with a good head on my shoulders. For some reason, as soon as you admit that you are a pervert (or have a good friend who is), all credibility is thrown out the window. That is the reason that during my years of living with my parents (even after we relocated from Minneapolis to the hipper and sexier San Diego), I saw no evil, heard no evil, spoke no evil. And that just made my perversion worse. Moving to California was the greatest moment of my young life. Granted, the first five years sucked ass. The culture shock was intense. Remember, I was coming from the Midwest, the Bible Belt, the farmer John-Boy "sheep at the edge of a cliff" type of place. I mean, I don't even think they knew where wool comes from in bleach-blond, surfer-dude, two-tacos-for-a-dollar 1980s San Diego.

After graduation, I moved to Los Angeles with the serious intention of attending the film department at Cal Arts. Somewhere between moving my belongings to Los Angeles and enrolling in classes, I lost my way a bit. I guess being studious during my high school days made my desire to party as much as possible a bit more intense than it should have been. I dropped out of art school and convinced my parents to support a less expensive three-year stint at a junior college. I made only about five of my classes during that first year, deciding to focus on Pot Smoking and Boy Chasing 101. I received an A for effort—and an A+ in my extracurricular activities, I might add. I lived in a great first apartment. I mean, all this space, all this time on my hands, and *no* parental supervision. It was awesome. And my two slutty roommates had to agree. I owe my sexual overexperimentation to them. I learned from the best. Something that really struck me was the amount of insecurities these girls had. I mean, these were beautiful girls, funny, easy to get along with, open-minded. But deep down, they were so sad. Maybe it came from their mothers. Both of them came from single-parent households, and their relationships with their mothers were anything but solid. I hate to say it, but their lack of self-love only made my desire stronger to love myself completely.

I think the first job everybody gets in Hollywood is a shady gig of some kind. Mine was customer service for a phone sex company. I was underage drinking at a local Sunset Strip rocker hotspot, screaming something about having no money because my parents had cut off support and I didn't know where my next meal was going to come from, when this incredibly hot guy caught my fall off the curb, saving me from an oncoming car. I was wearing a roommate-inspired miniskirt with black-and-white striped tights and a shitload of bangle bracelets (come on now, it was the early '90s) . . . ooohhhh, I thought I was the bomb that night, I'm sure. His name was Ryan, and if I hadn't been so drunk I would have pulled him behind the cars and given him a blow job right there. I gave a lot of blow jobs back then. I had the idea that blow jobs were much more innocent than full-blown intercourse as long as there was no penetration. There was no sex had here. Today I think it is called the Clinton Notion. Anyhow, he offered me a job at his company. And, not even really knowing what I was getting into, I joyfully accepted.

For about a year and a half I took perverts' credit card numbers and patched them though to what they were fooled into believing were hot, sexy singles just waiting to talk to them. Girls with 24-36-24 measurements, long, flowing, clean hair, dressed to the nines in their garters and fuck-me pumps, rolling around on red satin sheets. I was selling them the fantasies they wanted to believe was their reality, and it was for $4.95 a minute. Hundreds of minutes a day. Every once in a while I would get the lonely guy who hadn't paid his last month's credit card bill, whose card was declined, wanting to chat with me for a while. At first I wrote them off, reciting the prewritten script sitting in front of me: "I'm sorry, sir, I am with the Customer Service department . . . if you want to talk to one of the beautiful girls on the satin sheets, you're going to have to give me another credit card number." But after I moved to the graveyard shift and the calls came in pretty thin, my boredom got the best of me and I began to indulge the fuck out of these guys. I had quite a knack for it. I could dirty talk like no other, and I really loved the feeling of power it gave me. I was controlling the entire situation. These guys were mine. And when I told them to bend over and lick the floor, I honestly believe they were doing it. I know so, because I could hear the echo on their linoleum. I never felt any sexual satisfaction from these phone plays, but I did like the feeling of satisfying the male libido. That was incredibly sexy to me.

I think it was about then that I myself became somewhat of a slut. I was on a determined mission to create the New & Improved blow job. And, let me tell you, I wasted no time in perfecting my craft. The whole thing fit quite well with my "no sex" policy—you know, the one that allowed me to convince myself that I was still a good little Catholic girl you could bring home to Mom and Dad. Although, I was also the kind of girl that was eyeballing your father from across the dinner table trying to size his cock up. What a little hootchie I was when I look back on it!

Eventually Ryan's small phone sex company was bought out by a corporation, and I had no interest in continuing my career as a CSR. So I bailed out and found myself working as a cocktail girl at a strip club by LAX. Cocktail girl is a bit of a stretch—it was more like soda jerk, considering the club was completely nude and we didn't serve alcohol. I loved my job. I made way too much money for what I was doing. During a typical week I'd make $2,000, and I only worked three days a week. It was brilliant. Strippers are a unique bunch. I never had a negative thought about the fact they twirled around a pole naked for a dollar or two for six hours a night, and there was a huge part of me that was tempted to switch over to their side. Something about it seemed very empowering to me—dancing nude, imagining you were somewhere else completely, while men threw money at you. I was transfixed by the whole scenario. Many years later when I was broke and desperate, I would attempt the pole dancing myself. After missing my cue and walking out on stage during somebody else's set and then eating shit at the end of the stage, I retired my clear-bottom stripper shoes for greener pastures. I give those girls a lot of credit, though. Dealing with a bunch of civilians groping and groaning night after night is not a bowl of cherries, or chocolates, or even sex toys.

After random not-even-worth-mentioning jobs and years of trying to figure out what I wanted to do for the rest of my life, I came to the conclusion that I was just going to have to discover what my true calling was by trial and error. Being the TV junkie that I am, I've always had a serious addiction to commercials. The cheesier the better. My subscriptions to magazines were solely for the ads, which constituted 80 percent of the content anyway. That being said, I received a BA in advertising from the Advertising Arts College (now it's the Art Institute of California) in San Diego.

The number one thing I learned in school is that Sex Sells. Sex Sells Everything. They didn't necessarily teach us that—it's the silent truth. You've got a kitchen gadget to sell? If you have the model in your dime-budget infomercial wearing nothing but a cutsie apron and a hot pair of fuck-me pumps, that whatchamadoozie will *fly* off the shelves. And as an advertising copywriter, I could convince you with those tantalizing words paired with just the right colors that pull at the psychological heartstrings to buy, *buy,* BUY! Mind over matter. That, as well, applies to pretty much everything.

Once again I found myself packing my belongings and hitting the congested eight-lane yellow-lined trail up to Los Angeles, after graduating from college, pretty convinced that *this* time I would shine. I would be a star. I would be rich. I would take the advertising world by storm. Once again, disillusioned. Once again, my first job out of school was in adult entertainment. This time it was for a magazine I had never heard of. The magazine was *AVN—Adult Video News*—which I think is a starting point for the majority of the adult industry, talent or otherwise, and I was their new advertising designer. Here is where I truly discovered I had a bit of an obsession with porn. Gonzo was defined for me graphically, whether I liked it or not. Trannies and midgets and clowns galore graced the screen as I stared in awe, amazement, and horror. I dove head first into this curious industry. Fascinated by what I considered to be the security of these men and women to perform these sexual acts (most of which I did not know existed, much less had catchy names attached to them), I made sure I watched every film I could. *AVN* had this small closet filled to the rafters with screeners and novelty items: the porn closet. I helped myself quite often. So often that I began to feel guilty about it. To combat that guilt, I decided to give some of the movies away. This is about the time all my friends, new and old, officially labeled me a pervert. I noticed the lack of invitations to social events, especially when my friends' friends were involved. Whatever. I think the reason I have always had guy friends as opposed to girl friends is because boys not only embrace perversion, they require it.

When I'm in a group of guy friends I tend to talk a lot about sucking dick, especially when I'm drunk. Actually, I don't necessarily have to be drunk, but it's a good excuse for talking so much about fellatio. It gets me out of trouble with the girlfriends— mine *and* theirs. I tend to encourage the conversation to move toward sharing sexual experiences—likes and dislikes. I want to hear what the guys have to say. I want to hear something I have never heard before. I think more like a guy than like my nit-picking, oversensitive, catty female counterparts. I always have. Shit, I may as well have my own set of balls . . . and if I did, my hands would be all over them.

My next job in the industry was a complete 180 from my design job. I met a veteran director in the industry, Paul Norman, who had retired from directing and was now doing postproduction work. He took me under his wing and taught me the ins and outs of editing porn. I was thrilled. I mean, I had intentionally come to L.A. to be a filmmaker, so this was (in theory) what I really wanted to do. Right?

Now I was submerged in porno 24/7. Literally. I worked night and day. I think my favorite part of working with Norman was listening to his stories. And, shit, did he have stories. He was old-school, and with me being as new-school as new-school could get, I hung on every word he said. I was visualizing something close to what I saw in *Boogie Nights*: the pretty girls and guys with moustaches and cutoff shorts hanging outside by the pool in the San Fernando Valley, snorting drugs and engaging in unprotected orgies, all while sipping on margaritas and listening to great tunes blaring on the hi-fi. According to Norman, I was pretty close. I learned all about the porn edit formula: meeting, petting, girl oral, boy oral, insertion, fucking (position one), insertion, fucking (position two), optional position three, f.i.p. (that means "fake internal pop" for the softcore edit), and . . . drum roll please . . . the Money Shot. And, fade out. That pretty much sums up the pornography edit.

The great thing about editing was watching all of the stuff that doesn't make it to the final cut. The girls complaining about their feet hurting and their knees being sore from the hard floor. The newcomers freaking out about the male talent they are paired with in the scene because they know what kind of cock size they were dealing with. The men griping about the tardiness of the ladies. Bitching about house payments and car payments and their agents. The lack of ability to memorize three short lines and pronounce four-syllable words. Having to cut during a scene because the drugs or booze had really kicked in, and they couldn't finish the scene. The unfortunate event of wood loss. The overabundance of liquids, some expected and some not so expected. The reality of the whole thing. Because very little, if any, of what actually makes it to tape is reality. These directors create a fantasy world with their sets, their makeup and wardrobe, and their story lines. Porn is selling a fantasy. And fantasy is what the consumer is buying. Needless to say, I burnt out on editing pretty quickly. I think I was only there for about a year, if that. My creative frustration got the best of me. I was ready to do something different. I was at the point where I could recognize talent by their moans, even in fast forward. At that point it tends to sound like little purse-size dogs yelping. Very amusing, and very, very annoying at the same time. My boss continually rehashed the fact that the average porn viewer doesn't really want it artsy. They want it dirty. Dirty in a systematic way. Therefore, I decided it was time to create dirty artistically somewhere else.

It was around this time that I really started becoming comfortable with my body enough to finally let my sexuality come out of its shell. I didn't realize how much I had been keeping it under wraps. There were guys I dated here and there who had serious insecurity issues themselves, and to compensate for their own issues, they would tend to pick at my naked flaws. You know, my "birth-giving thighs," my "third nipple," my "velvety meat drapes." I had one boyfriend (if you could even call him that) who had me so insecure about my vagina that I was considering Vaginal Laser Rejuvenation. Basically, trimming my labia so it looked "prettier." What the hell was I thinking? That kind of insane consideration made me really start to question my own self-confidence. Have I been faking my security all this time? Is everybody fooled by my big smile and smart glasses? Am I trying to fool people? As confusing as it was, it was equally liberating. I began to get in touch with that sexual goddess inside that was hiding from the world, scared to come out because I was too concerned with what other people thought. Oh sure, I could talk the talk—blow jobs and anal sex and threesomes—but when it came to face-to-face, lights out, time to get naked, I could not walk the walk. Those devilish bedroom delights that danced in my head constantly zipped back up into the recesses of my mind, only to resurface as a dirty poem I wrote in my journal. And finally, I was slowly but surely becoming liberated enough to experiment sexually.

Right before I left my editing job I met my match, David. He was in the business as well, and that was a bit intimidating to me. Before meeting him, I preferred to engage the industry personally from afar. Stay behind the scenes. I just watched porno, edited porno, and created porno advertisements. He had porno friends and went to porno parties and had porno sex with porno chicks. Once again, my curiosity got the best of me and I dove into this porno relationship head first. I found a man who loved everything about me. My naked self was his piece of cake, and he ate it too. Enter my complete and unquestioned sexual revolution. There was nothing I didn't try. And by nothing, I mean *nothing*. Role play, golden showers, anal, threesomes, strap-ons, foursomes, four guys on one, yadda yadda. I fulfilled any fantasy I had had. Anything I saw in a video and wanted to try, we did. It was a beautiful thing. Granted, it had its ups and downs. It was emotionally testing at times. But it's during those emotional extremes that we really learn about ourselves. We don't know our limits until we test them. And shit, did I test them. Let's just say that only a handful of those games stayed in our sexual routine. The rest lost their appeal after the fourth or fifth time like a glow stick in the morning after an all-night rave. So exciting at first, and so boring and dull after the fun is over.

After two long, jobless years, I now find myself an art director at Pure Play Media. I spend my workday creating box covers and DVD wraps, catalogs, promotional materials, business-to-business and consumer advertising, collateral pieces, Web advertising, and other miscellaneous creative pieces with the intention to increase porno revenue dollar. Which is, as with any industry, the bottom line. The only difference in this industry is that we package and sell sex instead of perfume, clothing, music, or cars. Seventy billion dollars a year worth of sex, to be exact.

Before I became an art director, I was assistant to a brilliantly insane fine-artist who had been with a director by the name of Michael Ninn since the beginning. He helped me fine-tune my Photoshop skills, which is the key to being a successful artist in this industry. My first months of work consisted primarily of going through thousands of stills shot on set to create photo collections that would be used to promote the title, from the box covers and advertising to press pieces and media reviews. It's our job to make these girls flawless. Perfect, seamless skin devoid of wrinkles, moles, laugh lines, tummy folds, hair, blemishes, personality. Again, selling the idea of fantasy. To be honest, I was mortified at this process. I have always had an appreciation for those little things like laugh lines—to me, *that's* what makes a woman beautiful. But in this business, too many signs of reality on a box cover could kill the sale of a title.

My most difficult task was matching these cast-list names to a face. I would search the Internet (Google being my saving grace) for their image. I would find it, and still be left clueless. The face staring at me on their home page looked nothing like the stills I had in front of me. "Oh, that's her . . . no wait, she has blonde hair, green eyes, and thin lips . . . this girl is a brunette with blue eyes and big dick-sucking lips." It's amazing what a bottle of hair dye and a great makeup artist can do for the transformation of the girl-next-door to porn starlet. Eventually I figured that the key to proper porn star identification is the boobs. Especially if she's got a bad rack job. No amount of makeup or editing can conceal a bad "Ziploc bag look" boob job. No sir!

Over time, I have become incredibly familiar with every girl in the industry. Whether I like it or not. You know that saying, the eyes are the windows to the soul? I've seen into the souls of hundreds of these girls. The range of emotion I get is astounding. In the eyes of these young ladies I see these little girls filled with the same confusion and wonderment and curiosity that I felt at the birth of my self-discovery. The time when you begin to explore life and try new things to find your niche. They seemed caught between pleasure and pain. What a very precariously vulnerable place to be. Some of these girls are teenagers. And, speaking from experience, teenagers don't know shit. Although they all think they do. Nobody can tell them anything different from what they believe to be their truth. On a positive note, there were a good number of eyes that screamed, "I love being double-penetrated by gynormous phalluses and I wouldn't trade it for the world!" Over time, my concern for the well-being of the talent subsided. Basically, it comes down to the fact that life has to be experienced, trial and error, whether it is fucking on film and exploring your sexual limits for the world to see, or fucking around in junior college while exploring your drinking limits for all your friends to make fun of.

Unfortunately, I have come to a case of the Beauty Burnout, as I like to call it. Something about picking apart all these naked women and airbrushing them to perfection, correcting and revising and rebuilding them pixel by pixel, has caused me to be incredibly unimpressed by the beauty I see. Is that really what these people look like, or is it a fantasy somebody is trying to sell me? I know that game, or at least I think I do. But it's a fine line between fantasy and reality. Something which I question constantly. I may have a heads-up, but I, too, am fooled too often. My eye has been trained to find the "flaws," and as I work hard to undo that horrible programming, it hasn't happened yet. I tend to point out the crooked noses, the uneven eyes, the underarm skin, the neck wrinkles and the nonproportional torso of random hot girls crossing the street to whoever is willing to humor me. The lesson I've learned: there is no airbrushing or altering the beauty that is inside. And with each day that I discover my own beauty, I embrace those pesky flaws on the exterior even more.

Another concern I face is my desire to see the extreme. Nothing seems to shock me anymore. Yet another reason for my pervert-phobic friends to uninvite me to their Christmas parties . . . but I'm coming to the end of my "porn for entertainment value" phase. Refund please, because I am not entertained. I'm sure my feelings are shared by the majority of this industry. We've all seen it before.

I watched a trailer for a new feature the other day, and I was completely captivated by the unexpected violence that was juxtaposed against a calming atmosphere setting with a mesmerizing operatic female vocal audio. I was watching it with several other people I work with, and they were mortified by the entire scenario. Yet we all watched it over and over again. I made a mental note to myself to give props to the director for creating this catastrophe that completely satisfied that craving of mine to experience something new. A piece of adult entertainment that urged me to ask questions. Because if we don't ask questions, we never really learn. Then it hit me—what I was seeing on the monitor was nothing that I would ever attempt in my own sexual playtime. In all honesty, it was degrading to me as a female, but something about it caught me and still hasn't let go. It was the reality of emotions caught on camera when the director called "Cut!" and the tape kept rolling. From sexual fantasy to wakening reality in a split second. Life is just like that, I suppose. It is just rare to be able to rewind again and again and again.

I've only been in this industry for five years, and I will probably be here for a while longer. I embrace the open-minded thinking that encompasses the industry, and the togetherness we share as constant frontline fighters for our First Amendment rights. I've always believed in speaking my beliefs and opinions aloud, expressing my creativity freely, and sharing life experiences with others across a million mediums. On that same note, I like my opinions and beliefs to be challenged by louder voices than my own. It keeps me in check. And keeps me questioning things I don't know. My seasons in the porn biz have taught me to accept myself wholeheartedly and wear my perversion proudly. Embrace my naked flaws and slight insanity, because I truly know that these are the things that make me one of a kind and set me apart from every other piece of ass.

In life, if you don't ask questions, you never learn. This is my motto. You can't talk religion or politics or art with the majority of people. Sex is the one thing that you can talk about—the one thing everybody has in common. And, whether they admit it or not, they like to talk about it. When you discover that somebody shares something that you have always considered strange, weird, or alien, it is one step closer to finally being comfortable in your own skin. *That* is the difficult thing about our existence: finding true comfort in our own beautiful, imperfect skin.

ABOUT THE CONTRIBUTORS

Joanna Angel, writer, journalist, producer, model and adult film actress, is founder and owner of BurningAngel.com, an independent site that celebrates the intersection of sex and rock n' roll with hardcore photos and movies alongside her interviews with punk and indie bands including Marylin Manson, My Chemical Romance, the Bouncing Souls and Bad Religion, among many others. Referred to as the "queen of altporn," Joanna has been featured on *Playboy* TV's "Sexcetera," Fuse TV, KSEX Radio and in numerous editorials, including the *New York Times,* SCREW, XBIZ, Fleshbot, *AVN* and *Heeb,* which featured her on their cover and named her an "up and coming Jew." Joanna holds a B.A. in English from Rutgers University and is currently working on a book project—among her numerous professional and provocative roles, she considers herself a writer above all.

Many agree that **Danni Ashe** is the most successful woman in the history of adult entertainment. In the mid-1990s, she was among the first to recognize that the Internet had the potential to become a new, exciting medium for adult entertainment. In 1995, she taught herself HTML, built Danni's Hard Drive (www.danni.com) and launched the site with her own capital. In 2000, the *Guinness Book of World Records* named Danni Ashe the most downloaded woman on the Internet. As the company continued to grow, Danni's role shifted from being the site's primary model to driving the vision and direction of the company. Today, Danni's Hard Drive has expanded to become one of the world's most successful entertainment companies providing a full range of products well beyond its initial Internet offering. Under Danni's leadership, the company now encompasses a network of sites (including www.mishaonline.com, www.crystalklein.com and www.ericacampbell.com) a production company for adult films, a licensed consumer-products division and a global content-distribution channel. Danni continues to drive the company's future direction.

Juli Ashton and **Tiffany Granath** are the hosts of Nightcalls 411 on *Playboy* Radio.

Violet Blue is an author, editor, female porn expert and professional pro-porn pundit. She is the Assistant Editor at Fleshbot.com by day and a human blog by night. Violet has been a published sex columnist and trained professional sex educator since 1998, and lectures to students about human sexuality in UC's and community teaching institutions. She is the editor of four anthologies and the author of four books, two of which have been best-selling sex advice books since their release and have been translated into French, Spanish and Russian. Her influences are J.G. Ballard, David Sedaris, John

Waters, Emir Kusturica, Mark Pauline, A.M. Holmes and Patrick Califia. She has been interviewed, featured, and quoted as an expert by more magazine, web, television, and radio outlets than can be listed here, including *O (Oprah) Magazine*, NPR, CNN, *Wired, Esquire*, and Web MD. For more information visit her website, www.tinynibbles.com.

Jewel De'Nyle started her career in the sex industry and moved on to the world of adult not long after. Once she started in the adult industry it didn't take her long to make her mark. Within her first eight months in the business she won Best New Starlet at the Cannes Film Festival in 1999, Starlet of the year at the Nightmoves Magazine awards show, and in 2000, the XRCO awarded her Best New Starlet. Jewel's biggest acclaim to date happened in 2001 when she won two awards at the AVN Adult Awards show in Las Vegas where she was named Female Performer of the Year and also won for Best Girl/Girl Sex Scene. Jewel also has her own signature toy line with Las Vegas Novelties. Jewel shoots for Puritan, directing and starring in her very own series called *Babes in Pornland* and *Fresh Porn Babes*, and is also owner of Platinum X Pictures, which is starting to be one of the leading Gonzo companies in the adult business. Find out more about her at www.jeweldenyle.net.

Emily Dubberley has been a sexpert for over ten years. She studied psychology at university, specializing in sexuality, founded www.cliterati.co.uk, a text-based sex website for women, then created spin-off site www.bibibaby.com, a dating site for bi-curious women. She scripted the last three Lovers' Guide videos, and has written five books including *Brief Encounters: The Women's Guide to Casual Sex* (Vision) and *Things a Woman Should Know About Seduction* (Carlton). Emily was Founding Editor of UK-based sex-positive women's magazine, *Scarlet*, and also writes for publications including *Glamour* and *Men's Health*. She has regular radio slots and has been a sexpert for a number of TV shows, including the *Joan Rivers Position*. She's tested over 200 sex toys in the last two years.

Jane Duvall founded an internet resource guide to adult sites called JanesGuide.com in June of 1997. Since that time she's reviewed thousands of websites, in every area in the consensual and legal spectrum of sexuality. She's spoken extensively on the subject at various panels both adult and non. During the past years she has helped several friends as they start their own artistic/erotic web endeavors. She makes her home in the northernmost part of Washington State with her adored new husband Elliott, three daughters, and various pets underfoot.

Theresa Flynt, the Executive Vice President of Retail Operations, HUSTLER Entertainment, Inc., graduated from Mount St. Mary's College in Los Angeles,

California in 1997. She earned her B.A. in Business Administration with an emphasis in marketing. Since 1994, she has been involved in many aspects of the adult entertainment industry. Most notably, she used her marketing expertise to increase the sales of a diverse group of products for Larry Flynt Publications, Inc. In addition, Theresa conceptualized HUSTLER HOLLY-WOOD In 1998. HUSTLER HOLLYWOOD is the world-renowned erotic bou-tique located on Sunset Boulevard, which has become a blueprint for adult-theme stores throughout the world. With this unique upscale approach, she has redefined and established new trends in the retail industry. With the tremendous success of 10 current HUSTLER HOLLYWOOD stores, she has developed a catalog for consumers worldwide and has begun a plan to develop stores, both domestically and internationally. Theresa is also involved as an advisor and consultant to various new enterprises for LFP, Inc. Most recently, she created an international clothing line bearing the HUSTLER logo. With all of this, she continues to participate on many different levels of free speech and plans to continue on the legacy of her famous father, Larry Flynt.

Dana Harris is a senior writer and editor at *Variety*, where she writes about porn and many other entertaining topics. She is currently completing her first novel, *Nice Girl Like You*.

Twenty-one years into her career as a public advocate for sexual self-aware-ness, sanity, and literacy, **Nina Hartley** is just hitting her stride. An exhibi-tionist with a cause, she created a persona that was wholly new at its inception in1983 but is now part of the broader cultural lexicon: "feminist porn star." Ms. Hartley, first as a dancer in San Francisco and then as a per-former in adult videos, put her body on the line in support of her ideas about sexuality, feminism, personal liberation and social responsibility. A dedicated student of human sexuality for over thirty years, Nina Hartley began her career as an adult entertainer while an undergraduate in nursing at San Francisco State University, dancing weekly at the Mitchell Brother's O'Farrell Theater. Banding together with like-minded women during the "porn wars" of the mid-1980's, she was a founding member of the Feminist Anti-Censorship Task Force, whose impact on mainstream feminist thinking gave rise to a younger generation of sex-positive writers and activists. But it is undeniably as an entertainer that Nina Hartley has enjoyed her greatest success. Through the 600-plus video and film titles she has made, her two decades of dance tours and her thousands of personal appear-ances, she has become the most enduringly popular star in the history of the medium. Long before achieving a measure of mainstream notoriety with her casting in the hit movie *Boogie Nights*, Nina had become an inimitable head-liner. Her portrait, with an accompanying essay, is featured in photographer Timothy Greenfield-Sanders recent anthology *XXX: Porn Star Portraits*, from

Bullfinch/Time-Warner, 2004, introduction by Gore Vidal. At present, Ms. Hartley is completing *Nina Hartley's Guide to Total Sex,* a comprehensive book based on her video Guide series, for Avery, a division of Penguin Group, for Spring, 2006 release. Further information about Nina Hartley can be found at www.nina.com.

Linda Johnson is one fifth of the team that runs Club Jenna, the official company and website of Jenna Jameson. For more information, visit www.clubjenna.com.

A southern Californian native, **Joy King** got her start in the adult industry almost by accident. 20 years later King remains active and committed to bringing a strong female voice to the business side of the industry. Now working at Wicked Pictures (www.wickedpictures.com) as the Vice President of Special Projects, Joy has held positions overseeing the Sales department, Public Relations department, Internet department, and DVD Division as well as sales to mail order giant Adam & Eve. She has also assisted owner Steve Orenstein with Production and Marketing. King is best known for her role in helping catapult Wicked Pictures contract sensation Jenna Jameson to the top of the industry. By working with non-traditional media, King helped Jameson overcome some of the negative stereotypes that exist about the adult industry. An outspoken supporter of First Amendment Rights, Joy regularly works with the Free Speech Coalition by lobbying State Legislatures in the California State Capitol against unfair regulation and bills that could be harmful to the industry.

Seska Lee has her hands in many different pots. She is the creator and Webmaster of Seska's Amateur XXX Page (www.seska.com) , her personal porn site, as well as her erotic features website, Seska for Lovers (www.seska4lovers.com). She is a regular columnist at Homegrownvideo, a partner in the neo-burlesque troupe The Coral Lees, and is the Webmaster for the Coalition for the Rights of Sex Workers' website (www.lacoalitionmontreal.com). She was the first Internet Amateur who runs her own website to be featured on the cover of *AVN Online* magazine. She has been a featured speaker at McGill University and Concordia University on the topics of sex work and the Internet. Prior to her adventures in adult entertainment on the web, she was an educational consultant specializing in learning disabilities. Seska lives in Montreal (Canada) in a much too small apartment with her husband James and very old beast of a cat, Catamanga the cat with golden fur.

Laura Leu graduated from the University of Wisconsin-Madison in 2000 with a Journalism degree and a nasty hangover. Then, after a brief stint living in her parents' basement, she landed her first gig as a copywriter at a Minneapolis promotional marketing agency, where she wrote such glamorous headlines as "Three for the Price of One!" Now she's writing such prose as "Threesomes for

One!" as an editor at *Stuff* magazine. Besides the porn article, she has also written stories about spending the night at a brothel, hanging out with a cannibal serial killer and attending Coney Island Sideshow School (where she learned how to eat fire and swallow swords). Most recently, she created a line of women's underwear called UnderDares, which can be found at underdares.com.

Jodi Marie Lindquist is a graduate of the Art Institute of California with a B.A. in Advertising and currently works as the Art Director for Pure Play Media. Originally from Minneapolis, Minnesota, she moved to San Diego at the age of eight—a Midwest girl at heart with a Southern California attitude. After years of searching for the perfect profession, she entered into the Adult Industry in late 1999 as an Advertising Designer for *Adult Video News,* and has since remained in the post-production creative side of the Industry as an editor, designer, and Art Director. A writer since a young age, her fictional stories have appeared in Tattoo Flash Magazine and she has written free-lance articles for *Tattoo Savage, Screamer San Diego* ,and the *San Diego Reader.* Jodi's sexual escapades, reviews, photographs, artworks, musings, and ramblings are out in the open at www.venusenvi.com.

Regina Lynn writes the popular Sex Drive column for *Wired.com* and is the author of *The Sexual Revolution 2.0* (Ulysses Press, August 2005). She won the Western Publication Association's 2005 Maggie Award for Best Online Column, and she has been featured in the *New York Times,* NPR New Zealand, Digital Village on Radio Pacifica, and Midnight Sex Talk on Resonance 104.4 FM in London. Still, nothing delights her more than getting a column listed on FARK.com. Regina lives in Los Angeles with her dog, Jedi, and her fish, Squishy and Nigel. When not handcuffed to her computer, she can be found carving the canyons on her motorcycle or hanging out at the beach with inline skates and a boogie board. Her birthday is in May but she accepts presents year round.

Jennifer Martsolf began her career in the adult industry in 1991 and has since had the pleasure of exploring all sides of the industry from retail to wholesale, DVD to dongs, gift bags to gapers and everything in between. When she's not scouring the globe for goodies to get you off or occasionally appearing in Showtime's reality show Family Business, she's off riding horses and training for marathons. She is currently training with Team In Training and raising money for the Leukemia & Lymphoma Society. Members of the adult industry have contributed significantly to the cause and she would encourage you to do the same by contacting her at jennfst@yahoo.com. For more information on Pipedream Products, please visit www.pipedreamproducts.com.

Mason was a former child star on a very successful daytime television show. In 1998 she earned a degree in political science from Occidental College. After a period of disillusionment while studying law, and piqued by her sexual curiosity, Mason proactively investigated the world of pornography. Shortly afterwards she met porn director Rodney Moore, who offered her an apprenticeship as his cameraperson. Over the next three years she tutored herself in the technical craft of shooting and editing under his stewardship, with additional guidance from esteemed director Andre Madness. In 2001 Patrick Collins offered her the opportunity to direct exclusively for Elegant Angel. She directed the series *Lady Felatio* and *Dirty Trixxx* at Elegant Angel, and after her departure in 2003, she moved on to Platinum X Pictures where she directed *Sexual Disorder* and the critically acclaimed *Riot Sluts*. In 2003 she won the *AVN* awards for Best Vignette Video (*Dirty Trixxx*) and Best Oral Sex Scene (*Lady Felatio*). In 2004 she reclaimed the award for Best Vignette Video (*Dirty Trixxx 2*). You can learn more about Mason online at www.insidemason.com.

Lisa Massaro is the U.S. Editorial Manager for *Club, Club International,* and *Club Confidential* magazines and has been with the publications for 20 years. She has additional responsibilities with their website www.clubonline.com, as well as for Club DVD, a recently formed production company. She's a Connecticut native who says she's too honest and opinionated—as well as not rich or thin enough—to live in L.A. where the adult industry is based. Lisa is a reading junkie who loves music and movies but rarely deals with adult material other than on a work basis.

Hester Nash is the curator of www.retroraunch.com.

Known as the "glamour girl" of porn for her exotic Eurasian features and her background in mainstream international fashion modeling, **Tera Patrick** has won virtually every conceivable award in the adult business, clean sweeping every show and festival from *AVN* to Cannes with the coveted "best new starlet" awards and a virtual shoe in every year to win "fan favorite" from F.O.X.E. to the XRCO Awards. The only girl to appear on the covers of *Playboy* and *Penthouse*—where she's been named Pet of the Year in various countries—simultaneously, Tera has graced the cover of every major men's magazine in the world. She was also the former host and star of *Playboy* TV's Nightcalls 411, the network's top rated show, for two years. Tera owns and operates her Teravision, distributed by Vivid Video, which saw her first two movies under the brand, *Tera Tera Tera* and *Reign of Tera* become number one bestsellers. She also counts herself one of the prestigious Vivid contract girls. Tera is currently the publisher of *Genesis Magazine* (where she was named the number one porn star of The Hot 100 two years running), in addition to being a contracted cover girl for *Hustler.* Tera was also named *FHM* magazine's 36th sexiest woman in the world, while VH1 called her the 16th Hottest Rockstar Wife/Girlfriend! With a monthly sex column for *FHM U.K.*, a book deal, a best selling adult sex toy line through California Exotic Novelties (called The Tera Patrick Collection), and even her own adult talent management company, The Tera Patrick Agency, where she uses her success as a template to help women and men in the industry achieve their goals, Tera is certainly poised to stay on top for a long time to come! In her spare time, she is a loving stepmom to her husband's 10 year-old son, breeds toy fox terriers, and has started a foundation to help people find their lost pets. Presently, Tera splits her time between Los Angeles, New York City, Miami ,and London. Tera is presently on tour as the top drawing feature dancer in the world, and is continuing her pursuit of life, liberty, and shopping. For more information and exclusive content, visit Tera's official site at www.clubtera.com.

Sheila Rae is the proprietrix of Boston-area store Eros Boutique, which can also be found on the web at www.erosboutique.com.

Holly Randall was born in 1978 on September 5, her parents' first child. Though she grew up the daughter of a parental team of pornographers, she had the typically normal childhood filled with horses, books, and yes, photography. Holly took her first photography course at the age of 12, and the moment the print developed before her eyes in the tray she was hooked. A short while after she graduated from high school she moved to Santa Barbara, where she got a job as "the film girl" at Samys Camera. Soon her job there encouraged her to attend the prestigious photography school Brooks Institute, whose students her job forced to be constantly in contact with. After a year and a half of study, she was feeling restless and out of touch with the conservative nature of Brooks. Her parent's website, www.suze.net had just launched, and it was picking up with such alarming speed her parents begged her to move home and help them run things. When back in LA, Holly decided to also pursue her second obsession, literature. She enrolled in and graduated from UCLA in September 2003 with a degree in World Literature. Her new job at her parents' company first began with computer work—basic website maintenance and copyright enforcement. But a short while after working for the site, she had befriended models such as Aimee Sweet and Alexus Winston, and was encouraged to start shooting them. Soon after Holly immersed herself completely in photography, and has been producing work for www.suze.net ever since. Recently, after Suze launched her new DVD line, Holly took over directing and the second camera for all of the hot hardcore scenes Suze Randall Productions has been putting out this last year. In fact, the line was nominated for four AVN awards at the 2005 show, including best director! Her free website can be seen at www.hollyrandall.com.

Shane is a former performer and current adult movie director. Her official website is www.shane.tv.

Jill Sieracki is the Editor-In-Chief of *Playgirl* Magazine, a publication that is the internationally recognized source for women's adult entertainment. Recently promoted from Managing Editor, Jill's mission is to revamp the magazine in an effort to reach a broad, more contemporary readership. She has been charged with acquiring new writers, creating content aimed to inform and amuse, mandate design changes as appropriate and sign celebrity interviews. In addition, Jill will contribute scripts and write editorial for *Playgirl* TV, erotic programming created specifically for women, which can be seen on cable stations nationwide.

Katie Smith began her career in digital media in 1996, with the development of FrontierCoop.com, one of the first successful e-commerce sites in the holistic health food industry. In 1998, she joined *LA Weekly*'s advertising department and took a position as online marketing and sales representative, where she initiated a broad range of online advertising campaigns. Soon thereafter, she became brand manager for The Erotic Networks, where she was instrumental in the development strategy and marketing of several successful web sites, including TEN.com, which is widely considered one of the best broadband experiences online. In 2002 she was recruited by *AVN* and eventually served as director of corporate communications, where she managed the marketing and promotions for the company's magazines, tradeshows and network of web sites. Today she is the trusted adviser for (THROB) 3ob.com and holds a full-time position as Customer Acquisition and Retention for *Playboy*'s network of subscriptions sites and online VoD (Video on Demand). She is also affiliated and offers her guidance for companies such as WITI.com (Women In Technology International). Katie has been quoted in *The Wall Street Journal, Laptop Magazine, AVN Online* ,and *Maxim Magazine,* and produced the 04/05 seminar program for the world famous Internext Expo, and also develops seminars for Digital Hollywood, a respected mainstream digital media conference.

Lainie Speiser began her career in adult entertainment soon after getting her B.A. in journalism from School of Visual Arts in New York City and hasn't looked back since. After years of promoting stroke mags, *Gallery, Fox,* and *Lollypops,* Lainie finally hit the smut major leagues by becoming *Penthouse Magazine*'s publicity director in January 2003. She has repped famous porn stars such as Jill Kelly, Jewel De'Nyle, Anna Malle, Kylie Ireland, Tera Patrick, and *Penthouse Magazine* founder Bob Guccione. Throughout her 13 years in the porno biz she maintained her writing skills by penning silly, self-indulgent and tasteless columns for *Exit Magazine, Aquarian Arts Weekly, Downtown, Mojo10,* and *Sex and Guts Magazine.* When she isn't peddling smut, Lainie enjoys sharing a pint and a smoke with the boyishly handsome man of her choice, reading true crime books, buying platform shoes, and working out in the ghetto-fabulous gym Lucille Roberts. To catch up with Miss Lainie and her band of merry Pets on tour go to www.penthouse.com.

From humble beginnings in Baton Rouge Louisiana as a teenage stripper, **Stormy** (a.k.a Stormy Daniels or Stormy Waters) has done what no other woman in porn has ever accomplished: she is a successful contract performer, director and writer for a major label in the adult entertainment business, Wicked Pictures. With her relentless drive and voracious appetite for knowledge, this international sex symbol has learned to make the industry work for her, not just work for the industry. Stormy has paid her dues every step of the way as a house dancer, magazine cover model and centerfold. She's one of the most successful feature dancers ever on the circuit, and as a contract porn star, she became the winner of *AVN's* coveted "Best New Starlet" award in 2004. Stormy also has her own toy line through California Exotic Novelties, hosts the show "Contract Porn Star's" on KSEXRadio.com, and is the Sex Editor for *FHM-Mexico* magazine. Her official website is www.stormydaniels.com.

Dubbed "a local vocal legend" by the *San Francisco Bay Guardian,* **Jackie Strano** is a singer/songwriter that owns independent digital video production company S.I.R. Productions with her beautiful and multi-talented wife, Shar Rednour. S.I.R. Productions is the only lesbian owned and operated production and distribution house to win an AVN award for their title, *Hard Love & How to Fuck In High Heels.* They are also the creators of the best-selling and groundbreaking Bend Over Boyfriend series featured in media such as *Playboy* and *The Village Voice.* S.I.R. Productions has been featured on HBO's six-part documentary *Pornocopia,* KRON-TV's *History of Sex in San Francisco,* and their movies have played to sold out crowds in gay film festivals around the world including San Francisco, Los Angeles, Toronto, Montreal, Paris, London, Washington, D.C., New York, Berlin, Hong Kong, Milan, Vancouver, Barcelona, Sydney, Hong Kong, and Dublin. Their latest DVD project, *Healing Sex,* is a docudrama showing men and women on their path to recovery and reclaiming their sexual and intimate lives after surviving past abuse and trauma. For more information, check out www.sirvideo.com and www.healingsexthemovie.com.

Tristan Taormino is an award-winning author, columnist, editor, and sex educator. She is the author of three books: *True Lust: Adventures in Sex, Porn and Perversion* (Cleis Press); *Down and Dirty Sex Secrets* (ReganBooks/HarperCollins); and *The Ultimate Guide to Anal Sex for Women* (Cleis Press), winner of a Firecracker Book Award and named Amazon.com's #1 Bestseller in Women's Sex Instruction in 1998. She is director, producer, and star of two videos based on her book, *The Ultimate Guide to Anal Sex for Women* 1 and 2; the first video won two Adult Video News Awards and an XRCO Award in 2000. Tristan is series editor of eleven volumes of the Lambda Literary Award-winning anthology series *Best Lesbian Erotica.* She is a columnist for *The Village Voice, Taboo,* and *Velvet Park.* She is the former editor of *On Our Backs,* the nation's oldest lesbian-produced lesbian sex magazine. Tristan has been featured in over 200 publications, dozens of radio shows; she has appeared on CNN, HBO's *Real Sex, The Howard Stern Show, Loveline, Ricki Lake,* MTV, and The Discovery Channel. She lectures at top colleges and universities around the country, teaches sex and relationship workshops around the world, and does private coaching sessions for individuals and couples. Her official website is www.puckerup.com.

Jamye Waxman started in sex education as a Radio Producer for Eyada.com. While there, she absorbed herself in adult entertainment and began her pursuit of other sex-positive adventures. She currently writes the advice column "Sex Ed" for *Playgirl Magazine* and "Hot Wax," a sex and relationship column for *Steppin' Out Magazine,* where she examines her own habits when it comes to meeting, mating and dating. Jamye is the former radio producer of *Love-Bytes* with Bob Berkowitz, *The Joan Rivers Show,* and *The Alan Colmes Show,* and the former host of *Aural Fixation* on wsexradio.com. She was a producer of the popular Metro TV show *Naked New York.* In addition, Jamye is completing her masters degree in sex education at Widener University in Pennsylvania, and she is a sex educator at the world-famous sex shop Toys in Babeland in New York City. Jamye also teaches classes on oral sex, sex toys, and sex play. She is currently serving as President of Feminists for Free Expression. Jamye keeps a diary of her life and experiences on her website, www.jamyewaxman.com.

ABOUT THE EDITOR

Carly Milne, a former adult industry publicist and commentator, began her professional writing career at the age of 14 and hasn't looked back since. Her work has appeared in *Bitch Magazine, AVN Magazine, Rolling Stone, Playboy, Club, Hustler, Penthouse, High Society, Playgirl, EQ Magazine,* and more. She has also been interviewed by *MediaTelevision, Marketing Magazine, The Globe and Mail, Entertainment Weekly, Cosmopolitan, Glamour, Forrester Magazine, Black Book* and E!'s *True Hollywood Story* on Jenna Jameson, among many others. Milne has also had essays published in *Virgin Territory* (Three Rivers Press) and *Best American Sex Essays 2005* (Cleis Press). To learn more and read her regular blog blitherings, check out her website at www.carlymilne.net.